Adventure and Society

Simon Beames
Chris Mackie
Matthew Atencio

Adventure and Society

palgrave
macmillan

Simon Beames
University of Edinburgh
Edinburgh, UK

Chris Mackie
University of the Highlands and Islands
Inverness, UK

Matthew Atencio
California State University East Bay
Hayward, CA, USA

ISBN 978-3-319-96061-6   ISBN 978-3-319-96062-3   (eBook)
https://doi.org/10.1007/978-3-319-96062-3

Library of Congress Control Number: 2018960892

This Palgrave Macmillan imprint is published by the registered company Springer Nature Switzerland AG
The registered company address is: Gewerbestrasse 11, 6330 Cham, Switzerland

Foreword

Many readers of this book will, like me, have spent much of their lives engaged in adventurous activities. For me, these activities began when I was in Girlguiding and then Sea Rangers (a senior section of Girlguiding), and later included climbing, kayaking, skiing, and various forms of sailing. I have taught these traditional adventure activities both practically and theoretically. Currently my activities include windsurfing, SUPing (stand-up paddleboarding), and hiking. Many, unlike me, will have been introduced to these activities by family, The Duke of Edinburgh's Award or other national organizations, school, and/or be(coming) enthusiastic skateboarders, surfers, or sport climbers. There may well be some of you who have not experienced these forms of adventure but practice a wide range of other, perhaps less conventional, ones. You may be a social science student, sports studies student, or any other critical thinker. This book is for you, as well as for those of you taking outdoor adventure education or outdoor studies programmes.

When I was asked to write an 800-word foreword for *Adventure and Society* I agreed and avidly read the chapters in the book. The irony of this is that I was engrossed in a little-known TV comedy drama titled *800 Words*. The main character, a newly bereaved father and columnist, moves his reluctant teenage son and daughter from a large city to a small surf town. Although he wants to improve his surfing, he is trying to cope with the sudden death of his wife. He and his teenagers encounter a wide range of situations with the diverse members of the community, which take them on countless unexpected twists. There is pathos and comedy in the crises they encounter in the unexpected twists that are part of the day-to-day routine in this small surf town community. *Adventure and Society* draws attention to Becker's explanations that at the structural core of adventure is the 'interplay between crisis and routine' (p. 26). Adventure and society are inexorably intertwined, as represented in the *800 Words* drama, and, as we are shown in this book, adventure is complex, multifaceted, and deeply embedded in and shaped by society.

Although we might consider that many adventurers operate in isolation and find freedom through participating in risky pursuits, this simplistic notion, like many other popular (mis)conceptions, is explored and critiqued here. *Adventure and Society* provides readers with critical, scholarly understandings of what society is and considers how individuals and groups are both constrained and empowered in relationships within communities. The popular image of who can initiate and experience adventure is for the most part that of the White, middle-class, young, able-bodied male. Not only does this book help us to perceive things like this differently, but also it offers readers theoretical and narrative skills to see through stereotyping, resist taken-for-granted assumptions, and challenge inequalities in society and so in adventure.

We live in a world where consumption is overwhelming. In order for the few to profit many must labour and more must buy. This book prompts us to question how we engage in and consume adventures. What, and whose interests, are maintained by rampant production and consumption? Where once, years ago, we bought our walking, camping, and climbing gear cheaply and often recycled from ex-army shops, now vast numbers of different brands operate in the marketplace to gain our loyalty and get our money.

As Denzin (2010) opines, '[c]omplex discourses and ideological processes shape the rituals of cultural production and consumption. Each historical period has its racially preferred gendered self. These selves are announced and validated through these circuits of representation, identification and consumption' (p. xv). *Adventure and Society* offers readers the opportunity and knowledge needed 'to interrogate these formations and the circuits they forge'.

Social justice and environmental justice are inexorably interconnected. Challenging the abuse of people and the natural environment in meeting the wants of wealthy corporations and adventure seekers is crucial if future adventurers are to continue to live in a biodiverse world. Humans and the more than human are on the cusp of global disaster largely because of mindless consumption informed by neo-liberal ideologies or, more generously, by the unintended consequences of capitalism. We know that the oceans are becoming plastic; many beautiful coral reefs are now grey and lifeless. *Adventure and Society* brings these issues to our attention, but gives us hope by pointing to the many activist adventurers and others doing what they can at the local as well as global level for sustainable futures.

The authors of this book are offering you a wealth of knowledge to enable you to make sense of our complex fluid society, to challenge dominant ideologies, and to act sustainably and equitably in your adventures. Make it happen.

Barbara Humberstone
New Forest, UK

References

Becker, P. (2016). A German theory of adventure: A view on the Erlebnispedagogik. In B. Humberstone, H. Prince, & K. Henderson (Eds.), *Routledge international handbook of outdoor studies* (pp. 20–29). London: Routledge.

Denzin, N.K. (2010). Foreword. In J.A. Sandlin & P. McLaren (Eds.), *Critical pedagogies of consumption: Living and learning in the shadow of 'Shopocalypse'*. London: Routledge.

Preface

Before we get started, let us pause for a moment to make sense of what this book is going to be about; we aim to provide an accessible overview of the ways in which 'adventurous practices' influence, and are influenced, by the world around them. Compelling examples of this that are worth unpacking can be found in many places. For instance, please close the book and have another look at the cover. What do you see? Apart from a fantastic photograph of two skiers dropping into Number 3 Gully on Ben Nevis in Scotland, taken by Hamish Frost, what pieces of information can you glean?

First, specialist clothing and equipment is being used and it is probably quite expensive. Second, this activity—for most of the world's population—would seem pretty risky. Third, the top skier is wearing a GoPro camera on their helmet, in order to capture video of their descent which will likely be posted and shared online.

If those are the initial observations and assumptions that we can make, what might be some of the others? If you were a betting person, what social class, ethnicity, and gender would you guess these two skiers to be? They obviously have enough free time to travel to the mountains and spend the day climbing and skiing, and they are using and wearing costly pieces of technology—all of which come with a price; so, our skiers come from relative socio-economic and cultural privilege. It would, we think, be safe to assume that the two skiers take their pastime very seriously—so seriously that they watch lots of ski videos on YouTube, follow other extreme skiers on Instagram, and, as mentioned, contribute their own images to these and other social media sites. Being extreme skiers who participate in a community of like-minded others is part of who these two are.

Let us take our evolving, informal analysis a step further. From where do you think the raw materials for the ski equipment and clothing were extracted? Although purchased and used by individuals in a northern, developed nation, where do you think this gear was manufactured? By whom was it manufactured and under what conditions do these labourers work and live? Finally, it is worth considering the long term and what might happen to this equipment and clothing once they gather enough nicks, tears, and breaks, and need to be disposed of.

As they stand, the above questions and assumptions stemming from the vignette on the cover are no more than the kinds of topics we might discuss in a coffee shop or pub. This book aims to tackle these same issues, but with more precision and depth, through the use of recent scholarship and insightful theoretical frameworks. Our primary aim is thus to examine adventure practices from perspectives that we otherwise might not.

One of the most challenging aspects of writing this book was illustrating the interdisciplinary nature of how adventure and society interact; because each topic is connected to the others, it is hard to contain, for example, discrete discussions of social media, risk, identity, and equalities within the constraints of one standard chapter length. We have done our best to package the chapters into logical and relevant themes and have made plenty of links between the chapters in the text. Each chapter has discussion questions to personally contextualize the material and a case study to provide a rich illustration of the topic. We have also highlighted key readings at the ends of chapters, which you can pursue in order to gain further insight on certain topics.

We have left aside the conventional chapter-by-chapter summary and instead encourage you to take a look at the table of contents to get an overview of the topics that we will cover and then jump in wherever it works best for you. Although we recommend starting at the beginning, the chapters can be read in any order, and this may be useful for educators using this text in a variety of courses.

Finally, if we have a central wish for readers, it is that you come away from your time with this book motivated to undertake adventures that are more deeply considered. Whether your adventure involves meeting friends at the local climbing gym every Thursday night or training for a once-in-a-lifetime ascent of El Capitan in Yosemite National Park, it is our belief that having a richer scholarly, theoretical understanding of adventure practices will make these pursuits even more personally meaningful, less harmful to others, and perhaps even a force for positive social change.

Simon Beames
Edinburgh, UK

Chris Mackie
Inverness, UK

Matthew Atencio
Hayward, CA, USA
May 2018

Acknowledgements

We could not have written this book without the support of many people. We are grateful for the guidance from Palgrave Macmillan and their editorial staff. A number of international scholars reviewed chapters for this book. In no particular order, these are Tonia Gray, Jelena Farkic, Mary Louise Adams, Tommy Langseth, Rosa Murray, Eric Brymer, Kaye Richards, Peter Varley, Chris Loynes, John Kelly, Belinda Wheaton, Rebecca Olive, Mark Leather, Kass Gibson, Allen Hill, Jonathan Hearn, Becky Beal, and, of course, Barbara Humberstone. Jenny Hounsell brought her invaluable editing, referencing, and formatting skills to the project. Additionally, we were pleased to be able to collaborate with the photographer Hamish Frost, whose work provided the dynamic front cover for the book.

Professor Barbara Humberstone's outstanding research in the field of outdoor leisure and recreation has greatly influenced the ideas featuring within this book's chapters, and we are so pleased that she agreed to write the Foreword. Barbara, however, did more than write the Foreword: she also provided a chapter-by-chapter critique of the entire book, suggested literature to ensure that our discussions were up-to-date, and was hugely helpful in exposing weak arguments and assumptions unwittingly made by our gendered perspectives.

Finally, we are grateful to our friends and families for their continued support. Simon would like to thank Nancy for being a tower of strength and support to him, and to his colleagues in Edinburgh for tolerating his disappearances into the 'writing cave'. Chris would like to thank his wife Grace and son Seoras for their constant patience and encouragement. Matthew would like to thank his wife Lyndsey Mountain and daughter Eilidh Atencio for their support during this project.

Contents

Conceptualizing Adventure

© The Author(s) 2019
S. Beames et al., *Adventure and Society*, https://doi.org/10.1007/978-3-319-96062-3_1

1

Chapter Aims

After reading this chapter, you will be able to:

— Explain the masculine, capitalist roots of adventure
— Define adventure
— Understand how adventure is often associated with privilege
— Explain key features of adventurous activities
— Understand the relative nature of adventures
— Explain Lynch and Moore's 'adventure paradox'

1.1 Early Meanings of Adventure

Adventure and society have a long and fascinating shared history (Bell, 2016; Lynch & Moore, 2004). A book entitled *Adventure and Society* should begin by defining those two words, both of which have very broad meanings. The origins of the word 'adventure' have been traced back to the twelfth century and, over time, the English appear to have arrived at their own word, with its own spelling that is derived from French (which came from Latin).[1]

Zweig (1974) refers to universal 'adventure myths' from classical antiquity that comprise 'perilous journeys, encounters with inhuman monsters, ordeals of loneliness and hunger, descents into the underworld' (p. 3). The people involved in these stories usually did not choose to take part in these adventures, in the same way that Luke Skywalker and Frodo Baggins did not wake up one morning and decide to embark upon their epic journeys: the circumstances chose them, and they took part only because they saw no other course of action. Note that the actual term 'adventure' was not used in classical antiquity, but one can see how these ordeals were adventurous in nature.

The earliest actual use of the word adventure was in French: *aventure*. *Aventure* came to the fore in the middle ages (around the late 1100s) as part of a 'knightly' ideology. Knights of the court went on *aventures* in order to earn a livelihood, so that they could have a nice place to live and be an attractive marriage prospect. The big risk for a knight was not going on an *aventure* (Nerlich, 1987, p. 5), as that would have meant failure.

In the 1400s, in similar ways to knights venturing forth for personal gain, merchant adventurers sailed the seas. At this point these quests become more than personal, as they might involve ships with hundreds of men. Further, some of these expeditions would be blessed by the Crown and thus provide additional

---

1   The French word *aventure* and the Latin word *advenire*, which means 'to come' or 'to arrive', are both cited as precursors to our 'adventure'. However, this history of the word does not seem as helpful as the French 'courtly-knightly' origins, as explained above.

morality-free rationales for the 'exploration, subjugation, and exploitation' inherent in such profit-seeking adventures (Nerlich, 1987, p. 129).

These perilous journeys have been directly linked to what Michael Nerlich (1987) called the 'ideology of adventure'. In essence, Nerlich robustly argued that adventuring developed in the middle ages from the human desire to accrue capital: that is, to make money. Boje and Luhman (1999) explain how Nerlich's ideology of adventure 'makes the industrial revolution and enlightenment possible as a project of capitalism' (para. 2). Nerlich showed how the stories, literature, poems, and plays of the time promoted an 'adventure-mentality' that became 'appropriated in capitalistic commerce and production as adventure-practices' (Boje & Luhman, 1999, para. 2).

These myths, histories, and meanings of adventure can be associated with what Campbell (1949) called the mono-myth of the 'hero's journey'. Loynes (2003) explains how Campbell identified 17 stages of the hero's journey that will be very familiar to anyone who has read or watched epic stories like *Star Wars* or *The Lord of the Rings*. Bell (2016) further explains how the cultural production of today's adventurous and heroic individual is located within ongoing 'histories of imperialism and enforced inequalities' (p. 8). From this perspective, the socially agreed concept of what it means to be adventurous is built on stories, images, and ideas which are tied in with certain dominant cultural forces.

What is important to be aware of is that these narratives are very male oriented: the activities are physically strenuous and the principal protagonists are able-bodied young men. As such, historical notions of adventure have, to a large extent, marginalized women. Writing more than 20 years ago, Warren (1996) warned us that:

» the heroic quest is a metaphor that has little meaning to women. Each stage of a woman's journey in the wilderness is a direct contradiction of the popular quest model. A woman rarely hears a call to adventure; in fact, she is more often dissuaded … from leaving home to engage in adventurous pursuits. (p. 16)

Early adventuring did not only oppress women, but also everyone else (irrespective of gender) who was not part of this dominant adventure class. Consider for a moment the countless foreign lands (and the people who inhabited them) that were plundered and exploited for others' benefit. In summary, the roots of the word adventure are very much linked to centuries of male capitalist endeavour and colonization. Those reading a book on adventure and society should see that adventures in antiquity, the middle ages, the renaissance, and the industrial revolution were very much influenced by the social norms of their times.

1

1.2 Defining Adventure

While, on one hand, we can see that the word 'adventure' and its meanings have a long history, those meanings do not have the semantic precision required to grapple with our questions about adventurous practices in contemporary society.

According to the Oxford Concise Dictionary, an adventure is 'an unusual, exciting, or daring experience' (Soanes & Stevenson, 2008, p. 18). Colin Mortlock (1984), a British adventurer and educator, claimed in one of his influential early works that adventures involve 'a degree of uncertainty' (p. 14) and 'demand the best of our capabilities – physically, mentally, emotionally' (p.19). Indeed, most scholars seem to contend that uncertainty (or unpredictability, if you prefer) is a crucial feature of adventures. Some authors, such as Goldenberg (2001), claim that adventures should have inescapable consequences, but as we will see below, Mortlock and others emphasize the subjective and relative nature of adventurous experiences.

If we accept that adventures are challenging experiences, have a degree of unpredictability, and demand physical and mental skill to overcome, then let us put some of these features to the test.

❓ Discussion Questions

Discuss which of the following situations could be considered adventures and why.

1. Getting a flat tyre while driving alone in the middle of the night on a country road
2. Going to a huge city for the first time
3. Drag racing with another car on a backroad
4. Trying a new kind of food while on holiday
5. Going outdoor rock climbing for the first time
6. Spray-painting graffiti on the side of an office building
7. Losing electricity at one's home for 48 hours
8. Starting at a new high school

It is reasonable to suggest that all of the above circumstances could be considered adventurous. One crucial distinguishing factor in the above examples is the degree to which these circumstances were planned, expected, and desired. Seen this way, most people would not have foreseen, nor wanted to be inconvenienced by, a flat tyre or a power outage. Conversely, both trying an exotic dish and going climbing at a beautiful outdoor location might have been experiences that were very deliberately courted.

The kinds of adventure germane to this book are those on which one has wilfully chosen to embark. There are many inhabitants of planet earth who do not seek to add any uncertainty or challenge to their everyday lives. Can you imagine pre-industrial and traditional subsistence farmers—who were working the land day in and day out and surviving on the bare minimum of shelter, food, and water—discussing how they would like to climb to the top of the local hill after they finished 12 hours of grafting in a field? From this perspective, we can say that adventure is culturally relative (Beames & Pike, 2013).

The very idea of seeking adventure for adventure's sake might be, for some cultures, an absurd concept. Those living an agrarian life in a drought-ridden village in sub-Saharan Africa and those who have fled war-torn Syria and are living in squalid refugee camps probably do not seek experiences that are especially daring, exciting, or unpredictable; they seek stability, peace, shelter, clean water, food, jobs, and schools.

When we are fortunate enough to live in relative comfort and stability, the opposite of the everyday holds a special draw. It is not unusual for people in the dark of a northern hemisphere winter dream of Mediterranean sun; it is relatively common for office workers in a nine-to-five routine to seek uncertainty, spontaneity, and physical activity in fresh air. How much of this do you think is about the activity and the individual, and how much is about their everyday social setting? Our focus in this book is primarily on those lucky enough to undertake adventures more or less on their own terms. Indeed, if you are reading this book, you are most probably one of these people.

The late German sociologist, Georg Simmel (1919/n.d.), suggested that adventure has to do with leaving one's routines and doing something 'alien, untouchable, out of the ordinary' (p. 2). Simmel's compatriot, Peter Becker (2016), further explains that at the 'structural core' of adventure[2] is the 'interplay between crisis and routine' (p. 26). The space between the polar opposites of reasonably predictable day-to-day life and a full-on crisis is large, but there is some elusive territory within that space which attracts many of us. A crucial point to our foundational discussions on what constitutes an adventure is their relative nature. For example, skiing down a couloir high in the Rocky Mountains might be routine for a ski guide. For an intermediate 'resort' skier, standing at the top of that couloir would be a crisis. It is obvious, then, that 'what one person deems adventurous may not be to another person' (Beames & Pike, 2013, p. 2). As we will see in later chapters, relative adventure can be wonderful for individuals seeking that sweet spot where their skills meet the challenge that lies before them (see Lyng, 1990), but it can pose all kinds of problems for tour operators and outdoor education organizations, who might have one standardized product that must cater to a multitude of skills and abilities (Becker, 2016; Cater, 2006; Loynes, 1998).

---

2   Becker also discusses the closely related German term, *erlebnis*.

1

With these items of cultural and individual relativity addressed (for the meantime), we can expand our working definition of adventures to also include a certain element of *desirability*. Adventures, then, are actively sought and therefore planned to a greater or lesser extent. It follows that adventures are *planned, challenging experiences that feature a degree of unpredictability and which demand certain physical and mental skills to undertake*.

Having an agreed definition of adventure may be well and good, but there remains one caveat which needs to be highlighted, and that surrounds the anti- or pro-social nature of the activity (Beames & Pike, 2013). We can see how skateboarders hanging out and pulling tricks on the steps of a city hall might fall within what we would label adventurous. While this can be understood as an act of resistance against private and political control of urban spaces (Borden, 2001), we can still say that the skaters are principally concerned with challenging themselves to respond to, and move creatively through, a dynamic environment. Furthermore, there are growing instances where activities like skateboarding are practised and even supported by communities in pro-social ways, for the common good (Atencio, Beal, McClain, & Wright, 2018). Conversely, there may be elements of adventurousness inherent in some forms of anti-social behaviour, such as hopping a fence and spray-painting the side of an office building. When the activities' central aims focus on harming people or property through bullying or vandalism, however, it is difficult for us to include them in our discussions on adventure and all-encompassing terms such as 'adventure sports'. We will revisit the subject of adventure being used to change behaviour in ▶ Chap. 9.

To a large extent, the kinds of pro-social adventure with which we are concerned are what Breivik (2010) labelled 'adventure sports'. Midol (1993) referred to this trend towards adrenaline-fuelled pastimes as 'whiz sports'. Another French writer, Loret (1995), called these sports—which seemed to share the common feature of sliding along snow or water—as *sports de glisse*. Rinehart (1998) has written extensively on the X-Games and how powerful commercial forces have institutionalized and popularized these alternative sports. Indeed, as captured in Booth and Thorpe's (2007) volume, the whole notion of 'extreme sports' made for television covers fascinating sociological ground, which we will examine in ▶ Chap. 5.

A label that has become very common in the academic literature is that of 'lifestyle sports', which was developed by scholar Belinda Wheaton (2004, 2013). Wheaton herself, along with Robinson (2008), has noted that it is probably not that productive to get caught up in the terms themselves, and suggests that it is of greater importance to focus on the meanings ascribed to them.

Norwegian scholar Gunnar Breivik posits that adventure sports share certain features:

1. Have elements of challenge, excitement, and (in most sports) risk;
2. Take place in demanding natural or artificially constructed environments;
3. Are more loosely organized than mainstream sports;
4. Represent a freedom from or opposition to the dominant sport culture;
5. Are individualistic pursuits but tend to build groups and subcultures around the activity. (2010, p. 262)

Breivik's five defining characteristics of adventure sports, combined with our Mortlock-inspired definition of adventure, together provide a useful platform for forthcoming discussions on adventure and society. As we have seen, many different labels have been ascribed to the kinds of adventures that we are discussing. While we will use these terms somewhat interchangeably, we will refer to them predominantly as adventure sports.

1.3 What Is Society?

So, what about the 's' word: society? What do we mean by society? In the most general terms, we can assert that societies comprise sets of human beings and their complex, ever-changing relationships. Defining society beyond this very vague assertion invariably attracts critics! Fear not, readers, as we will endeavour to gain more precision on this term.

A society is effectively a large web of individuals. Usually, societies are much too large for people to have direct contact with each other. For example, Matthew Atencio is part of American society, but he has not interacted with most Americans. Understanding what a society is may be helped by also understanding what communities are. Communities—whether bounded by geography, built around a common activity, or connected across continents through technology and social media—usually feature a stronger sense of identity, interaction, common ways of thinking and acting, and belongingness than do societies (McMillan & Chavis, 1986). Societies can comprise countless communities and these can come in hugely contrasting sizes and status, such as the Greater Toronto Area, which comprises upwards of 5 million people, or those few who dare to BASE jump (Building, Antenna, Span, or Earth skydiving) within the boundary of Yosemite National Park (where the sport is outlawed).

At each of these levels, from societies down to the smallest communities, individuals' actions and behaviours interact with social structures. There are many different ways to understand the

1

reciprocal flow of influence between individual actors and society depending on which sociological perspective you use to look at the world, and three key terms that will help you to use some of these different perspectives to understand adventure in society are *culture*, *values*, and *norms*.

According to Giddens and Sutton (2017), the 'values, norms, habits and ways of life characteristic of a coherent social group' (p. 995) can be characterized as that group's *culture*. These groups can be of any scale, geographically dispersed, and have a membership consisting of individuals who also belong to other social groups but are united by the culture which their members hold in common. Let us take surfing as an example to illustrate these terms. There are distinct forms of art (e.g. films and music), ways of dressing, language, and important places with which many surfers identify: they are produced and consumed by surfers. This is surf culture, which is representative of the everyday practices and ideas that most people who identify as surfers participate in and value.

These ways of doing things are linked to the *values* of creative individual expression, connection with nature, travel, and (increasingly) clean living, which the surfing community identifies as important. These values are maintained through social *norms*, such as the unspoken etiquette of the 'line-up', where informal queuing and respect for more competent surfers ensure that waves do not go unridden. Surfers do not 'snake' the line-up or 'drop in' on someone who is already standing up on a wave and, if they do violate these norms, may face sanctions specific to the local setting. For example, some surf breaks have histories of violent localism, while at other spots you might get some friendly advice or simply be branded a 'kook': someone who poses as a surfer, but does not act 'authentically'.

❓ Discussion Question

To which cultures (or social groups) do you belong and what are the unwritten values and norms of each of these groups?

At a certain level, debates about what makes a society a society become unhelpful. What we are interested in is how groups of people—whether card carrying members of the International Orienteering Federation or a gang of skateboarders doing tricks at a local park—influence individuals. The flipside of that is equally important, of course: how individuals influence groups of people.

This reciprocal influence between individuals and groups of people is, in essence, the study of sociology, as put forward by early sociologists like Durkheim, Marx, and Weber.[3] This book is

---

3   See introduction to sociology textbooks, such as Giddens and Sutton (2017), for more information on sociology's origins.

chiefly concerned with another reciprocal tension, which is that between adventure and society. At one end of the spectrum, we seek to more deeply understand how larger structural forces such as governments, the media, and multi-national companies influence the adventurous practices of individuals in the Global North.[4] At the other end, there are single people and small groups who have transformed the way certain activities are practised and given currency within our society. Take parkour, for example: the popular emergence of parkour has influenced the way millions of (mostly) young people use their bodies in urban spaces. It is an adventurous activity that has been directly shaped over decades by the geographical, physical, cultural, and political circumstances in which it was located.[5] Adventure and society are thus influencing each other.

1.4 Adventure as Escape

From our discussion in this first chapter alone, we hope you will agree that the broad topic of adventure and its symbiotic relationship with our social world is complex and multi-faceted. Cohen and Taylor (1992) discuss the different forms of 'escape attempts' that people make to cope with the constraining, predictable routines of everyday living. This is more complicated than it seems, Rojek (1993) argues, because our values are so tightly intertwined with society that our escape attempts themselves are artificial: so, escape is not possible! A simpler way of explaining this paradox is that while we might feel like our adventures provide freedom, they are still 'tightly determined and modified by cultural, social and economic settings' (Lynch & Moore, 2004, p. 2).

What cannot be emphasized enough is that most—but by no means all—of the adventure practices that we are interrogating are those undertaken by people in positions of relative privilege. Quite often, it is those who have high-enough paying jobs to have the money to buy specialist technical equipment, coupled with the holiday to use it. Seen this way, adventures are 'romanticised as escape' (p. 2) from, and a 'psychological palliative' (p. 3) against, the trials of late modern life (Lynch & Moore, 2004).

Pip Lynch and Kevin Moore (2004) label this the 'adventure paradox' that features, on one hand, 'the crucial role of adventure ideology in the historical development of the modern, industrialised world and economy' and, on the other hand, 'the current promotion of adventure as the romantic escape from that world'

---

4   The Global North is used to describe what might otherwise be considered the 'developed' or 'first' world—a world of relative privilege.
5   See Atkinson's chapter on 'The quest for excitement in parkour' in Pike and Beames, *Outdoor Adventure & Social Theory* (2013)

1

(p. 2). While these and other discourses are about leaving behind one reality temporarily to visit another (Becker, 2016) or to enter the unknown (Nerlich, 1987), this binary is probably too simplistic for most of our discussions. It may be more useful to think about temporary, adventurous separations from quotidian life on a spectrum of how 'in the moment' or 'in the adventure reality' one is. Naturally, this will be different for each of us.

This fictional case is, we believe, entirely plausible. Jane's story reflects all of the key themes in this first chapter. First, it shows how the term 'adventure' is a relative concept (see Beames & Pike, 2013). For Jane, indoor climbing at the gym is not adventurous, when compared to a major unforeseen travel disruption on the other side of the world. Second, it shows how the climbing lifestyle (see Wheaton, 2004) is mediated by consumptive behaviour, as revealed by their clothing and holiday choices. Indeed, Jane and her friends have the financial power to buy adventure-related goods and experiences. Third, they see climbing as an escape from their relatively banal day-to-day existences (see Lynch & Moore, 2004). For Jane and her pals, climbing is a central organizing feature of their lives.

Case Study

Jane is a 27-year-old Scottish woman. She works as a bank teller in Edinburgh and is a serious sport climber. Jane loves climbing so much that she goes climbing at the gym at least three times during the week and once on a weekend, when she can drive out of town to a crag.

Most of Jane's closest friends are also climbers. When not at the office, all of them wear a similar style of clothing that seems to come from the same few manufacturers who make trousers, shirts, and fleece tops specifically for climbers. As well as spending their leisure time together, they also speak a language that few outside of the climbing community would understand. On some evenings they get together and watch videos that feature sponsored, professional climbers tackling cliff faces in exotic parts of the world. In the last four winters, they have gone to a different venue in southern Europe for a holiday on 'hot rock'.

Jane and her friends do not think that climbing is at all adventurous. For them, pushing their bodies to the limit on steep, artificial walls and taking roped leader falls is an inherent part of each session on the plastic. It is normal and routine, and provides a welcome escape from their highly predictable, indoor, sedentary, screen-based jobs. The biggest adventure in Jane's recent memory is the time she lost her passport in Thailand, missed her flight, and ended-up having to miss ten days of work, while she arranged for a new passport, had her mum send her enough money to buy another air ticket, buy the ticket, and fly home.

Chapter Summary

There are five key themes that we have covered in this chapter and which should be summarized. First, we highlighted how the myths and recorded histories associated with adventure often have at their common root men embarking on perilous journeys with the principal aim of gaining wealth, capital, and status.

Second, although the word 'adventure' seems easy enough to define, we have seen that there are important nuances in its meaning that need to be articulated. While it may be reasonable to accept that adventures feature unpredictability, and demand some daring and mental and physical skill, our notions of adventure also involve an element of agency, where we have deliberately chosen to embark on them. Further, they do not seek expressly to harm people or property.

The third theme that needs emphasizing is the relative nature of the term 'adventure'. We understand that there may be many people in the world who do not seek additional adventures in their lives; the implication here is that anyone who does actively seek adventure inhabits a world of relative privilege, since they have the time to spend doing this rather than earning money, growing food, or seeking shelter, for example. On a more individual level, what we perceive to be adventurous is also highly relative. A terrifying and possibly harmful experience for one person might be a normal, everyday, and even banal experience for another.

Next, we briefly introduce what is meant by the term 'society'. In a nutshell, it is a large group of people who are networked at some (albeit distant) level. Societies are often quite diverse and feature people who have not necessarily chosen to be part of it; they have been born into it. Societies can comprise innumerable communities, and these can contrast greatly in terms of size, mission, and regulation.

Finally, we outlined how adventure sports are often seen as escapes from the stresses, rigidity, social norms, and institutionalization that are features of late modern society in the Global North. The next chapter outlines central features of society alongside some key sociological concepts, which will together arm us with the language necessary to have deeper and more meaningful discussions about adventure in subsequent chapters.

Key Readings

Beames, S., & Pike, E. (2013). Outdoor adventure and social theory. In E. Pike & S. Beames (Eds.), *Outdoor adventure and social theory* (pp. 1–9). Abingdon, UK: Routledge.

Lynch, P., & Moore, K. (2004). Adventures in paradox. *Australian Journal of Outdoor Education, 8*(2), 3–12.

Wheaton, B. (2004). Introduction: Mapping the lifestyle sport-scape. In B. Wheaton (Ed.), *Understanding lifestyle sports: Consumption, identity and difference* (pp. 1–28). London: Routledge.

1

References

Atencio, M., Beal, B., Wright, E. M., & McClain, Z. (2018). *Moving boarders: Skateboarders and the changing landscape of urban youth sports.* Fayetteville, AR: University of Arkansas Press.

Atkinson, M. (2013). The quest for excitement in parkour. In E. Pike & S. Beames (Eds.), *Outdoor adventure and social theory* (pp. 55–65). Abingdon, UK: Routledge.

Beames, S., & Pike, E. J. (2013). Introduction. In E. Pike & S. Beames (Eds.), *Outdoor adventure and social theory* (pp. 1–9). Abingdon, UK: Routledge.

Becker, P. (2016). A German theory of adventure: A view on the Erlebnispedagogik. In B. Humberstone, H. Prince, & K. Henderson (Eds.), *Routledge international handbook of outdoor studies* (pp. 20–29). London: Routledge.

Bell, M. (2016). The romance of risk: Adventure's incorporation in risk society. *Journal of Adventure Education and Outdoor Learning, 17*(4), 280–293.

Boje, D., & Luhman, J. (1999). *The knight errant's ideology of adventure.* Presentation to the Academy of Management session on 'Reclaiming Indigenous Knowledge'. Retrieved from https://business.nmsu.edu/~dboje/knight.html

Booth, D., & Thorpe, H. (2007). The meaning of extreme. In D. Booth & H. Thorpe (Eds.), *Berkshire encyclopedia of extreme sports* (pp. 181–197). Great Barrington, MA: Berkshire.

Borden, I. (2001). *Skateboarding, space and the city: Architecture, the body and performative critique.* Oxford: Berg.

Breivik, G. (2010). Trends in adventure sports in a post-modern society. *Sport in Society, 13*(2), 260–273.

Campbell, J. (1949). *The hero with a thousand faces.* Princeton: Princeton University Press.

Cater, C. (2006). Playing with risk? Participant perceptions of risk and management implications in adventure tourism. *Tourism Management, 27*(2), 317–325. https://doi.org/10.1016/j.tourman.2004.10.005

Cohen, S., & Taylor, L. (1992). *Escape attempts: The theory and practice of resistance to everyday life* (2nd ed.). London: Routledge.

Giddens, A., & Sutton, P. (2017). *Sociology.* Oxford: Polity Press.

Goldenberg, M. (2001). *Outdoor and risk educational practices.* Washington, DC: ERIC Clearinghouse.

Loret, A. (1995). *Génération glisse: Dans l'eau, l'air, la neige; la révolution du sport des 'années fun'.* Paris: Éditions Autrement.

Loynes, C. (1998). Adventure in a bun. *The Journal of Experimental Education, 21*(1), 35–39.

Loynes, C. (2003). Narratives of agency: The hero's journey as a construct for personal development through outdoor adventure. In J. Koch, L. Rose, J. Schirp, & J. Vieth (Eds.), *Bewegungs: Und korperorientierte ansatze in der sozialen arbeit* (pp. 133–143). Marburg, Germany: BSJ/Springer VS.

Lynch, P., & Moore, K. (2004). Adventures in paradox. *Australian Journal of Outdoor Education, 8*(2), 3–12.

Lyng, S. (1990). Edgework: a social psychological analysis of voluntary risk taking. *Am J Sociol. 95*, 851–856.

McMillan, D., & Chavis, D. (1986). Sense of community: A definition and theory. *Journal of Community Psychology, 14*, 6–23.

Midol, N. (1993). Cultural dissent and technical innovations in the 'whiz' sports. *International Review for the Sociology of Sport, 28*(1), 23–32.

Mortlock, C. (1984). *The adventure alternative.* Milnthorpe, UK: Cicerone Press.

Nerlich, M. (1987). *Ideology of adventure: Studies in modern consciousness* (Vol. 1 and 2, pp. 1100–1750). Minneapolis: University of Minnesota Press.

Pike, E., & Beames, S. (2013). *Outdoor adventure and social theory.* Abingdon, UK: Routledge.

Rinehart, R. (1998). Inside of the outside: Pecking orders within alternative sport as ESPN's 1995 'The eXtreme Games'. *Journal of Sport and Social Issues, 22*, 398–414.

Robinson, V. (2008). *Everyday masculinities and extreme sport: Male identity and rock climbing*. Oxford: Berg.

Rojek, C. (1993). *Ways of escape: Modern transformations in leisure and travel*. Basingstoke, UK: Palgrave Macmillan.

Simmel, G. (1919/n.d.). The adventurer (trans: Kettler, D.). In G. Simmel (Ed.), *Philosophische Kultur* (pp. 7–24). Leipzig, Germany: Kröner. Retrieved from http://www.osea-cite.org/tourismworkshop/resources/Simmel_The_Adventurer.pdf

Soanes, C., & Stevenson, A. (Eds.). (2008). *Concise Oxford English dictionary*. Oxford: Oxford University Press.

Warren, K. (1996). Women's outdoor adventures: Myth and reality. In K. Warren (Ed.), *Women's voices in experiential education* (pp. 10–17). Dubuque, Iowa: Kendall Hunt.

Wheaton, B. (2004). Introduction: Mapping the lifestyle sport-scape. In B. Wheaton (Ed.), *Understanding lifestyle sports: Consumption, identity and difference* (pp. 1–28). Abingdon, UK: Routledge.

Wheaton, B. (2013). *The cultural politics of lifestyle sports*. Abingdon, UK: Routledge.

Zweig, P. (1974). *The adventurer: The fate of adventure in the Western world*. Princeton, NJ: Princeton University Press.

Adventure and Contemporary Society

© The Author(s) 2019
S. Beames et al., *Adventure and Society*, https://doi.org/10.1007/978-3-319-96062-3_2

2

Chapter Aims

After reading this chapter, you will be able to:

- Understand broad concepts of *agency* and *structure*
- Explain key concepts associated with late modernity
- Understand key concepts that explain how adventure sports typically transform from positions of obscurity to the mainstream
- Understand how the places where adventure practices occur are 'sites of struggle' for the participants

2.1 Social Theory 101

Before we can have an in-depth examination of adventure sports, it is important to understand the social and historical contexts in which they have developed and currently take place.

From this perspective, let us take rock climbing as a compelling socio-historical example. In 2020, speed climbing will be an official sport at the Summer Olympic Games in Tokyo. How did this form of indoor artificial rock wall climbing come to be? After all, people have not always climbed like this. Climbing was first formally practised by the British from the 1880s, as a means to prepare for larger mountaineering expeditions in the Alps. Indeed, some critics at the time thought that this kind of gymnastic training on boulders and shorter rock climbs, and the guidebooks in which these routes were described, was somewhat unsporting, as the level of adventure to be had in the mountains would be reduced (Gilman & Gilman, 2001).

The path from (mostly) rich, White men of privilege climbing in their leisure time[1] in the UK's Lake District to the Tokyo Summer Olympic Games in 2020 is winding and fascinating. Ultimately, the ways that people climb today have been shaped by countless people over the last 150 years; this idea that a current adventure phenomenon evolves through historical processes will be addressed later through the work of Norbert Elias (1978). For now, it suffices to say that people's attitudes and actions in adventure have been directly shaped by the structural influences that exist within society. When sociologists talk about society's structures, they are referring to over-arching, stable, and enduring patterns of social relations, such as culture, gender roles, and divisions of labour (Hearn, 2012). Structures can also come in the form of institutions and organizations. All structures, in some way, serve to guide, govern, and limit what people think and do. The ways in which these forces constrain people's lives are called *structural*

---

1   Every single member of the 823 admitted to the (British) Alpine Club between 1857 and 1890 were university-educated and from the upper-middle class (Isserman & Weaver, 2008).

determinism. Within all social interactions, there are what sociologists call *agents.* An agent (or an *actor*) is an academic term for human beings who intentionally take action to pursue their goals (Hearn, 2012).[2]

Many sociologists like to examine issues pertaining to human agency and structural determinism. The inherent, perpetual tension between the two considers the forces exerted by individuals upon structures and vice versa. Sociologists do not necessarily aim to resolve these tensions; rather, they attempt to expose the ways in which individuals are influenced by, for example, cultural institutions, peer groups, as well as dominant customs and, of course, how these same individuals exert influence on their prevailing social networks and norms. Unsurprisingly, most social arrangements tend to favour some people more than others, and this will be a thread that runs throughout the book while being examined in greater depth in ▶ Chap. 7.

If we return to the above climbing example, the key point to recognize is that climbing practices today have been morphing steadily over time and that ways of climbing have been influenced by myriad features of social life throughout history. These contextual features might include equipment innovations, having more leisure time, increasing disposable income, national governing bodies, government policy, and the media. Thus, given these constraints, what are the opportunities for individuals to innovate and create personal forms of practice? Put simply, in what ways are individuals' agency limited or enhanced by these broader social conditions?

Society's agents and the structures that envelop them exert mutual influence over each other. What is thus intriguing is trying to understand how and why these processes have happened (and continue to happen) in the worlds of adventure we inhabit. We see throughout this chapter that social theories give us analytical power to understand or make sense of daily phenomena occurring within human activities (Macdonald et al., 2002). Theoretical frameworks are thus used to shed a more focused light upon adventure practices throughout this book. In the next section, we highlight key theoretical concepts that help explain the ways in which broader society has been defined by scholars seeking to understand the conditions in which we live; of course, these conditions directly influence the nature and scope of adventure practices.

---

2   Agents can act alone, of course, but as we see later, they can also work together through networks of people, and these can come in countless forms—from political groups to associations of mountaineering instructors.

2

2.2 Modernity, Rationalization, and Late Modernity

In the last 30 years, sociologists have disagreed on the label they give to the times in which we live. Some say we no longer exist in the era of modernity but are instead in a time of *postmodernity* (e.g. Lyotard, 1984). Others say that we are still at the tail end of modernity, in what can be called *late modernity* (e.g. Giddens, 1991) or, more recently, *liquid modernity* (Bauman, 2007)—which reflects the increasingly fluid and unstable nature of life.

The period of modernity effectively began in the mid-1800s, when factories emerged and people migrated to cities to work in them. The moderns (as some called them) were rather obsessed with calculability and control (Lupton, 2013; Ritzer, 1993). They assumed that 'the social and natural worlds follow laws that may be measured, calculated and therefore predicted' (Lupton, 2013, p. 6). More than 40 years ago, Lyotard's work dismissed these universally believed assumptions about how the world worked when he claimed that the notion of humans having predictable futures was outdated. He referred to a 'grand narrative' that includes such predictable (and eventual) desirables as going to university and getting a steady job, marrying and having children, buying a house, retiring on a pension, and so on. We know, even more so today, that this grand narrative (also called meta-narrative) is no longer of use to many of today's young people who inhabit a vastly different world than their parents and grandparents. Contemporary youths have rapid access to new and shifting information, as well as diverse lifestyles, in unprecedented ways (Wright, 2004).

2.3 Our Changing World

We all know how the world is markedly different from 100, 50, or even 30 years ago. As we have seen, it probably is not hugely important what exact label we give to today's era. It is vital, however, that we understand its principal features. With these features articulated, we are then better able to discuss and debate the ways in which our adventures are shaped by the social circumstances in which they are located. We now introduce four key features in turn: *uncertainty, technology, mobility,* and being *networked*.

■ Uncertainty

The first feature of late modernity (as we will call 'our time' for now) is that it is marked by uncertainty. Compare your career possibilities with those of your grandparents. For most of you, your grandparents and great-grandparents had only one or two jobs and lived in one or two dwellings throughout their lives. Today, it is estimated that those born between 1995 and 2010 will have at least 17 different jobs and move 15 times in their career (McCrindle, 2014).

Uncertainty as a sociological concept refers to much more than jobs and homes, however. Uncertainty in late modernity is something that imbues all aspects of human life (Giddens, 1991). For example, it is no longer regarded as an almost absolute certainty that snow will come at Christmas time in the north, that music concerts will be free from bombings or shootings, or that one's pension will exist 20 years from now. This uncertainty is directly related to what Beck (1992) calls the 'risk society', where humans are obsessed with minimizing the chances of bad things happening to them.

Furedi (1997) refers to this as a 'culture of fear', where humans tend to fear being harmed or losing things of value. A parenting example of this would be the increases in children being driven to school (rather than walking) and decreases in children's unstructured and unsupervised time. Taking up this idea of parents' aiming to mitigate risk, Atencio, Beal, Wright, and McClain (2018) have shown that formerly street-based adventure activities like skateboarding have been reinterpreted by these adults so they may occur within safe, comfortable conditions, such as municipal skate parks.

We talk more about risk and society in ▶ Chap. 4. For the time being, what you need to remember is that people's feelings of uncertainty and their concerns about the future together serve to influence what they do for work and play.

■ Technology

It is arguable that technology has always existed in some form or another. Indeed, some say that the canoe is such a great piece of technology that its design has not changed in a thousand years! What characterizes today's technology is the high rate at which it changes; it is a very fluid concept. Consider how often we have to update the software on our phones and computers. It seems constant. Of course, these same pieces of hardware are often obsolete after three years, or even less.

The above examples of high-tech evolution are also evident with outdoor equipment, such as the weight of climbing protection, parabolic skis, the dramatic shortening of white-water kayak lengths, and the advent of single chainring fat bikes. It can be difficult and very expensive to always have the latest and best equipment on the market, and one of the tricks for consumers of all kinds may be to discern between which new products will make a significant difference to performance and enjoyment and which ones will not. It has already been argued in the broader sports world that technology is pushing the boundaries of what constitutes fair play and equitable competition, since some practitioners

2

undoubtedly have more resources to obtain certain technological advances than others (Ryall, 2013). We talk more about equipment in ▶ Chap. 5 when we discuss the influence of capitalism.

■ Mobility

The third feature of late modernity is mobility (Elliot & Urry, 2010) and, in particular, international mobility. There are two kinds of mobility. The first is the kind that many of us who live in relative privilege are accustomed to: we can fly to a far-away place for a weekend city break, do a work placement in a different country, and commute to offices that are thousands of miles away from our homes. Most of us choose to be mobile and do it on our own terms, as a way of enriching our work and personal lives. Some of us might be adventure tourists who spend a week mountain biking in a different country; others might be what Holly Thorpe (2014) calls 'seasonal migrants' who spend extended periods of time honing their craft in exotic destinations around the globe.

There are also many people in the world who live mobile lives but have not chosen to. Millions of people each year leave their homes to escape poverty, war, and natural disasters. Indeed, statistics from the United Nations Commission on Human Rights report that, in 2016, 65.6 million people were forced to leave their homes 'as a result of persecution, conflict, violence, or human rights violations' (UNHCR, 2017, p. 2). Think of the Syrians who have fled to Europe through the Turkish border, the Africans who have crossed the Mediterranean in search of a better life, the Rohingya Muslims who have left Myanmar, and those from storm-flattened Caribbean islands who headed to the southern US. These people have probably endured lengthy and perilous journeys and given their last funds and possessions to crooked opportunists.

■ Being Networked

The fourth key feature of today's social world is that most humans are highly networked. Although we are all, as Manuel Castells (2000) first explained in the early 1990s, part of an increasingly technologically networked society, even he might be surprised with the ways humans are now able to connect with each other through digital information networks. Thanks to handheld mobile devices and wifi/4G, many of us are able to contact others (and be contactable) almost 24 hours a day with video calls. We are also able to constantly update our own social media profiles while monitoring those of others. Being networked is arguably one of the most defining features of those born between 1995 and 2010 (Boyd, 2014; McCrindle, 2014). This notion of always being connected to each other through our handheld devices (particularly for younger people) has especially strong links to ▶ Chap. 8 on identity.

An interesting point to note with all of the above features of contemporary social life is that if one possesses a certain wealth, one can negotiate the features much more freely. For example, if one can draw on financial resources it is much easier to guard against uncertainty by buying insurance, keep up with technology by buying the latest smart phone, travel from place to place through multiple modes of transport, and stay networked through purchasing global roaming data plans. We revisit some of these ideas later in ▶ Chap. 5, when we discuss the impact of social media on adventure practices.

Keep the above four features in mind as we continue to explore how society's corporations, governments, informal groups of people, and institutions influence how the average citizen goes adventuring.

? **Discussion Question**
To what degree does each of the four defining features of late modernity exist in your day-to-day life?

2.4 From the Fringes to the Mainstream

Having discussed the social backdrop through identifying major features of contemporary society, we now turn towards how their influence has shaped adventure practices as we know them today. History has shown that many, if not all, adventure sports started life as obscure, esoteric pastimes that were practised by small numbers of people (Atkinson, 2013; Tracey, 2013). Freestyle kayaking, bouldering, and skateboarding are three examples of sports that were to a large degree initially practised by those wanting to break away from the mainstream and undertake their own kinds of adventure practices beyond the public gaze and corporate influences. However, as these leisure activities become popularized, the players' demands for improved equipment, followers' desires to be identified with the activities, and entrepreneurs' eyes for an emerging market, together conspire to cement an accepted and normal set of cultural practices.

As quickly as new adventure sports emerge, others are being subsumed into the mainstream and regulated by mediators such as online norm-setting forums and international rules for standardized competition (see, e.g. Coates, Clayton, & Humberstone, 2010). Snowboarding and BMX are two examples of adventure sports that now feature in the Olympic Games, and climbing, surfing, and skateboarding will follow suit in 2020.

Three concepts can help us understand more deeply how this journey from the obscure fringes to the mainstream of an adventure society can happen. They are *rationalization,* the *figurational perspective*, and *hegemony.*

2

■ Rationalization

The German sociologist Max Weber wrote extensively about what he called rationalization, bureaucratization, and regulation (1922/1968). Varley (2013) explains how these processes, which are so necessary to capitalism, 'pervade an ever-increasing proportion of our everyday lives', and goes on to argue that these are manifest in the increasing 'provision of outdoor instructor schemes, the accepted practices and policies of national governing bodies and the widespread availability of reliable, replicable adventure experiences' (p. 41).

Drawing on Weber's key concepts, American sociologist George Ritzer wrote a classic book in 1993, in which he showed how life was 'increasingly provided as standard, dependable, and safe products just like the McDonald's hamburger' (Loynes, 1998, p. 35). His McDonaldization framework highlighted how human existence was becoming increasingly defined by features of efficiency, calculability, predictability, and control. Rationalization, then, is the 'systematic, measured application of science to work and everyday life' (Varley, 2013, p. 35). This idea is utilized later on in the book, when discussing the influence of technology in ▶ Chap. 6 and tourism in ▶ Chap. 10.

Writing in 1998, Englishman Chris Loynes voiced his concern over a corporate approach doing to 'outdoor adventure what it has done elsewhere, that is to disassociate people from their experience of community and place' (p. 35). One can see how it is often in organizations' best interests to mitigate the loss of money, power, and prestige through minimizing the influence of events over which they have little control (Beames & Brown, 2014). Some adventure operators can increase the predictability (and thus control) of their products and services by actually moving their outdoor activities, such as skiing and climbing, indoors (see Beames & Brown, 2017). Dutch researchers Maarten van Bottenburg and Lotte Salome (2010) have called this the 'indoorization' of outdoor sports. Similarly, there are instances where skateboarding has been moved to the more predictable and controlled confines of a purpose-built venue, as found in Atencio et al. (2018) description of California's largest skate park in San Jose. This trend of housing such activities within what Beames and Varley (2013) have called 'adventure cathedrals' will be expanded upon in ▶ Chap. 5, which looks at capitalism.

❓ Discussion Questions

1. Consider the ways in which your favourite adventure sport has become more bureaucratized in the last 20 years. Examine the degree to which aspects such as membership, qualifications, competitions, rankings, rules and policies, and levels of office management are part of how it is organized.
2. List some activities that used to be outdoor sports but which can now be done entirely indoors.

■ **Norbert Elias' Figurational Perspective**

Writing in the 1930s, German sociologist Norbert Elias (1978) advocated for a *figurational* or *process* perspective of sociology, which challenged the traditional divide between society and the individual. Elias suggested that people comprise multiple social webs or figurations, which led to the evolution of certain practices and experiences over time. Writing much more recently in 2013, Atkinson suggests that Elias would encourage parkour practitioners (and by extension all adventure sports practitioners) to see themselves as part of an 'historically developing network or web of interdependent actors' that spans across time and is specific to certain geographic spaces (pp. 56–57). As Atkinson puts it, our adventure practices have extensive histories of relationships that shape current practices; they did not 'simply emerge out of the social dust accidentally' (p. 57) and are thus part of a constantly developing network of human interaction.

If we accept that our adventure sports did not magically appear out of nowhere, but instead evolved over decades (if not centuries) of practice, then we should also be willing to accept that they will continue to develop over a long period of time, in terms of their locations, equipment, rules, and so on. For instance, the practice of kayaking existed long before any of us were born (as a means for northern coastal peoples to hunt on the ocean) and will exist long after we are gone, in ways we probably cannot imagine. Kayaking, as an evolving web of social activity, is also supported by (and supports) many diverse practitioners who share a multitude of beliefs and ways of practising; these practitioners constitute, and are constituted by, 'figurations with others at different levels of integration, identification, cooperation and competition' (Connolly & Dolan, 2012, p. 493).

■ **Hegemony**

The third concept that we introduce to explain how activities on the fringe have become socially influential is Gramsci's idea of *hegemony*. There are two kinds of hegemony: the first is through force and the second—far more interesting for a sociologist—is through consent (Gramsci, 1999/1971). Gramsci explained how manufacturing consent from those who oppose the views of the ruling powers can be cleverly done by making those who are marginalized feel like the social and political arrangements imposed on them are in their best interests. This is akin to getting people to consume the opiates supplied by the ruling powers. It is important to note, however, that hegemony is not necessarily about domination through deception; it can be used by leaders to obtain consent for morally good reasons too.

In 1977, sociologist Raymond Williams used Marxist and Gramscian theory to explain how 'emergent cultures' start at society's margins, and often in opposition to the dominant cultures of a given time and place. Over time, however, a particularly well-

2

organized dominant culture trying to maintain its power (for 'good' purposes or not) might deliberately change to become more attractive to these emergent cultures. Tracey (2013) explains how this fluid practice of domination can operate in the world of adventure activities:

>> this pattern starts with an alternative counter-cultural activity that is initially developed by pioneering practitioners. The new form of sports practice then becomes adopted and virtually taken over by commercial interests, who use it as a marketing tool and may promote it to a broader audience as the latest 'craze'. In time, a core of serious exponents emerges, whose spectacular exploits can threaten to undermine the image and status of an associated major sport. The response to this situation is a process of absorption, through which the alternative activity becomes re-invented as a new discipline within the established structures of formal sport. (p. 48)

The concept of hegemony (as it is popularly used) is useful because it helps us understand how those with power manufacture consent from the people they dominate. In a commercial sense, it is now logically accepted by many practitioners that they 'need' to own a helmet-mounted camera or the latest kitesurfing rig, in order to live adventurously. This notion of domination by consent is a fascinating one, as it explains how obscure and emergent adventure sports can be lured, subsumed, and institutionalized by influential social forces.

As a seminal sociological theory, Gramsci's (1971) description of hegemony offered one of the earliest and most enduring explanations of why the widespread revolution of workers that Marx and Engels (1848) predicted never happened: dominant cultures have continually reshaped the social and working arrangements so that opposing emergent cultures never deemed them oppressive enough to completely challenge. In ► Chap. 5, we will revisit the concept of hegemony in order to illustrate corporate influences on adventure practices, lifestyles, and identities.

This current chapter has featured theoretical concepts that range from rationalization to hegemony. A point that must be emphasized is that none of these concepts is better than another; rather, they can each be more or less suited to analysing a given set of social circumstances. These theories have been introduced for a good reason: they can help us make sense of adventure phenomena. For example, keeping in mind that 'actions, values or the attitudes of particular social actors in relation to others' (Connolly & Dolan, 2012, p. 493) continuously shape adventure practices, the figurational perspective help us understand how open canoeing has shifted from being a vessel for transport, fur trading, and colonization, to an activity that is the bastion of summer camp life in southeastern Canada. Equally, Weber's concept of rationalization could be particularly useful for shining an analytical spotlight on how the bungy jumping world strictly calculates and controls each participant's experience. Few organizations and institutions are immune to the forces of bureaucratization, and the world of adventure sports is no exception, despite the common perception that these are often organic, free-flowing, informal activities.

Case Study: The Olympicization of Adventure Sports

In 2020, surfing, skateboarding, and sport climbing will be included in the Summer Olympics. These activities follow BMX and freestyle snowboarding, in what Thorpe and Wheaton (2011) describe as the 'highly complex and contested process' (p. 44) of incorporating adventure sports into Olympic programmes. Competition has always been a component in these activities, but the counter-cultural characteristics, dynamic environments, and creative nature of many adventure sports have historically led participants to resist the rationalization, bureaucracy, and corporate relations associated with competition in mainstream sports.

We can now watch professional surfers riding ten-point waves at World Surf League events live-streamed from Indonesia, see where our favourite surfer sits in the Championship Tour ranking (including how many hundreds of thousands of dollars they have earned in a season), and even play Fantasy Surf League (see ▶ www.worldsurfleague.com). The progression from grassroots, volunteer-run settings, and organizations through various degrees of corporate sponsorship and endorsement to this global fantasy level, which is so far removed from most recreational surfers' experiences, can be explained by concepts, such as rationalization and hegemony, which are outlined in this chapter.

One way of looking at this is that, in order to be considered on the same level, capitalize on popularity, and receive the same funding and media attention as traditional sports, a new kind of officially legitimized surfing— where the aim is to meet the assessment criteria laid out by judges and fit within commercial breaks—has developed. TV companies sign deals to show the competitions, and commentators build up the hype. To facilitate this, a bureaucracy has emerged, where a hierarchy of qualifications, memberships, and governing body rules dictate who may participate and on what terms.

With the variety of surfing forms, surfers can choose to engage with and consume these 'Olympicized' formats, or resist or ignore them by identifying with freer aspects of their sport. In some ways, this can strengthen cultural identification. For example, when *Thrasher* magazine asked professional skateboarders how they felt about skateboarding being included in the Olympic programme, Ishod Wair—who skates in the Nike-sponsored Street League Word Tour—responded, 'It's gonna happen regardless. So many people have their own takes on skateboarding. It's going to bring it to more places around the world and make it bigger. But then if you are into the core skate shit, the Olympics will be irrelevant to you.'

2.5 Adventure as Sites of Social Struggle

Following the above case study, we can see that all adventurers— whether they be kitesurfers, extreme skiers, or high-altitude mountaineers—do not think alike. Further, there are heated debates within these communities regarding regulation, the ethics of certain practices, and relationships with government and corporate bodies.

Using language from French sociologist, Pierre Bourdieu (1989), the places where agents interact and compete with one

2

another can be viewed as 'fields' which can be described as 'structured, social contexts that are comprised of rules and practices that engender particular ways of being and thinking' (Beames & Telford, 2013, p. 82). Sea kayaking, cake baking, salsa dancing, and municipal government politics are all examples of social fields, and will each feature accepted ways of doing things—protocols, habits, rituals, and rules—that form a social order that will in turn influence (almost) everyone in that field (see, e.g. Urquía, 2005).

As we will see, some agents have more influence in these fields than others. It may be that these individuals have especially deep understandings of what Bourdieu (1977) refers to as 'the rules of the game', or the unwritten norms that structure how people behave within particular fields. These understandings can help agents modify their attitudes and actions in a way that improves their position and influence within these social contexts. Telford and Beames (2016) explain that '[p]ositions of power within a field are directly proportionate to the possession of whatever stakes are held by the field to be valuable' (p. 487). Items regarded as valuable might be one's high skill level, financial resources, or fame. Irrespective of what is deemed valuable in a field by a social group—and thus lends power to individuals—Bourdieu (1986) sees them all as forms of 'capital'. The fields that we highlighted above are effectively sites of struggle, where people compete with one other through various forms of capital.

Much of the research surrounding activities such as skateboarding, surfing, and snowboarding has connected Bourdieu's theoretical ideas with the notion of subcultural 'authenticity' (see, e.g. Atencio, Beal, & Wilson, 2009; Beal & Weidman, 2003; Coates, Clayton, & Humberstone, 2010; Wheaton, 2017). It has regularly been found that men are highly represented in these types of cultural fields, and have accordingly accrued various types of social, cultural, and economic benefits in the form of fame and sponsorship, for example.

At the same time, recent work also expands upon this subcultural capital idea, showing that the mass participation in these activities has introduced a wider demographic of stakeholders who are seeking their own forms of capital within these expanding fields. It is thus not simply a matter of a counterculture or subculture activity that opposes the mainstream; the cultural fields in adventure activities make for a very fluid social arena where diverse actors are seeking to participate in ways that are meaningful and beneficial to them. Examining skateboarding, which now increasingly occurs within specially constructed parks that serve as 'Urban Platforms for Capital', Atencio et al. (2018) contend that many newcomer participants, even those formerly considered 'inauthentic' (often females, ethnic minorities, and families), can now shape and even contest the previous social norms that guided this activity. In this way, they can re-work established codes and practices in order to create more favourable conditions that then serve to benefit them as well, and thus gain, in Bourdieu's language, capital.

Chapter Summary

This chapter has covered a lot of theoretical territory. We began with a brief outline of the key concepts of structure and agency. It is probably most accurate to think of social life as many different agents (and groups of agents) interacting with, negotiating their way through, and creating layers of social structures (Hearn, 2012). We then continued by proposing four central features of contemporary social life. These were uncertainty, technology, mobility, and being networked. Uncertainty reflects how our futures are perceived as being less predictable when compared to past generations. This often leads to people obsessing about the risk of something bad happening to them, and thus trying to mitigate risk. The dominance of technology in our lives is matched only by the rapid rate at which it changes, and by human desires to keep up with the times. Whether global mobility is chosen for work or play, or forced upon us by war, it is a defining feature of contemporary human existence. And finally, most people in the developed world are highly connected to each other and their publics through various devices and forms of media. But how do all of these characteristics influence our adventure practices?

In order to understand how these influences operate at a theoretical level, we introduced four major concepts: rationalization, figurations of people, hegemony, and field and capital (two for one!). Rationalization is a broad-reaching term that captures the tendency for organizations to become increasingly focused on calculating the variables that impact them, in order to have greater predictability and efficiency, and also to control their futures. The theory of figurations reminds us that the way we do things now is part of a much wider historical narrative, with a rich and dynamic history, networks of current participants, and a future that is largely unknown. Hegemony—and, in particular, the strand of hegemony that focuses on domination by consent—explains how dominant members of society can make the very social arrangements that give them power over others seem acceptable to all. Finally, Bourdieu's concepts of field and capital were introduced as a means of illustrating how adventure practices can be seen as sites of struggle, within which agents jostle for power and status.

2

As you can imagine, we have really only scratched the surface layer of these social theories, but we hope you will see that they prove their worth over the chapters that follow. Perhaps the greatest gift of these concepts is the exact language they provide, which in turn allows us to have more precise and meaningful discussions about adventure and society's reciprocal influences.

Key Readings

Bauman, Z. (2007). *Liquid times: Living in an age of uncertainty*. Cambridge, UK: Polity Press (Chapter 1: Liquid modern life and its fears).

Beames, S., & Brown, M. (2016). *Adventurous learning: A pedagogy for a changing world*. Abingdon, UK: Routledge (Chapter 3: Socio-cultural backdrop).

References

Atencio, M., Beal, B., & Wilson, C. (2009). The distinction of risk: Urban skateboarding, street habitus and the construction of hierarchical gender relations. *Qualitative Research in Sport and Exercise, 1*(1), 3–20.

Atencio, M., Beal, B., Wright, E. M., & McClain, Z. (2018). *Moving boarders: Skateboarding and the changing landscape of urban youth sports*. Fayetteville, AR: University of Arkansas Press.

Atkinson, M. (2013). The quest for excitement in parkour. In E. Pike & S. Beames (Eds.), *Outdoor adventure and social theory* (pp. 55–65). Abingdon, Oxford: Routledge.

Bauman, Z. (2007). *Liquid times: Living in an age of uncertainty*. Cambridge: Polity.

Beal, B., & Weidman, L. (2003). Authenticity in the skateboarding world. In R. Rinehart & S. Sydnor (Eds.), *To the extreme: Alternative sports inside and out* (pp. 337–352). New York: SUNY Press.

Beames, S., & Brown, M. (2014). Enough of Ronald and Mickey: Focusing on learning in outdoor education. *Journal of Adventure Education and Outdoor Learning, 14*(2), 118–131.

Beames, S., & Brown, M. (2017). Disneyization and the provision of leisure experiences. In K. Spracklen, B. Lashua, E. Sharpe, & S. Swain (Eds.), *Palgrave handbook of leisure theory* (pp. 855–871). London: Palgrave MacMillan.

Beames, S., & Telford, J. (2013). Pierre Bourdieu: Habitus, field, and capital in rock climbing. In E. Pike & S. Beames (Eds.), *Outdoor adventure and social theory* (pp. 77–87). London: Routledge.

Beames, S., & Varley, P. (2013). Eat, play, shop: The disneyization of adventure. In S. Taylor, P. Varley, & T. Johnston (Eds.), *Adventure tourism: Meanings, experience and learning* (pp. 77–84). Abingdon, UK: Routledge.

Beck, U. (1992). *Risk society: Towards a new modernity*. London: Sage.

Bourdieu, P. (1977). *Outline of a theory of practice*. Cambridge: Cambridge University Press.

Bourdieu, P. (1986). The forms of capital. In J. Richardson (Ed.), *Handbook of theory of research for the sociology of education* (pp. 241–258). Westport, CT: Greenwood Press.

Bourdieu, P. (1989). Social space and symbolic power. *Sociological Theory, 7*(1), 14–25.

Boyd, D. (2014). *It's complicated: The social lives of networked teens*. New Haven, CT: Yale University Press.

Castells, M. (2000). *The rise of the network society* (2nd ed.). Oxford: Blackwell.

Coates, E., Clayton, B., & Humberstone, B. (2010). A battle for control: Exchanges of power in the subculture of snowboarding. *Sport and Society, 13*(7), 1082–1101.

Connolly, J., & Dolan, P. (2012). Re-theorizing the 'structure-agency' relationship: Figurational theory, organizational change and the Gaelic Athletic Association. *Organization: The Interdisciplinary Journal of Organization, Theory and Society, 20*(4), 491–511.

Elias, N. (1978). *The civilizing process*. Oxford: Basil Blackwell.

Elliot, A., & Urry, J. (2010). *Mobile lives*. Abingdon, UK: Routledge.

Furedi, F. (1997). *The culture of fear: Risk taking and the morality of low expectations*. London: Cassell.

Giddens, A. (1991). *Modernity and self identity*. Cambridge: Polity Press.

Gilman, P., & Gilman, L. (2001). *The wildest dream: Mallory – His life and conflicting passions*. London: Headline.

Gramsci, A. (1999/1971). *Selections from the prison notebooks of Antonio Gramsci* (trans: Q. Hoare and G.N. Smith (Eds.)). London: Elecbook.

Hearn, J. (2012). *Theorizing power*. Basingstoke, UK: Palgrave MacMillan.

Isserman, M., & Weaver, S. (2008). *Fallen giants: A history of Himalayan mountaineering from the age of the empire to the age of extremes*. London: Yale University Press.

Loynes, C. (1998). Adventure in a bun. *The Journal of Experimental Education, 21*(1), 35–39.

Lupton, D. (2013). *Risk* (2nd ed.). London: Routledge.

Lyotard, J. F. (1984). *The postmodern condition: A report on knowledge*. Manchester, UK: Manchester University Press. (French original version 1979).

Macdonald, D., Kirk, D., Metzler, M., Nilges, L. M., Schempp, P., & Wright, J. (2002). It's all very well, in theory: Theoretical perspectives and their applications in contemporary pedagogical research. *Quest, 54*(2), 133–156.

Marx, K., & Engels, F. (1848). Manifesto of the Communist Party.

McCrindle, M. (2014). *The ABC of XYZ*. Bellavista, Australia: McCrindle Research.

Ritzer, G. (1993). *The McDonaldization of society: An investigation into the changing character of contemporary social life*. London: Pine Forge Press.

Ryall, E. (2013). Conceptual problems with performance enhancing technology in sport. *Royal Institute of Philosophy Supplement, 73*, 129–143.

Telford, J., & Beames, S. (2016). Bourdieu and alpine mountaineering: The distinction of high peaks, clean lines and pure style. In B. Humberstone, H. Prince, & K. Henderson (Eds.), *Routledge international handbook of outdoor studies* (pp. 482–490). Abingdon, UK: Routledge.

Thorpe, H. (2014). *Transnational mobilities in action sport cultures (Migration, diasporas and citizenship)*. London: Palgrave Macmillan.

Thorpe, H., & Wheaton, B. (2011). 'Generation X Games', action sports and the Olympic Movement: Understanding the cultural politics of incorporation. *Sociology, 45*(5), 830–847.

Tracey, J. (2013). Antonio Gramsci: Freestyle kayaking, hegemony, coercion, and consent. In E. Pike & S. Beames (Eds.), *Outdoor adventure and social theory* (pp. 45–54). Abingdon, UK: Routledge.

United Nations Committee on Human Rights. (2017). *Global trends: Forced displacement in 2016*. Geneva, Switzerland: UNHCR.

Urquía, N. (2005). The re-branding of salsa in London's dance clubs: How an ethnicised form of cultural capital was institutionalised. *Leisure Studies, 24*(4), 385–397.

Van Bottenburg, M., & Salome, L. (2010). The indoorisation of outdoor sports: An exploration of the rise of lifestyle sports in artificial settings. *Leisure Studies, 29*(2), 143–160.

Varley, P. (2013). Rationalization and new realms of the commodity form. In E. Pike & S. Beames (Eds.), *Outdoor adventure and social theory* (pp. 34–42). Abingdon, UK: Routledge.

2

Weber, M. (1922/1968). In G. Roth & C. Wittich (Eds.), *Economy and society: An outline of interpretive sociology*. Los Angeles: University of California Press.

Wheaton, B. (2017). Subcultural formation and lifestyle sporting practices. In M. Silk, D. Andrew, & H. Thorpe (Eds.), *Routledge handbook of physical cultural studies* (pp. 102–110). London: Routledge.

Williams, R. (1977). *Marxism and literature*. Oxford: Open University Press.

Wright, J. (2004). Critical inquiry and problem-solving in physical education). In J. Wright, D. Macdonald, & L. Burrows (Eds.), *Critical inquiry and problem-solving in physical education* (pp. 19–31). London: Routledge.

Daily Adventure Practices

© The Author(s) 2019
S. Beames et al., *Adventure and Society*, https://doi.org/10.1007/978-3-319-96062-3_3

3

Chapter Aims

After reading this chapter, you will be able to:

- Understand how adventure activities are part of people's daily lives and social interactions
- Characterize a range of key motivators which lead people to undertake daily adventures
- Understand that daily adventures are complex and diverse activities that go beyond simplistic extreme sports stereotypes
- Begin to see how daily adventure practices link with identity formation and one's sense of self

3.1 My Daily Buzz

It is not uncommon for people to go for a quick spin on their mountain bike or go kayaking in their favourite hole on their way home from work. Indeed, riding skateboards after school or work over diverse urban terrain while attempting complex manoeuvres or getting in the surf for an invigorating session in the water before heading to the office are examples of how adventure is increasingly becoming woven into the everyday fabric of people's lives. But, as Stephen Poulson (2016) asks in the title of his book on mountain bikers and triathletes, *Why would anyone do that*?

This chapter consequently delves into why individuals might choose to regularly incorporate this type of adventure into their worlds. Poulson (2016) describes how mountain bikers and triathletes used these adventure activities to keep their sanity, so to speak, in relation to regular jobs and life responsibilities. Where banal patterns in people's daily lives become entrenched and routine, adventure activities can thus be viewed as an antidote to established patterns and predictability (see Elias & Dunning, 1986). This brings us back to the idea highlighted by New Zealanders Lynch and Moore (2004) that '[t]he popularity of adventure recreation and adventure education has arisen, in part, from an assumption that adventure experiences are radically different from those of everyday life in modern societies' (p. 3).

When contemplating what seems to be missing from contemporary living, it has been suggested by many current scholars that the notion of risk-taking is critical to many of these daily adventure activities (e.g. Atencio, Beal, & Wilson, 2009; Thorpe, 2004). Brymer and Oades (2009), in their study of such pursuits as BASE (building, antenna, span, earth) jumping, waterfall kayaking, and solo rope-free climbing, tell us how '[t]ypically, participation is considered to be about crazy people taking unnecessary risks, having "no fear" or holding onto a death wish – why else would someone willingly undertake a leisure activity where death is a real potential?' (p. 114).

Thus, while it might be said that all leisure and recreational practices offer chances to engage in non-traditional life practices, it could also perhaps be argued that adventure episodes, even much less extreme ones than those described by Brymer and Oades, feature some of the unpredictability, daring, and risk-taking that are not demanded in other parts of people's lives. Of course, it could also be the case that daily adventurers do not seek *too much* uncertainty—just a measure more than they have in their ordinary day-to-day pattern of existence. Our discussion in this chapter focuses on those daily practices that are more like hobbies and where riding the fine line between life and death is not a participant's primary objective. (We discuss notions of risk more deeply in ▶ Chap. 4.)

There is a danger in simply viewing daily adventure in terms of individuals just searching for 'something else' and navigating higher states of unpredictability and risk-taking in order to obtain the personal kudos that may result from their 'collection of achievements' (Shoham, Rose, & Kahle, 2000, p. 248). In this chapter, we demonstrate through both theoretical concepts and practical examples how daily adventure practices reflect participants' multi-faceted experiences, interests, and motivations. There are numerous reasons why people come to participate in adventure on a daily basis.

In this discussion of daily adventure and its regular practitioners, we also explain how, to varying degrees, being an adventurer often involves belonging to a social community or 'tribe', as Maffesoli (1996) has described temporal collectives of people who ascribe to a certain shared lifestyle and mindset. These groups may gather online or in person. Together, these ideas regarding daily adventuring, and the fundamental social relationships that underpin these regular activities, are examined further in this book's chapter on identity formation (▶ Chap. 8).

Finally, it is important to contemplate how *all* participants, both experienced and newer ones, come to engage with a range of adventure activities. While many scholars have addressed core or established participants, Lori Holyfield (1999) indeed reminds us that many novice adventurers, too, have become attracted to activities such as white-water rafting, for social, emotional, and psychological reasons. We now explain several key concepts within adventure research that pertain to the reasons why participants embark upon adventures in the first place.

3.2 The Need to Escape and Be Free

Brymer and Schweitzer (2013) reinforce the belief that participants in adventure activities are searching for new and exciting experiences that allow them to escape and feel unrestrained from the everyday work, school, and social schedules typified by modern living in Western societies. This means that adventure is often envisioned as taking a person away from the typical routines and constraints found in ordinary life, as 'a way of freeing themselves' (p. 220).

The surfing mums group in New Zealand, that features in Spowart, Burrows, and Shaw's (2010) paper, explains how surfing was not only regarded by participants as a source of fun or pleasure, 'but rather as a way of living' (p. 1192) that diverged from expected parenting roles and responsibilities held within mainstream society. Roy (2014) provides another surfing example, suggesting that for its practitioners, 'surfing instigates feelings of freedom' (p. 48). She goes on to tie this idea of freedom specifically with the experience of *stoke*. Stoke experiences, according to Wheaton (2013), refer to being lost or consumed in the thrill or buzz of the moment, and are discussed next.

Roy's (2014) paper offers an illustrative conversation from her research data where one surfer is asked, 'Why do you surf?' This surfer eventually responds,

» You can't put your finger on it, it's called the stoke isn't it?
   That's what they call it. There is no other word. The one thing
   that actually makes you think. Like, on a good day, there's literally, nothing else better, in life. (p. 41)

This type of embodied yet indescribable thrill experience, of being stoked, was also recounted to us by professional soccer player turned surfer, John O'Brien. He explained that 'the thrill of riding a wave' and 'the alternative culture – where all that matters is getting a good wave and feeling stoked' were vital aspects of his surfing adventures (personal communication with Matthew Atencio, October 14, 2017).

Moreover, Della Fave, Bassi, and Massimini (2003) highlight how what has been deemed *flow* can be achieved through rock climbing participation. They focus upon 'the quality of the experience' (p. 83), which refers to the body of flow work from Csikszentmihalyi (1990, 1996). In this flow framework, optimal experience is achieved through the combination of challenge, opportunities for action, as well as high states of personal attention, well-being, and control – all of which lead to personal satisfaction and a sense of reward. States of flow are common in athletes, in particular, who find themselves 'in the zone', where they feel as though they can do no wrong. Typically, one loses the flow when the challenge is too low or too high in relation to the individual's skill level (Nakamura & Csikszentmihalyi, 2002). It is easy to see how kite surfers to solo climbers to free skiers see their chosen craft as rich sites for seeking flow states. Della Fave et al. (2003) explain how, as their abilities increase, athletes will 'search for higher challenges to be faced with more refined skills' (p. 83).

These ideas about the stoke and flow mental states achieved through adventuring have also been examined by John Kerr and Susan Houge Mackenzie (2012), who collected data about various adventure participants and their experiences. One of their research subjects, a river surfer named Jody, told them that it's '[o]ne of the best feelings in the world! It's just adrenaline. You're just stoked' (p. 652). Jody further explained that there was an accompanying 'sense of achievement' obtained by envisioning a goal and achieving it through skill mastery:

>> It's the adrenaline, but it's also everything else leading up to it which enabled you to be able to do it properly, like the skills that you have or the hard work that you've done . . .

Therefore, the notion of achievement and being capable skill-wise was crucial to her sense of adrenaline pumping and being stoked and is closely related to what other researchers in the field of adventure have called *efficacy*, which stems from Bandura's seminal work on self-efficacy in 1977. Indeed, this idea has been described by Shoham et al. (2000) as acquiring and mastering skills during the frequent practice of adventurous activities. They suggest that 'the need for efficacy is a motive for continuous involvement' (p. 239). Kerr and Houge Mackenzie (2012) thus conclude that 'Jody experienced a strong emotional reward in the form of excitement when, for example, she successfully negotiated rock hazards and rapids at high speed while riversurfing downstream' (p. 652).

Within this discussion on deeply personal states such as stoke and flow occurring during adventure activities, it is important to emphasize the distinction between an emotional buzz (which could come from a commercially operated bungy jump) and flow, which is a product of a very careful balance between challenge and skill. Nakamura and Csikszentmihalyi (2002) clearly explain this idea of flow in their own words:

>> The flow state is intrinsically rewarding and leads the individual to seek to replicate flow experiences; this introduces a selective mechanism into psychological functioning that fosters growth. As people master challenges in an activity, they develop greater levels of skill, and the activity ceases to be as involving as before. In order to continue experiencing flow, they must identify and engage progressively more complex challenges ... A flow activity not only provides a set of challenges or opportunities for action but it typically also provides a system of graded challenges, able to accommodate a person's continued and deepening enjoyment as skills grow. (p. 92)

We can see how, in regard to flow, more practice leads to higher levels of performance, which can lead to more enjoyment, and so on. This can be seen as a kind of positive feedback loop, 'where

3

challenge and mastery lead to the seeking of further challenges and the development of more complex skills' (Beames & Brown, 2016, p. 96).

When these ideas of stoke and flow are both taken into consideration, we can see why adventure participants, both veterans and newcomers, may be compelled to gravitate towards these kinds of activities. Indeed, regular adventure practice is associated with experiencing desirable emotional states resulting from performing at a level of skill that aligns with the challenges presented. In this regard, Lori Holyfield's study of white-water rafting (1999) also reminds us that novices and veterans may approach and experience adventure phenomena in unique ways, because their skill levels are so differentiated. Thus, for example, 'the very activities that an experienced risk taker might disdain, become, for the novice, the essential ingredients for adventure' (p. 27).

3.3 Spirituality and Nature

More recently, scholars have examined the ways in which spirituality plays a role in adventure practices, particularly as these often take place in natural, outdoor environments. Brymer and Oades (2009) contend that spiritual experiences are found in adventure participation, which also engenders individuals with a profound sense of personal transformation. Marsh (2008) conducted a study of 63 backcountry skiers, telemarkers, and snowboarders, in order to address the research question: What do people mean when they describe backcountry adventure experiences as being spiritual? Marsh found that, overwhelmingly, nature and the backcountry setting were crucial to those participants having a spiritual experience. Taylor (2007) also examines this type of spirit-nature idea, and highlights how '[f]or some, surfing is a religious experience, and it does not take long analyzing material surf culture or its associated rhetoric to see its spirituality-infused nature' (p. 924). Furthermore, for Taylor, there is a close link between the notion of spirituality and that of being immersed in, and respectful of, nature.

Taylor (2007) goes on to suggest that surfing provides a 'sense of belonging to nature' and has inspired 'environmentalist values and action among some surfers' (p. 937). This idea of spirituality and respect for nature being integrally linked has been furthered by Brymer, Downey, and Gray (2009), who have challenged interpretations of adventure sports as being simply 'battles against nature' (p. 200), as these experiences have been typically characterized. They thus challenge the popular idea that seeking adrenaline has driven these adventurers 'to conquer, compete against or defeat natural forces' (p. 193). Brymer et al. consequently suggest that adventure activities can foster deep, caring relationships between people and the natural. This type of connection, they argue, can overcome our current estrangement from nature, and eventually engender important transformations of the self.

Likewise, in what could be seen as a more Scandinavian perspective, where 'nature is home' and something that nurtures us (see Henderson & Vikander, 2005), there are strong numbers of adventurers who seek what Shoham et al. (2000) call a 'communion with nature' (p. 240). The word *friluftsliv* is literally translated as 'free air life', and was explained by the Norwegian eco-philosopher, Arne Naess, as being necessary to counteract 'the ills of an increasingly industrialized society' (Pedersen Gurholt, 2014, p. 233). For Scandinavians and Finns, outdoor pursuits with friends and family may 'be based on simple natural pastimes involving the harvesting of local resources, such as berries, fish and game, and/or pleasurable hiking in nearby environments' (p. 239). While this motivation for participation lies in stark contrast to those who regard nature as some kind of objectified sparring partner, Kirsti Pederson Gurholt (2008) has highlighted that these traditional understandings of *friluftsliv* are historically rooted in gendered and nationalistic assumptions that exclude women's experiences of outdoor living and do not reflect the heterogeneity of contemporary Nordic society.

This profound personal connection to the natural element of adventure practices can be illustrated by two actual adventurers. In discussion with Matthew Atencio in 2017, sailor Duke Austin described how he had 'always loved being in the outdoors, connecting with the environment in a more natural state'. He added that 'Being on the water is similar for me. The cities are crowded with people and concrete, but the ocean feels open, wild, and untamed'. Another conversation that Atencio had with surfer John O'Brien in 2017 revealed how 'being connected with nature, the feel of the water, paying attention to tides and winds' were crucial elements of this person's meaningful surf adventures. We can therefore see that adventurers like these closely connect to their 'natural' environments, as this experience can provide deep emotions, an aesthetic sensibility, and a feeling of authentic experience (Holyfield, 1999, p. 4).

Looking ahead, beyond motivations for adventuring such as achieving states of stoke or flow, or even connecting to nature, adventurers are also drawn to the feelings of belongingness that come from being part of a like-minded community.

❓ Discussion Questions

1. Make a list of the different types of adventure activities that you have tried, or some that are popular in your community.
2. How might participation in each of these activities mirror the key concepts of flow, stoke, and spirituality in nature?

3.4 Social Relationships and a Sense of Community

Although the stereotype of a lone adventurer in the wild is a popular one, adventure activities are undoubtedly social in nature. Being part of a group is an important motivator for many adventure practitioners. Wheaton (2013) even tells us that, within different adventure activities, whether based in the street, mountain, or water, participation is marked by the need for a group identity. Furthermore, this group identity is maintained 'by a range of symbolic markers, extending from the specialist equipment used and clothing worn, to musical taste and the vehicles driven (such as the long-term status of the VW kombi van in surf culture)' (p. 32). This idea of group identity connects with our discussion of Bourdieu's theory in ▶ Chap. 2, whereby people's 'authentic' participation in adventure-specific cultural 'fields' may lead to certain benefits. In a similar vein, Shoham et al. (2000) have highlighted the intriguing concept of *communitas* as being especially important to adventure practitioners; this concept represents a sense of meaningful camaraderie that exists during these adventure activities. These scholars suggest in the following extended statement that:

» Communitas develops when shared experiences transcend the drudgery of everyday life and provide shared rituals or extraordinary experiences. Group members recognize the irrelevancy of external roles and develop expertise and specialized roles within the community, maintaining the separation between the everyday world and the extraordinary risky sport experience. (p. 239)

This type of communal experience has been found with many adults undertaking activities such as mountain biking, as Kerr and Houge Mackenzie (2012) once found in their study, when describing one particular practitioner named Sarah. They contend that, for Sarah, 'there was also a social side to her participation' which motivated her to take part in the activity. She eventually characterized her motivation to participate in these terms:

» The people I meet. The lifestyle – opportunities to travel to new and different places. I quite like travelling now. It's a really cool crowd that you hang around with. My friends are racers from all around the world. (p. 653)

For many young people, the social aspects of their participation in adventure activities are as important as the bodily experience of the activity itself. It follows that many adventure activities, especially those that are inherently youth-centric and socially connective, such as skateboarding, surfing, snowboarding, and parkour, have gained more cultural relevance than ever before.

While some of these social activities, especially skateboarding, were formerly associated with counter-cultural and even perhaps outlaw youth constituents, it is clear that these activities profoundly shape many young people's lives in unprecedented ways. Statistics from the United States, for instance, point to the daily aspect of youths' skateboarding participation. From a survey sample of 15,770 individual and 26,593 household surveys, it was found that, for children between the ages of 6 and 17, skateboarding was considered their third most favourite outdoor activity by frequency, behind only running/jogging and riding bikes. Skateboarders in the US averaged 58 outings per year for a total of 220 million outings nationally (Outdoor Foundation, 2013).

The everyday popularity of youths' adventure activities like skateboarding highlights the vital nature of their social relationships. For instance, Atencio, Beal, Wright, and McClain (2018) have found that several skateboarding locations in the San Francisco Bay Area provided opportunities for youth to make meaningful, trusting relationships that ultimately led to social capital generation.[1] The authors suggest that, when left to their own devices, the young skateboarders were able to create friendships with diverse others and help each other while a sense of camaraderie was fostered. In one skate park scene that was described, from San Jose, California, the authors found that several youths spoke about social bonds and mutual support that emerged through their everyday rides. For instance, one youth skater here felt that this particular skate park was the best place in the world, because lots of people went there to hang out and they knew each other. He also mentioned that this San Jose skate spot was cool and relaxed as well as motivating because youths would assist each other by giving advice when it came to trying out new tricks.

Furthermore, groups of people with similar interests, who are engaged in tasks (of any kind) in each other's company, can be said to be part of what Lave and Wenger (1991) called 'communities of practice'. We can see how those who gather at the BMX park are all ultimately there for similar reasons (e.g. the stoke, pleasure, communion with nature) and this binds them together to varying degrees. McMillan and Chavis' (1986) seminal paper on defining what elicits a sense of community cites *membership, influence, integration and fulfilment of needs*, and *shared emotional connection* as

---

1   According to Beames and Atencio (2008), outdoor adventure activities can provide substantial social capital to participants. This means that these activities generate social relationships that are marked by elements of trust, reciprocity, and volunteerism.

four key features. Membership refers to feelings of belonging; influence is about feeling that individuals matter to the group (and vice versa); integration and fulfilment of needs covers having one's personal needs being through group membership; and shared emotional connection encapsulates 'the commitment and belief that members have shared and will share history, common places, time together, and similar experiences' (p. 9).

It is not difficult to see how groups of people engaged in the same activity would feel part of a community. McMillan and Chavis' four-pronged conceptual framework can be a helpful way of examining the adventure communities of which we are a part.

❓ Discussion Question

Using McMillan and Chavis' four concepts consider one of the communities of practice in which you are involved. Score your chosen community out of ten for each of membership, influence, integration, and fulfilment of needs, and shared emotional connection. (ten being high levels).

N.B. Your community does not have to be adventure-related. It could be a sports team, religious group, or club of some sort.

Next, we provide a case study which illustrates how one adventure practitioner, Paul Carpenter, exemplifies several key concepts raised above. Paul currently rides to work and back home each day while taking part in several California Triple Crown cycling events that exceed 200 miles. In the past, he would ride a few 12-hour events per year as well as a few 24-hour events, while occasionally taking part in major races that involved riding across the entire United States or its West Coast.[2]

Paul Carpenter's case study speaks to several of the key concepts discussed throughout this chapter. First, it demonstrates how gaining a sense of achievement, related to one's unique abilities to overcome great adversity, is of central importance to regular adventure practice. Paul's daily rides to work and home can be tiring, and certainly his long-distance rides demand the best of his mental and physical capacities. This story also illustrates how social connection is important to adventure practice. While Paul does his daily work rides alone, he greatly enjoys the camaraderie that comes from being an integral part of several riding groups and organizations. Further, Paul appreciates that rides allow him to be immersed in nature, with many of his rides being conducted in wild and natural areas found across the United States, at all times of the day and night.

---

2   These races are known as Race Across the West (RAW) and Race Across America (RAAM); the latter is branded as the world's most difficult bicycle race.

Case Study

Paul Carpenter described how local and long-distance rides offer immense personal challenge to him, while also providing him with feelings of camaraderie and social contribution. Paul has been an active leader in his various social networks, including one ultra-cycling association. He also appreciates being immersed in nature during his rides.

'My cycling is a daily event. In any given year I'll ride over 300 days and ride 20,000+ miles. Much is commuting miles, although my commutes can take the indirect route to work and back so can range from 12 miles to 100+ miles.'

'During my peak involvement I'd do several 12-hour events each year, 2 or 3 24-hour events, one 500 mile race and perhaps one 500 mile + race.'

'Part of the motivation is testing my physical and mental limits. How far/hard can I push myself? There is a sense of self-reliance and certainly a great deal of satisfaction from achieving something that few people can contemplate let alone do.'

'There is also a social element in that the group of people doing these events is small and I know many riders personally ... For many races I will carpool with other riders and there is a sense of the joy of a "road trip".'
(Personal correspondence with M. Atencio, October 4, 2017)

Chapter Summary

In this chapter, we have drawn on work from a range of social science contexts to demonstrate how, for both new and experienced daily adventure practitioners, there are several key motivating features of their practice. For some, there is a sense of escape from their daily lives, where they experience feelings of freedom from the schedules, demands, and fast pace of contemporary life. We then explained how the experience of stoke, as well as the state of flow, can be important to adventure practitioners. Stoke refers to having a buzz in the moment; the concept of flow also implies being lost in the moment, but under deep focus and with immediate feedback and goal achievement taking place. Importantly, these adventure activities can be accompanied by feelings of self-efficacy from the challenges successfully negotiated by the performer's particular skill, knowledge base, and judgement. For the adventure practitioner, then, there is normally a sense of working towards a goal, and developing skill, knowledge, and judgement on the path to that end.

Connecting with nature, in perhaps spiritual or authentic ways, was also another identified factor that can impact upon daily adventure practices. For some, the peace, solitude, and more direct connection with the natural world or a higher plane of existence is an enormous pull to the trails, rivers, crags, and couloirs (and we discuss more of these motivations in the following chapter on risk). Finally, we suggested that some adventure practices have become attractive because of their highly communal attributes, for both adult and youth participants found within diverse activities ranging from skateboarding to ultra-cycling.

3

Key Reading

Spowart, L., Burrows, L., & Shaw, S. (2010). 'I just eat, sleep and dream of surfing': When surfing meets motherhood. *Sport in Society, 13*(7–8), 1186–1203.

References

Atencio, M., Beal, B., & Wilson, C. (2009). The distinction of risk: Urban skateboarding, street habitus and the construction of hierarchical gender relations. *Qualitative Research in Sport and Exercise, 1*(1), 3–20.

Atencio, M., Beal, B., Wright, E. M., & McClain, Z. (2018). *Moving boarders: Skateboarding and the changing landscape of urban youth sports.* Fayetteville, AR: University of Arkansas Press.

Bandura, A. (1977). Self-efficacy: Toward a unifying theory of behavioral change. *Psychological Review, 84*(2), 191–215.

Beames, S., & Atencio, M. (2008). Building social capital through outdoor education. *Journal of Adventure Education and Outdoor Learning, 8*(2), 99–112.

Beames, S., & Brown, M. (2016). *Adventurous learning: A pedagogy for a changing world.* New York/London: Routledge.

Brymer, E., Downey, G., & Gray, T. (2009). Extreme sports as a precursor to environmental sustainability. *Journal of Sport & Tourism, 14*(2–3), 193–204.

Brymer, E., & Oades, L. (2009). Extreme sports: A positive transformation in courage and humility. *Journal of Humanistic Psychology, 49*, 114–126.

Brymer, E., & Schweitzer, R. (2013). The search for freedom in extreme sports: A phenomenological exploration. *Psychology of Sport and Exercise, 14*(6), 865–873.

Csikszentmihalyi, M. (1990). *Flow.* New York: Harper and Row.

Csikszentmihalyi, M. (1996). *Creativity: Flow and the psychology of discovery and invention.* New York: Harper Collins.

Della Fave, A., Bassi, M., & Massimini, F. (2003). Quality of experience and risk perception in high-altitude rock climbing. *Journal of Applied Sport Psychology, 15*(1), 82–98.

Elias, N., & Dunning, E. (1986). *Quest for excitement: Sport and leisure in the civilizing process.* Oxford, United Kingdom: Basil Blackwell.

Henderson, B., & Vikander, N. (2005). *Every trail has a story: Heritage travel in Canada.* Toronto, Canada: Natural Heritage/Natural History.

Holyfield, L. (1999). Manufacturing adventure: The buying and selling of emotions. *Journal of Contemporary Ethnography, 28*(1), 3–32.

Gurholt KP. Joy of nature, friluftsliv education and self: combining narrative and cultural–ecological approaches to environmental sustainability. J Adventure Educ Outdoor Learn. 2014;14(3):233–46.

Gurholt KP. Norwegian Friluftsliv and ideals of becoming an 'educated man'. J Adventure Educ Outdoor Learn. 2008;8(1):55–70.

Kerr, J., & Houge Mackenzie, S. (2012). Multiple motives for participating in adventure sports. *Psychology of Sport and Exercise, 13*, 649–657.

Lave, J., & Wenger, E. (1991). *Situated learning: Legitimate peripheral participation.* Cambridge, UK: Cambridge University Press.

Lynch, P., & Moore, K. (2004). Adventures in paradox. *Australian Journal of Outdoor Education, 8*(2), 3–12.

Maffesoli, M. (1996). *The time of the tribes: The decline of individualism in mass society.* London: Sage.

Marsh, P. (2008). Backcountry adventure as spiritual development: A means-end study. *The Journal of Experimental Education, 30*(3), 290–293.

McMillan, D., & Chavis, D. (1986). Sense of community: A definition and theory. *Journal of Community Psychology, 14*, 6–23.

Nakamura, J., & Csikszentmihalyi, M. (2002). The concept of flow. In C. Snyder & S. Lopez (Eds.), *Handbook of positive psychology* (pp. 89–105). New York: Oxford University Press.

Outdoor Foundation. (2013). Outdoor participation report 2013. *Outdoor Foundation, 37*. Retrieved from http://www.outdoorfoundation.org/pdf/ResearchParticipation2013.pdf

Pedersen Gurholt, K. (2008). Norwegian friluftsliv and ideals of becoming an 'educated man'. *Journal of Adventure Education & Outdoor Learning, 8*(1), 55–70.

Poulson, S. (2016). *Why would anyone do that?: Lifestyle sport in the twenty-first century*. New Brunswick, NJ: Rutgers University Press.

Roy, G. (2014). Taking emotions seriously: Feeling female and becoming-surfer through UK surf space. *Emotion, Space and Society, 12*, 41–48.

Shoham, A., Rose, G., & Kahle, L. (2000). Practitioners of risky sports: A quantitative examination. *Journal of Business Research, 47*, 237–251.

Spowart, L., Burrows, L., & Shaw, S. (2010). I just eat, sleep and dream of surfing': When surfing meets motherhood. *Sport in Society, 13*(7–8), 1186–1203.

Taylor, B. (2007). Surfing into spirituality and a new, aquatic nature religion. *Journal of the American Academy of Religion, 75*(4), 923–951.

Thorpe, H. (2004). Embodied boarders: Snowboarding, status and style. *Waikato Journal of Education, 10*, 181–201.

Wheaton, B. (2013). *The cultural politics of lifestyle sports*. Abingdon, UK: Routledge.

Adventure and Risk

© The Author(s) 2019
S. Beames et al., *Adventure and Society*, https://doi.org/10.1007/978-3-319-96062-3_4

4

Chapter Aims

After reading this chapter, you will be able to:

— Define the terms *risk* and *hazard*
— Understand how the term *risk* has evolved over time
— Understand ten factors that are behind most people's motivations for participating in adventure practices
— Explain why extreme adventurers do not generally regard themselves as risk-takers
— Explain how playing 'close to the edge' may bring more recognition within adventure subcultures
— Understand the problems associated with providing adventure activities perceived as risky to groups with varying backgrounds and needs

One January day in Edinburgh, 2018, we witnessed a teenaged boy 'pulling a wheelie' on an old commuter-type bicycle. What was extraordinary was how the rider's skills allowed him to travel close to 100 metres on his rear wheel alone and—astonishingly—across several lanes of traffic. What fascinates many of us is why a person would deliberately choose to put him or herself at risk in this manner. We could change the example from riding a bicycle in a low-income part of the city to freeriding down a couloir in the Alps on a snowboard, but the question remains the same.

4.1   Risk: Definitions and Historical References

Historically, adventure and risk have been seen by many people as closely associated—both in theoretical discussions and everyday society. We have already shown that adventure is a concept which is culturally constructed and relative: it means different things to different people, depending on their experiences. In this chapter we begin with an examination of the meaning of the word 'risk' and how sociologists have described its prominence in contemporary society. We then explore the question asked by so many journalists of so many adventurers: 'Why do you do it?' There are several answers to this question—all of which are fascinating. Indeed, why would anyone want to deliberately increase the likelihood of him or herself being harmed?!

As the chapter progresses, we show how, although risk can be objectively calculated to some degree, in terms of the likelihood and consequence of something happening, it is highly subjective and often socially mediated. We then outline different perspectives that have been used to understand the role that risk plays in voluntary adventurous activities, and which characterize risk in very contrasting ways. Some writers have stated that risk and adventure are inseparable, while other researchers position risk as something which people consciously seek out to feel alive, or, increasingly, for skilled performers, as a minor component within a complex system of experiences and motivations.

Before we go any further, we need to distinguish between two terms: *hazard* and *risk*. This will enable us to have a more precise discussion. A *hazard* is something that can harm us, whereas *risk* refers to the likelihood and severity of being harmed by the hazard. So, if we were considering swimming across a river full of alligators, the alligators are not the risk: they are the hazard. Before taking the plunge, we will need to assess the likelihood of being attacked by an alligator (based on our prior experiences and skill) and, if we did get attacked, how severe this might be. Seen this way, risk is two-pronged.

In historical terms, the very idea of risk is a relatively recent concept. People in the middle ages did not obsess about risk. Indeed, if bad things happened (due to a natural disaster), they were accepted as acts of god. Prayer and ritual were the principal means of trying to avoid being the recipient of bad luck (Lupton, 2013). Lupton explains how it was in merchant shipping where notions of risk came to the fore, as companies began to buy insurance in case the valuable contents of their trading ships were lost at sea. Even at this point, however, ideas of blame and human error were not part of the discussion. It was during the industrial revolution, which gathered steam in the early 1800s, that humans sought to comprehensively assess levels of risk through what Reddy (1996) termed, the 'myth of calculability' (p. 237). For Reddy, this notion of control over a 'radically indeterminate cosmos' was (and is) a myth, because human lives, and the enterprises in which they are engaged, are so complex that it is impossible to fully identify all of the hazards one might encounter and then mitigate against being harmed by them.

At a most fundamental level, none of us live hazard-free lives (Martínková & Parry, 2017). Even if you wanted to be super-safe and decided to stay in bed, drink kale smoothies, and watch Netflix all day for the foreseeable future, there would always be the possibility that your apartment might catch fire, that an earthquake could take place, or (if you did this for years on end) that you might suffer in the long term from some kind of physical or emotional problem that arose from never leaving your room.

If we accept that it is impossible to live a life that is free from being exposed to hazards, then we can see how, through our daily lives, we are constantly making small decisions about the likelihood and severity of being harmed by all kinds of banal things, such as the rain that has made the moss on the sidewalk slippery, the hot sun that could burn your skin, your creepy neighbour who you might bump into on your way out, or the car that you will get into to drive to work. By the time we are adults, most of us are making countless decisions every day—all of which have to do with reducing the risk of being harmed. Furthermore, we are not usually even aware that we are going through these continuous cycles of risk assessment.

For almost 30 years, sociologists like Ulrich Beck and Anthony Giddens have posited that contemporary society is obsessed with notions of risk and taking increasing care to minimize the possibility of being harmed physically and emotionally, or of losing something valuable. The title of Beck's (1992) book was *Risk Society* and Giddens (1991) argued that we live in a 'risk culture'. Writers like Frank Furedi (1997) continued this line of scholarship and claimed that we live in a 'culture of fear', where many of us in the Global North spend a disproportionate amount of time and energy worrying about negative things happening to us and our loved ones, despite statistics showing that most of us are living much healthier, cleaner, and crime-free lives than before: '"Be careful" dominates our imagination' (Furedi, 1997, p. viii).

It is generally accepted that, since the turn of the millennium, life has featured rapidly evolving technology, global migration, and general uncertainty (Elliot & Urry, 2010; Young, DaRosa, & Lapointe, 2011). These feelings of uncertainty may stem from a wide range of fears, such as pension funds collapsing or terrorist attacks. Of course, people's fears are increasingly driven by the media, which affects how we perceive risk. Is not it interesting that although 32 people died from terrorism on US soil in 2014, we seem more conditioned to remember them than the 33,599 people who died from domestic firearm use in the same year? (CNN, 2016).

If you read ► Chap. 1, you might be asking yourself about the apparent contradiction between the fact that, despite living in uncertain times, late modern life is actually highly predictable for many of us. We would argue that, in the face of myriad uncertainties, humans have done everything they can to render the day-to-day features of their existences more devoid of risk than at any period in history. We can buy a myriad of insurance policies and breakdown cover to mitigate the effects of uncertainty and worry, and make increasingly informed decisions based on the wealth of advice and data at our fingertips.

The world is an increasingly uncertain place, but humans have worked hard to remove as many of those uncertainties as possible (Lupton, 2013). For the most part, we seem to want a life that is largely predictable except within certain boundaries that we determine.

❓ Discussion Questions

1. What do you worry about losing or getting damaged?
2. Is it material (e.g. your phone or your savings) or is it symbolic (e.g. your reputation)?
3. What specific measures do you take to mitigate against the thing you worry about getting lost or damaged?

4.2 · Motivators for Engaging in Adventurous Activities: Is Risk a Factor?

49

4

As we can see, we all live with some degree of fear or anxiety about losing something that we value. Humans in the twenty-first century are relatively risk-averse when compared to previous generations, and on the whole would rather protect what they have (e.g. money and health), rather than risk-losing it in pursuit of something more. Indeed, as Max Roser (n.d.), curator of Our World in Data highlights, humans have never had it so good in terms of health, education, security, and prosperity. This 'social fact' becomes even more interesting when we consider why some people in our society go to great effort and expense to participate in what the general public might consider a risky activity.

Why would anybody in their right mind jump off a cliff with a small parachute, cut a hole in the ice just to go swimming, or hurtle down a narrow, forested path on a bicycle? It is these motivational drivers to which we now turn.

4.2 Motivators for Engaging in Adventurous Activities: Is Risk a Factor?

There are a number of plausible reasons why human beings might voluntarily accept a higher likelihood of being harmed, and they motivate people to differing degrees. While this is by no means a systematic literature review, we have identified ten key factors that may motivate people to participate in adventures which might involve a higher degree of risk, whether they be in educational, touristic, sporting, or recreational contexts. If you have read ► Chap. 3 on daily practices and ► Chap. 10 on adventure tourism, you will see that many of these motivators resonate both with people's regular, habituated adventurous outings and with the commercialized experiences of adventure tourists.

The first reason for undertaking 'risk activities' is that, because everyday life is so banal, predictable, and unstimulating, some people seek to add an additional level of challenge and excitement to it (Elias & Dunning, 1986; Langseth, 2011). Second, since participation in these sorts of activities is relatively uncommon, participants possess a certain distinguishing *caché* that separates them from non-adventurers (Bourdieu, 1984; Kane, 2012). The third factor is the status and recognition within the activity's socio-cultural *milieu* that comes from this type of skilful performance (Atencio, Beal, & Wilson, 2009; Booth & Thorpe, 2007; Fletcher, 2008; Langseth, 2012).

Our fourth reason that people participate in adventure sports is the membership of a certain community of like-minded others, and the sense of belonging which comes from that (Boyd, 2012; Langseth, 2012). A fifth reason is the embodied, sensory pleasure that individuals might get from the cold air rushing past their faces while skiing or the quietness and peace that free-divers might feel from swimming unencumbered by SCUBA gear (Evers, 2009; Humberstone, 2011; Rossi & Cereatti, 1993; Zuckerman, 2000). The sixth motivating factor we suggest is that through participation in a given adventure sport, one's identity—how we think and feel about ourselves—is shaped and even transformed (Miles & Wattchow, 2015; Wheaton, 2004). The seventh reason is that one's physical and mental health can be improved by taking part in these activities, which are often practised in natural environments (Carpenter & Harper, 2015). The connection to the natural environment that some people experience through adventure practices is the eighth factor which we see emerging from the literature (Brymer & Gray, 2009; Humberstone, 2013).

As noted in ▶ Chap. 4, engaging in an activity where one's skills perfectly align with the challenges presented is referred to as *flow* (Cziksentmihalyi, 1975), and flow can be experienced by people of all abilities. Finally, some people seek the thrill or buzz that comes from participating in the activity (and possibly from completing it) (Brymer & Oades, 2009; Cater, 2006; Wheaton, 2013). These last two motivators, when experienced simultaneously by more skilled performers, have been referred to as *rush* (Buckley, 2012).

❓ Discussion Question

Consider one of your favourite adventure sports (or even your favourite leisure activity). Which of the following ten factors lie behind your reasons for participating in your chosen activity?

1. It is an exciting diversion from everyday banality
2. It sets you apart from other 'normal' people in society
3. Your skilful performances earn you higher status with your peers
4. It gives you membership of a community
5. You enjoy the feelings associated with moving itself and moving in specific environments
6. It makes you feel more like you are who you want to be (or become)
7. It improves your physical and mental health
8. You feel more connected to nature
9. You enjoy the feeling of flow that comes from matching your skills to the challenge
10. You enjoy the buzz and thrill of performing the activity

Through reading the above paragraphs, thinking about adventurers you know and have watched online, and considering your own circumstances, you will probably have come to the same conclusion that we have: most people will have a unique combination of these ten factors that drive them to take part in their favoured activities—whether it is going to the climbing gym three

4.2 · Motivators for Engaging in Adventurous Activities: Is Risk a Factor?

51

4

nights a week after work or rowing across the Atlantic. There are also probably more than ten motivating factors too. Can you think of any more?

Despite our relatively straightforward account of why people might choose to take part in adventure activities, the public, as well as sociologists, remain fixated on those individuals who partake in activities that are located at the extreme end of adventure sports, where one minor miscalculation can result in death. Adventure sport has a sub-category of what many refer to as *extreme sports*, and which Brymer and Oades (2009) define as 'leisure activities where the outcome of a mismanaged mistake or accident is death' (p. 114). Research into these sorts of sports has, until recently, used sociological and psychological theories to explain people's participation in them. Extreme sports and risk scholar, Eric Brymer (2010), summarizes this below:

» From a social standpoint participants are seduced by the glamorous image of adrenaline and risk to voluntarily go beyond the edge of their control. From a psychological viewpoint participants are either adrenaline seekers fulfilling a need for uncertainty, novelty, ambiguity, variety, and unpredictability or they are pathological with unhealthy, narcissistic tendencies. (pp. 225–226)

As we will see, these notions surrounding risk-taking are increasingly being developed, critiqued, and informed by new ways of understanding people's experiences of extreme sports, and may align more appropriately with the motivating factors that we argue influence adventure in the more general sense. First, though, we need to understand some of these key concepts which have informed discussions of risk and adventure up to the present.

A seminal piece of sociological research in the area of extreme sport was conducted by Stephen Lyng in 1990. Lyng's research with skydivers revealed that they were a group of ultra-cautious, meticulous planners, who left nothing to chance. The skydivers were particularly obsessed with occupying a space that only those with consummate knowledge, skill, judgement, and mental strength could. Without being armed with these attributes, death was much more likely. Lyng called this practice of carefully operating at the limits of one's capacities 'edgework' and the term has since entered the adventure sports vernacular as a means of helping to explain how, to those involved in pursuits that the general public regards as idiotic or even suicidal, participation is not regarded as risky at all. The participants' argument is that, yes, the consequence of something going wrong would be death, but due to their skill, planning, and presence of mind, the likelihood of something going wrong is incredibly low. Being able to operate along these 'edges' sets

4

people apart from the rest of society and allows them a sense of escape from everyday reality (Lyng, 2005).

Lyng (1990) claimed that there was one particular skill possessed by those engaging in edgework and that was 'their ability to maintain [mental] control over a situation that verges on complete chaos, a situation most people would regard as entirely uncontrollable' (p. 859). Lyng draws a parallel to Tom Wolfe's (1979) ethnography on test pilots who have 'the right stuff', as demonstrated by their ability to maintain mental control in the face of severe hazards. This part of the edgework concept is reflected in climber Alex Honnold's comments. Honnold is renowned for his solo rope-less ascents of huge vertical rock faces such as Half Dome and El Capitan. He has explained the relative nature of risk in his climbing in the following way:

» I don't like risk. I don't like passing over double yellow. I don't like rolling the dice … I always call risk the likelihood of falling off. The consequence is what will happen if you do. So I try to keep my soloing low-risk – as in, I'm not likely to fall off, even though there'd be really high consequences if I did. (Honnold, 2015, p. 11)

Writing more recently on what has been called the 'most extreme' of adventure sports, BASE jumping, Langseth (2012) confirmed what Lyng (1990) and Laurendeau (2006) had found years before in studies on skydiving: that those who die while engaging in extreme sports are more likely to be blamed for their deficiencies in skill or mental control (i.e. 'it was not the activity that killed the person – it was their own fault'). Thus, practitioners are able to maintain their belief that harm will not come to them because they possess the attributes required for a successful performance. Laurendeau also found that when this lack of skill and mental control could not adequately explain the circumstances, individuals explained deadly accidents as flukes—thus maintaining what Lyng (1990) called an 'illusory sense of control' (p. 872).

Although this last paragraph may cover uncomfortable subject matter, it is hopefully clear throughout this chapter that there is widespread agreement that adventurers—whether everyday folk like us or superstars like Alex Honnold—do not aspire to seriously hurt themselves or die. Avid mountain biker and scholar/consultant Kath Bicknell also tells us that technology and sports gear increasingly enable riders to maintain a sense of control in their fast-paced and obstacle-laden environments and that in actuality, these 'activities may appear to contain a higher level of risk or sensation-seeking to outsiders than they do to insiders' (2016, pp. 239–240).

Indeed, if the sole aim of participating in an activity was to increase the likelihood and severity of seriously hurting oneself, there would be no point in putting the surfboards on the roof rack and driving to the beach. All we would need to do is go to the side of a busy road, put on a blindfold, and start walking across. Such an adventure—apart from not lasting a long time—would not be responding to any of our ten motivating factors.

The emphasis in our understanding, as outlined above, draws primarily on social theory and sociological perspectives, as these are what we are most familiar with, but voluntary engagement with risk has also been explored from a range of psychological perspectives, such as bio-social and evolutionary standpoints. An important example of this is Marvin Zuckerman's (1994) concept of a 'sensation-seeking' personality trait, which is 'defined by the seeking of varied, novel, complex, and intense sensations and experiences, and the willingness to take physical, social, legal, and financial risks for the sake of such experience' (p. 27), has been applied to a wide range of social contexts over the last 50 years (Zuckerman, 2007).

More recently, 'ecological dynamics approaches', which critique perspectives that focus solely on personality, are increasingly being used to explore how people, task, and environment interact in specific adventure activities (Brymer & Davids, 2014; Immonen et al., 2017; Peacock, Brymer, Davids, & Dillon, 2017). In an adventure tourism context, for example, stepping out of everyday life and travelling to a new place in order to engage in a novel activity open tourists up to a wider range of potential *affordances* than they are used to. An affordance is an opportunity for an individual to interact with the environment in meaningful ways (Gibson, 1979) and is perceived differently depending on personal experience, physical, intellectual, and emotional ability and the task at hand. This is one way to explain how, although all the participants on a whitewater rafting trip are engaged in the same experience, they might be there for a wide variety of reasons and gaining very different outcomes from the trip (Immonen et al., 2017).

For the most part, barring psychiatric illness for example, the literature suggests that human beings deliberately expose themselves to additional hazards with the very firm intent of living to tell the tale, having similar encounters over the decades that follow, and for living life to the fullest. Indeed, some extreme athletes tend to claim to have a 'life wish' rather than a death wish (Brymer, 2005; Brymer & Schweitzer, 2017). It is arguable that attitudes to risk exist on a 'consequence spectrum', with extreme sports featuring high/deathly consequences for mistakes at one end, and lower consequence sports at the other, where risk may even have a somewhat playful character.

Tommy Langseth's 2012 paper looked at BASE jumping at Lysefjorden in Norway, which is an international BASE destination. Langseth puts forward a number of findings, but he quite starkly highlights how levels of prestige and recognition are afforded to members of the small subculture of BASE jumpers.

Langseth's 12 informants revealed that, despite BASE jumping being statistically many times more dangerous than skydiving, one cannot be considered a 'real' BASE jumper if one only does high jumps or pulls their chute early. More status is afforded to jumpers who are the first to go off objects and who purposely fly close to walls. Langseth shows how there are distinctions between those who are BASE jumpers and those who are not (and who do not understand the game), and power struggles between members of the relatively small BASE jumping culture.

Using Bourdieu's (1984) terms, Langseth explains how within the BASE subculture, performances that involve, for example, flying close enough to 'lick the wall' (p. 164) earn jumpers *symbolic capital*. This kind of capital is highly prized within its particular subculture or field and can afford a person with a kind of a reputational currency that is more highly valued than economic capital. It is the only kind of capital that can be gained through bestowal from others.

Symbolic capital can also come from other related actions, such as the first ascent of a climb or descent of a couloir. Fletcher (2008) refers to 'the first' as the gold standard in adventure sports, and one that is particularly highly valued by corporate sponsors.

Langseth also found that in his study, men were often more interested in seeking higher recognition through risk-taking than women. In 2009, using a similar Bourdieusian lens to look at skateboarders, Atencio, Beal, and Wilson arrived at a similar conclusion: the men were generally much more interested in distinguishing themselves through engaging in especially risky practices.

What kinds of symbolic capital are apparent in your adventure and/or recreational circles?

4.3 Risk Beyond the Individual

Up until now, our conversation in this chapter has centred primarily on the motivations and actions of individual agents who are taking part in adventures as part of their personal leisure time. As we will see, as soon as adventure becomes a service or product that is bought and sold and facilitated by others, discussions of risk become laden with problems.

Let us concentrate on adventure education and adventure tourism for the moment. The central problem for these two sectors is highlighted in ► Sect. 1.2 of ► Chap. 1: risk is individually relative. So, if you, as the instructor, are taking ten 14-year-olds on a high ropes course (aka challenge course), you need to be capable of managing ten people's varying fears of being harmed. Similarly, if you are the white-water rafting guide, you need to manage the same kinds of anxieties for the six clients in your boat.

Once adventure becomes a packaged, re-usable product that can cater to a wide variety of audiences, it then loses some of what makes it inherently adventurous, as it becomes denuded of uncertainty (see Beames & Brown, 2016; Loynes, 1998). It follows that, for the adventure educator and guide alike, one of the key skills is being able to match the challenges presented by the terrain, weather, and activity with the skills and abilities of each individual within the group.

An educational or tourist organization whose activities occasionally result in their clients getting seriously harmed or dying will not stay in business for very long. In the world of commercial adventure tourism there appears to be a fascinating paradox where clients are expected to feel simultaneously safe and at risk. Fletcher (2010) explains how this simultaneous maintenance of 'contradictory perceptions' is done through the construction of what he calls a 'public secret' which is 'commonly known but not articulated' (p. 6).

While we will look at this notion of feeling safe but at risk in more detail in ▶ Chap. 10 on adventure tourism, this also features prominently in outdoor education practice. Martínková and Parry (2017) call this same kind of contradiction 'safe danger', while Beames and Brown (2016) go a step further by stating that deliberately exposing young people to harm for its own sake has no part in any educational enterprise. As will be discussed in forthcoming chapters on adventure and personal development, and adventure tourism, most activities are primarily chosen for their developmental, educational, or tourism-related aims. Once those aims have been established, appropriate risk management plans can be put together that will guard against participants being seriously harmed by any unforeseen hazards.

Chapter Summary

As we can see, everyday adventurers like most of us, and adventure heroes like Steph Davis (who flies in her wingsuit most days), are motivated by a number of the ten factors that we highlighted earlier. Although we know adventures are relative and that we can choose how 'close to the edge' we want to play, there is a strong body of literature claiming that people do not participate in adventurous activities primarily because they want to take risks. It may be, of course, that certain pressures to maintain sponsorship with an equipment manufacturer might require playing very close to the edge and filming oneself in the process, but, at this level, performers use their knowledge of the task and the environment to control the risks (Brymer, 2010). Conversely, a group of friends who want to ski the famous Haute Route in the French/Swiss Alps might hire a mountain guide to ensure that (despite their skill and experience) they do not unwittingly go too close to the limit of their abilities in an unfamiliar setting. For them, the holiday is about participating in their favourite sport, in novel and beautiful surroundings with their friends. These skiers are not actively seeking risk; risk is an inherent part of the holiday they have chosen, and they are managing it appropriately.

4

The above examples once again illustrate how, in the world of adventure sports, there is a vast array of performers who take part for a wide variety of reasons. Indeed, before writing this chapter, we only noted a handful of motivating factors that might drive an individual's appetite for adventure, but we ended up finding ten different ones in the literature.

There are a couple of key elements within the extreme sports and risk literature that stand out and should be recapitulated. First, despite public opinion, most athletes who are involved in extreme sports (where a small mistake can lead to death) (Brymer, 2005) take great care when planning logistics, managing equipment, and considering weather conditions (Lyng, 1990). These are highly skilled, meticulous planners, not irrational and impulsive risk-takers. Most extreme athletes shun the idea of taking risks.

The second element of theory that is important to remember is that in many adventure communities (not just the extreme sports), higher status and recognition are conferred on those who have played very close to the edge. Athletes' reputational gains come not only from the exceptionally high levels of skill they possess, but from the mental control they exercise in order to stay calm in circumstances when the smallest of errors would be penalized in the harshest of ways.

As will be increasingly apparent as this book progresses, separating adventure phenomena into discrete chapters is very challenging and often not particularly helpful, as many key themes inherently overlap. Take, for example, risk, capitalism, and the media. In relation to these concepts, Coates, Clayton, and Humberstone (2010) describe how the media actively dramatizes and glorifies risk, which in turn pushes adventure athletes into taking increasingly higher risks, as that becomes their principal route to earning a living and gaining recognition. This kind of pressure on athletes exemplifies how a capitalist, media-driven agenda can overshadow athletes' own motivations for adventure practice (as outlined in ▶ Sect. 4.2, above), as well as their personal safety.

Key Readings

Langseth, T. (2012). B.A.S.E. jumping – Beyond the thrills. *European Journal for Sport and Society, 9*(3), 155–176.

Lyng, S. (1990). Edgework: A social psychological analysis of voluntary risk taking. *American Journal of Sociology, 95*, 851–856.

References

Atencio, M., Beal, B., & Wilson, C. (2009). The distinction of risk: Urban skate-boarding, street habitus and the construction of hierarchical gender relations. *Qualitative Research in Sport and Exercise, 1*(1), 3–20.

Beames, S., & Brown, M. (2016). *Adventurous learning*. New York: Routledge.

Beck, U. (1992). *Risk society: Towards a new modernity*. London: Sage.

Bicknell, K. (2016). Equipment, innovation and the mountain biker's taskscape. In H. Thorpe & R. Olive (Eds.), *Women in action sport cultures: Identity, politics and experience* (pp. 237–258). London: Palgrave Macmillan.

Booth, D., & Thorpe, H. (2007). The meaning of extreme. In D. Booth & H. Thorpe (Eds.), *Berkshire encyclopedia of extreme sports* (pp. 181–197). Great Barrington, MA: Berkshire.

Bourdieu, P. (1979/1984). *Distinction* (trans: Nice, R.). Cambridge, MA: Harvard University Press.

Boyd, J. (2012). Lifestyle climbing: Toward existential authenticity. *Journal of Sport & Tourism, 17*(2), 85–104.

Brymer, E. (2005). *Extreme dude: A phenomenological exploration into the extreme sport experience*. PhD Thesis, Faculties of Education and Psychology, University of Wollongong. Retrieved from http://ro.uow.edu.au/theses/379

Brymer, E. (2010). Risk taking in extreme sports: A phenomenological perspective. *Annals of Leisure Research, 13*(1–2), 218–238.

Brymer, E., & Davids, K. (2014). Experiential learning as a constraints-led process: An ecological dynamics perspective. *Journal of Adventure Education and Outdoor Learning, 14*(2), 103–117.

Brymer, E., & Gray, T. (2009). Dancing with nature: Rhythm and harmony in extreme sport participation. *Journal of Adventure Education and Outdoor Learning, 9*(2), 135–149.

Brymer, E., & Oades, L. G. (2009). Extreme sports: A positive transformation in courage and humility. *Journal of Humanistic Psychology, 41*(1), 114–126.

Brymer, E., & Schweitzer, R. (2017). *Phenomenology and the extreme sport experience*. New York: Routledge.

Buckley, R. (2012). Rush as a key motivation in skilled adventure tourism: Resolving the risk recreation paradox. *Tourism Management, 33*, 961–970.

Carpenter, C., & Harper, N. (2015). Health and wellbeing benefits of activities in the outdoors. In B. Humberstone, H. Price, & K. Henderson (Eds.), *Routledge international handbook of outdoor studies* (pp. 59–69). Oxon, UK: Routledge.

Cater, C. (2006). Playing with risk? Participant perceptions of risk and management implications in adventure tourism. *Tourism Management, 27*, 317–325.

CNN. (2016). American deaths in terrorism vs. gun violence in one graph. Retrieved from, http://edition.cnn.com/2016/10/03/us/terrorism-gun-violence/index.html

Coates, E., Clayton, B., & Humberstone, B. (2010). A battle for control: Exchanges of power in the subculture of snowboarding. *Sport in Society, 13*(7–8), 1082–1101.

Cziksentmihalyi, M. (1975). *Beyond boredom and anxiety*. San Francisco: Jossey- Bass.

Elias, N., & Dunning, E. (1986). Quest for excitement in leisure. In N. Elias & E. Dunning (Eds.), *Quest for excitement: Sport and leisure in the civilizing process* (pp. 63–90). Oxford, UK: Basil Blackwell.

Elliot, A., & Urry, J. (2010). *Mobile lives*. Abingdon, UK: Routledge.

Evers, C. (2009). 'The point': Surfing, geography and a sensual life of men and masculinity on the Gold Coast, Australia. *Social & Cultural Geography, 10*(8), 893–908.

Fletcher, R. (2008). Living on the edge: The appeal of risk sports for the professional middle class. *Sociology of Sport Journal, 25*(3), 1–23.

Fletcher, R. (2010). The emperor's new adventure: Public secrecy and the paradox of adventure tourism. *Journal of Contemporary Ethnography, 39*(1), 6–33.

Furedi, F. (1997). *Culture of fear: Risk-taking and the morality of low expectation.* London: Cassell.

Gibson, J. (1979). *The ecological approach to visual perception.* Boston: Houghton Mifflin.

Giddens, A. (1991). *Modernity and self identity.* Cambridge, UK: Polity Press.

Honnold, A. (2015). *Alone on the wall: Alex Honnold and the ultimate limits of adventure.* New York: Macmillan.

Humberstone, B. (2011). Embodiment and social and environmental action in nature-based sport: Spiritual spaces. *Leisure Studies, 30*(4), 495–512.

Humberstone, B. (2013). Adventurous activities, embodiment and nature: Spiritual, sensual and sustainable? Embodying environmental justice. *Motriz: Revista De Educacao Fisica, 19*(3), 565–571.

Immonen, T., Brymer, E., Orth, D., Davids, K., Feletti, F., Liukkonen, J., et al. (2017). Understanding action and adventure sports participation – An ecological dynamics perspective. *Sports Medicine - Open, 3*(1), 18.

Kane, M. (2012). Professional adventure tourists: Producing and selling stories of 'authentic' identity. *Tourist Studies, 12*(3), 268–286.

Langseth, T. (2011). Risk sports: Social constraints and cultural imperatives. *Sport in Society, 14*(5), 629–644.

Langseth, T. (2012). B.A.S.E. jumping – Beyond the thrills. *European Journal for Sport and Society, 9*(3), 155–176.

Laurendeau, J. (2006). 'He didn't go in doing a sky dive': Sustaining the illusion of control over an edgework activity. *Sociological Perspectives, 49*(4), 583–605.

Loynes, C. (1998). Adventure in a bun. *The Journal of Experimental Education, 21*(1), 35–39.

Lupton, D. (2013). *Risk* (2nd ed.). London: Routledge.

Lyng, S. (1990). Edgework: A social psychological analysis of voluntary risk taking. *American Journal of Sociology, 95*, 851–856.

Lyng, S. (2005). *Edgework: The sociology of risk-taking.* New York: Routledge.

Martínková, I., & Parry, J. (2017). Safe danger: On the experience of challenge, adventure and risk in education. *Sport, Ethics and Philosophy, 11*(1), 75–91.

Miles, B., & Wattchow, B. (2015). The mirror of the sea: Narrative identity, sea kayak adventuring and implications for outdoor adventure education. *Australian Journal of Outdoor Education, 18*(1), 16–26.

Peacock, S., Brymer, E., Davids, K., & Dillon, M. (2017). An ecological dynamics perspective on adventure tourism. *Tourism Review International, 21*(3), 307–316.

Reddy, S. (1996). Claims to expert knowledge and the subversion of democracy: The triumph of risk over uncertainty. *Economy and Society, 25*(2), 222–254.

Roser, M. (n.d.). *Our world in data.* Retrieved from https://ourworldindata.org/

Rossi, B., & Cereatti, L. (1993). The sensation seeking in mountain athletes as assessed by Zuckerman's sensation seeking scale. *International Journal of Sport Psychology, 24*, 417–431.

Wheaton, B. (2004). *Understanding lifestyle sports: Consumption, identity, and difference.* London: Routledge.

Wheaton B. The cultural politics of lifestyle sports. Abingdon: Routledge; 2013.

Wolfe, T. (1979). *The right stuff.* New York: Farrar, Straus, and Giroux.

Young, N., DaRosa, V., & Lapointe, J. (2011). On the origins of late modernity: Environmentalism and the construction of a critical global consciousness. *ANTROPOlógicas, 12*, 2–8.

Zuckerman, M. (1994). *Behavioral expressions and biosocial bases of sensation seeking.* New York: Cambridge Press.

Zuckerman, M. (2000). Are you a risk taker? *Psychology Today*, November/December, 130.

Zuckerman, M. (2007). *Sensation-seeking and risky behaviour.* Washington, DC: American Psychological Association.

Adventure, Capitalism, and Corporations

© The Author(s) 2019
S. Beames et al., *Adventure and Society*, https://doi.org/10.1007/978-3-319-96062-3_5

Chapter Aims

After reading this chapter, you will be able to:
- Understand the significant impacts of capitalism upon adventure practice
- Explain key concepts related to corporate 'authentic' branding and consumerism in the adventure world
- Use the concepts of *hegemony* and *discourse* to explain the complex arrangements inherent in adventure consumption
- Understand how the production of adventure goods may damage the planet and take advantage of people living in dire conditions who are desperate to work
- Conceptualize what is *neo-liberalism* and how this has led to corporations deliberately fostering public initiatives for positive social change
- Begin to understand how corporate involvement in adventure also supports new technological advances in adventure

5.1 The Origins of Capitalism

Using money to buy and sell goods is an integral part of our daily lives that often goes unnoticed. Most of us take it for granted, but using money generated from a job to buy goods that were produced by someone else is a relatively new phenomenon in human history. Of course, throughout history there have always been wealthy people who have employed others to cook, clean, build, and tend livestock. However, the circumstances whereby a person could employ people to produce specific surplus capital or goods—which would then be sold at a profit—have only existed for the last 200 years or so.

According to Scottish philosopher and economist, Adam Smith, who was writing in the late eighteenth century following the industrial revolution, rational and self-interested individuals would specialize production in order to create a surplus of goods that could be sold to others (2000/1723–1790). In this arrangement, a successful business would seemingly foster mutually beneficial exchanges in society through transactions of surplus goods for money. In essence, this is supposed to be a 'win-win' situation. Yet, as we shall see below, this capitalistic system has, in many cases, been criticized for benefiting the owners themselves. And, crucially, business owners who have the means to produce and profit from surplus specialized goods pay another (much larger yet less compensated) group of people to do the physical labour necessary to create these goods.

Accordingly, there is also a critique that capitalism exploits the majority to benefit the minority who will consistently accumulate more and more wealth. The roots of this critical literature on capitalism are very strongly connected to Karl Marx and his writing partner, Friedrich Engels. Marx and Engels were particularly concerned with the low wages and poor work conditions that the workers were forced to accept because they had few other options. They posited that, when stripped to its very core, economics and the ways people went about making money played the central role in organizing their social lives. Marx and Engels' (2004/1848) principal issue was that the bourgeoisie (the owners) and the proletariat (the workers) had unequal access to resources. Further, they argued that the bourgeoisie continuously shifted arrangements so that they retained a much larger share of profits than their employees. These changing social arrangements allowed some people in society to amass significant capital while being enabled by others' labour.

At this point, you may be asking: What does any of this discussion of capitalism and Marxist thought have to do with adventure? The short and simple answer is 'everything'! Now that you have had a brief introduction to these economic concepts, we will move on to critically examine how today's big business is inextricably intertwined with adventure practices—for better and for worse. This examination will deepen as these three key sociological concepts are introduced: *hegemony*, *discourse*, and *neo-liberalism*. After highlighting some socio-economic concerns and inequalities resulting from corporate-infused adventure, our discussion will then turn to the ways in which corporations may potentially advance 'social good' and develop helpful technologies.

5.2 Corporations and Big Business

The influence of capitalism in its many forms on adventure cannot be overemphasized. Daily adventurers, we suggest, are directly immersed within a myriad of capitalist practices. Indeed, it is difficult for adventurers to escape the influence of capitalism which is so influential in our current era of globalization. Take The North Face Corporation, for example. Once an equipment manufacturer started by adventurers who needed better gear, in 2015 the company's revenue was over 12.4 billion US dollars and its products have potentially become more akin to those of a fashion emporium. Moreover, adventure activities such as skateboarding, which were once simply considered niche hobbies for select enthusiasts, already comprise huge markets that are buoyed by sales of decks, shoes, and protective gear. On its own, the global skateboarding equipment market is expected to exceed 5 billion USD by 2020 (Maida, 2016). These two examples show how there is money to be made, not just from people who need specific items of equipment, but from people who want to wear garments that suggest that they have membership of a larger 'tribe' that possesses certain values and ideals.

5

Arguably, an adventure lifestyle is now being embraced and constantly lived, to the point that scholar Belinda Wheaton (2004) actually refers to pastimes like windsurfing, wave surfing, and skateboarding as 'lifestyle sports', as they are so much more about fostering a particular social identity that pervades much of one's life. As we will discuss in ▸ Chap. 8 on identity, much of what we think and what we do is influenced simply by what we buy.

Increasingly, then, we can see how the adventure lifestyle is inextricably linked with big business in various ways—particularly in relation to the free-market's idealization and targeting of young people. Holly Thorpe (2016) describes the process of how many adventure activities originally became linked with late 1990s corporate strategizing focused upon a lucrative youth market. This meant that products ranging from energy drinks to credit cards were promoted and sold via 'cool' surfers, skateboarders, and snowboarders (p. 92).

Scholars Robert Rinehart and Synthia Sydnor (2003) add to this discussion, claiming that many seemingly youth-centric adventure activities are now an everyday part of our lives, as 'they decorate our backyards, streetwear, language, lunch boxes, the Worldwide Web, MTV, ESPN, and advertising of every sort' (p. 1). Magazines and websites for outdoor recreators are full of advertisements promising everything from stronger and lighter ice axes to more remote and daring guided expeditions. From this standpoint, clever marketing can shape what becomes desirable and important, which consequently determines what adventurers wear to work and play, discuss on online forums, choose for their equipment, and deem to be righteous or spiteful (see Wheaton, 2004).

In one sense, then, this chapter picks up on ▸ Chap. 2's discussion on the professionalization and mainstreaming of adventure. Unlike 20 years ago, when adventure could be a lonely and unpaid pursuit, it is now possible to make a living as a sponsored adventure athlete who is contracted by multinational companies to undertake daring feats while wearing appropriately branded technical garments and being videoed (see, e.g. Puchan, 2005).

Furthermore, the influence of capitalism on professional adventure practice is clearly reflected in the shifting nature of modern activities themselves. The previously niche practices of rock climbing and white-water paddling, for instance, have been cleansed, standardized, and re-packaged through Disneyized, gladiator-style competitions such as the X Games (see Rinehart, 1998, 2008). Moreover, today there is the mainstream recreational phenomenon of adventure activities based in artificial indoor environments, whereby 'Typical outdoor lifestyle sports such as surfing, snowboarding, skydiving and rock climbing, which used to be exclusively practised in natural environments, are now being offered for consumption in safe, predictable and controlled artificial settings, such as snowdomes' (Salome, 2010, p. 69).

This notion of indoor and/or artificial environments being used to house adventure activities is a fascinating one, as it demonstrates how, on one hand, market forces are responding to a perceived opportunity to generate income, while on the other hand, activities that were once only available to a very narrow slice of the population have become increasingly attractive and accessible for people from other historically under-represented groups (Salome, 2010).

More recent work on the 'Disneyization of adventure' (Beames & Brown, 2017; Beames & Varley, 2013) has drawn attention to the increasing 'indoorisation of adventure' (van Bottenburg & Salome, 2010), where people can come to 'adventure cathedrals' and eat, shop, and play under one roof. In these venues, adventure and consumption can be viewed as being Disneyized, as they resonate with Bryman's (2004) four features of: theming (where an overall narrative envelops the activity, like Irish pubs in airports); hybrid consumption, which entails being able to buy products during the leisure activity; merchandising, where one can purchase branded goods; and performative labour, which refers to employees following scripts that govern what they say and do. We will revisit these ideas of Disneyization in ▶ Chap. 10, which looks at adventure tourism.

The world of adventure tourism is closely linked to the adventure leisure market, and both have developed along a pathway that is principally based on the exchange of services for money. Participants at all levels regularly traverse national boundaries in their search for adventure. As we will see in ▶ Chap. 10, Kane and Zink (2004), among others, highlight contemporary tourists' abilities to purchase adventure through a marketplace that is full of opportunities that are effectively laid out on a menu—from the cheap, accessible thrills of a zipline park through to bespoke guided heli-skiing trips. At the extreme end of this, one only has to look back to the mid-1990s, when a handful of companies began offering guided ascents of Mount Everest, to see how the market responds to and encourages customer demand.

As we look at this chapter so far, we can see how the influence of capitalism has given rise to proliferating types of adventure practices and lifestyles. Indeed, there are now more and more practitioners ranging from unpaid hobbyists to well-paid celebrities. In parallel, under conditions of globalization, there is the phenomenon of transnational markets that cater to all kinds of adventurers. These markets are expanding and catering to new international audiences that are often youth-oriented. In ▶ Chap. 2, we highlighted certain ideas about modern capitalistic society. However, one decides to categorize our current socio-economic conditions, as late or liquid modernity or even post-modernity, what is undeniable is that we currently live under conditions of capitalism with its accompanying consumerist way of being. We explain how these ideas structure contemporary adventure practice in the following sections.

5

5.3 Adventure Sponsorship, Corporate 'Authenticity', and Global Marketing

As we have noted throughout this book, many adventure activities have been preoccupied with notions of 'authentic participation by the core members' (Donnelly, 2006, p. 220). Today, pronounced corporate involvement has implications for the ways in which adventure is conceptualized and experienced by these practitioners. This relationship is increasingly perceived as necessary and symbiotic, with corporations and participants often relating to each other through their mutual claims to 'authenticity'. For example, Poulson (2016) describes how triathletes, road cyclists, and mountain bikers are often expected to make appropriate consumer choices, in terms of how they purchase, display, and utilize gear, to be considered authentic.

Corporations keenly understand (and promote) this underlying aspect of authentic adventure participation. Red Bull, for example, has gone to great lengths to be considered by adventure participants as authentic, so that their products are loyally consumed and promoted by participants and supporters. Red Bull famously sponsors numerous elite athletes that represent authentic adventure values too. In ▶ Chap. 6, we will hear more about how corporations like Red Bull use social media and digital technologies to promote these athletes in relation to youth cultures and adventure communities (see Thorpe, 2017). The profound involvement of multinational corporations in adventure practices also reflects a burgeoning global audience for these activities—the worldwide youth market, in particular, is considered a trendy and profitable one that these corporations and institutions are targeting, with significant investment now being made in newer markets such as Asia, Central and South America, and other parts of Europe (Bradstreet, 2016).

One example of Red Bull's high-profile adventure sponsorship is snowboarder Shaun White's Project X. In 2009, Red Bull built White, who is now a three-time Olympic gold medallist, his own private half-pipe that was carved into the mountains of southwest Colorado. Instead of the United States Olympic Committee (USOC) financially backing the athlete, the private sector heavily intervened to prepare White for the 2010 Winter Olympics, with this company being publicly seen as a leader in snowboarding. With recent acceptance of adventure sports such as surfing, skateboarding, snowboarding, and snow climbing, the International Olympic Committee (IOC) is simultaneously trying to embrace lifestyle sports and be considered relevant and appealing to a market that is typically driven by privately sponsored adventure mega events such as the X Games and Dew Tour.

The cultural legitimization and institutionalization that hallmark the inclusion of lifestyle sports in the Olympic programme is further evidence of how adventure sports are positioning themselves closer to traditional sports. It is capitalism that is largely responsible for taking what has been 'play' to many people and turning this into more a formally institutionalized practice. If we accept that play involves elements such as occupying its own time and space, costing nothing, and being unproductive (Callois, 1961), then one can see how mountain biking, kite-surfing, and ice climbing have now become 'sportified'. That is, these activities now have additional levels of rules, competitions, and rankings, and organized media exposure is used to make these activities look and feel 'proper' and official, thus gaining mainstream (and corporate) acceptance.

Adventurers can engage with, or even promote, this type of institutionalization and formalization, or they can take up more oppositional stances. Indeed, adventure subcultures now abound: there is no longer one accepted way of 'doing adventure'. In an oversimplified way, it could be that individuals can be part of a group that embraces the commercial packaging of an activity or participate in a group that resists it. Furthermore, as we shall see, capitalism can serve to blur this distinction between assimilation and contestation in terms of people's everyday adventure practices.

So, looking ahead, how exactly do people engage with the ideals of both capitalism and adventure, in an everyday sense? In the following section, we take up this line of inquiry by revisiting the concept of *hegemony* and introducing the terms *discourse* and *neo-liberalism*.

5.4 Theory Time: Hegemony, Discourse, and Neo-liberalism

We have explained how adventure practices are simultaneously supported by numerous global industries and their consumers. But what does this burgeoning adventure market actually mean for everyday practice? The concept of *hegemony* was introduced in ▶ Chap. 2. As first defined by the Italian Antonio Gramsci, hegemony is a particularly helpful theoretical cornerstone to understand how powerful forces like capitalism can influence what people think and do in their regular adventures. Gramsci wrote during the era of fascist Italy in the 1930s, and extended Marx's ideas about the power of economic production.

In his book *Prison Notebooks*, Gramsci (1971/1999) explained how individuals can be coerced by dominant civil institutions and their preferred cultural ideologies into doing what those in power want them to do. This coercion occurs either by force or consent. Domination by force is just as one might think. For example, it has been argued that Africans from Ghana were actually keen surfers back in the pre-slavery days, although this stopped when the slave trade appeared and prevented this practice through physical violence (Kaplan, 2012). Domination by consent, on the other hand, is more implicit and yet just as influential (or perhaps more). In another example, African-American television host Sal Masekela, who commentated for over a decade at the X Games, once noted that racism exists in surfing because of the ideology that all African-Americans play ball sports and do not swim (*The Inertia*, 2014). This pervasive racist ideology can be internalized by young African-Americans and prevent them from taking part in adventure activities like surfing. These two related examples illustrate the different ways that people act and invest in certain practices. And, this latter idea about how people consent to and internalize specific beliefs, often through coercion, is of central importance when it comes to capitalism and adventure practice.

This idea of hegemony through ideologies circulated within society was developed further by French sociologist Michel Foucault (1978). He outlined how power in today's societies rarely functions in a 'top-down' manner between rulers and the ruled, or the state and the governed, in the traditional hierarchical relationship maintained by physical domination. Instead, Foucault contends that power, which aligns with dominant values or 'truths' in society, is present in *all* of our relationships and life practices. Power and knowledge thus exist in a web, rather than something exercised from the top-down. From this perspective, we can see how certain corporate ideologies circulating in the media and in our daily social interactions can cause us to act in certain ways and believe in certain things. This is explained by Foucault through the concept of *discourse*, whereby individuals enact particular life practices and identities based on dominant ideologies.

Moving ahead with the theoretical ideas of Gramsci and Foucault, if we consider adventure to be integrally linked with capitalism, then we must understand how capitalism creates certain cultural values, ideologies, and power networks that influence everyday adventure practices.[1] To do this, we next look to the concept of *neo-liberalism*, and demonstrate how this political ideology (or reproduced system of cultural beliefs) has the power to foster new types of adventurers and their practices, by prioritizing corporate involvement and values.

---

1   According to Pringle (2005), although there are some differences at times between Foucauldian and Gramscian concepts, there are key similarities pertaining to the 'workings of power' (p. 272). Furthermore, he suggests that 'Researchers who combine Foucauldian and Gramscian concepts such as discourse and hegemony should be encouraged to carefully reflect on the theoretical coherency of such combinations …' (p. 272).

Neo-liberalism refers to a broad set of ideas that favour deregulation in economics, politics, law, religion, health, and education, among many other sectors. Born mainly through policies of UK Prime Minister Margaret Thatcher and US president Ronald Reagan in the late 1970s and early 1980s, neo-liberalism espouses the rule of the market, by cutting public expenditure for social services, reducing government regulation, and privatizing state institutions (Martinez & Garcia, 1998).

Today's cultural activities, including adventure ones, are without doubt influenced by the neo-liberal belief system, especially in most Western societies. This prevailing trend, driven by government policies, has engendered private sector intervention and authority deep into our social lives and personal affairs. For instance, we can see how private corporations and donors are considered necessary to provide funding and resources for the skateboarding public (Atencio, Beal, Wright, & McClain, 2018). This shift towards the private sector supporting everyday citizens' lives parallels the rapid globalization and post-industrialization that has occurred in Western societies to a greater or lesser extent since the late twentieth century.

How does neo-liberalism directly impact the lives of adventurers and influence them to enact certain ways of being? Neo-liberalism calls for individuals to embrace free-market values of self-sufficiency and responsible choice-making, which in turn point towards a more individualistic and entrepreneurial way of existence. Quite simply, rather than relying upon state support, in neo-liberal times individuals are each held responsible for supporting the capitalistic economy by making 'appropriate' choices about how they live their everyday lives (Hamann, 2009). This means, for example, participating in self-maintenance practices through health, fitness, and sport lifestyles, which also requires one to avidly consume associated products. Likewise, choosing to partake in adventure activities and their accompanying market is also considered an appropriate lifestyle choice under current neo-liberal conditions. Quite simply, being a capitalistic adventurer is culturally valued in neo-liberal times.

An exemplar of the neo-liberal ethos and its influence upon how individuals exist in society can be found in Recreational Equipment Incorporated (REI) and their advertised guide to climbing basics. Here we can see how corporations compel individuals to specifically act in self-sufficient ways, in order to epitomize a healthy, trendy, and consumerist lifestyle:

» If you're looking for fitness, fun and a healthy dose of adrenaline, then rock climbing is a worthy pursuit. Though it attracts its share of daredevils, rock climbing is also enjoyed by legions of everyday adventurers. If you're reasonably fit and get yourself proper equipment and instruction, you, too, can become a rock jock. (REI, 2018, para. 1)

5

Once again, the idea of participant authenticity, associated here with the 'rock jock' stereotype, remains highly meaningful to corporations as well as mainstream and core participants alike. In many adventure cultures, the ideals of being 'cool' and 'hip' are deliberately propagated and reinforced (see Atencio & Beal, 2011). Thus, given the presence of adventure corporations in these networks, both corporations and participants synergistically create certain culturally valued identities, styles, and belief systems.

The above REI example highlights how the private sector idealizes a certain way of being in modern society: fit and healthy, cool and adventurous, self-reliant and responsible, and immersed in the techniques of daily self-practice. This way of life advocated by REI is, of course, enhanced by active consumerism: this specific guide to rock climbing is actually supplemented by numerous shopping links under the website's call to 'gear up'. Potential adventurers are expected to purchase a range of items, such as climbing clothing, rock shoes, helmets, harnesses, chalk bags, carabiners, belay devices, ropes, and climbing protection. It should now be clear that being an adventurer requires being an active participant in a highly consumerist lifestyle, which essentially means embracing the free-market ethos. Adventure pursuits are thus considered crucial cultural contexts where neo-liberal values are reproduced; here, individuals can seemingly achieve acceptable happy, healthy, and fulfilling lifestyles by being avid consumers in the global economy.

❓ Discussion Questions

1. List some corporations and businesses that you patronize or admire as part of your daily sport and physical activity practices.
2. Consider how these corporations and businesses promote and reproduce certain cultural values.
3. Examine the degree to which you do (or do not) live your life according to these values.

5.5 Power to the People: Agency and Negotiating Corporate Adventure

As we have seen, the dominant forces and ideologies of capitalism greatly influence human social activities, and adventure activities are no exception. An important question to ask is how individuals might evade or even contest the prevailing capitalistic belief system. Are we simply dupes that just follow and consume the latest corporate-inspired trends?

While both Gramsci and Foucault talk about dominant societal 'truths' and the subsequent coercion of individuals within modern capitalistic societies, all human beings possess a degree of agency—and 'capacity for free thought and action' (Bruce & Yearley, 2006, p. 7)—to contest private sector values. Thus, while dominant cultural values and ideologies are indeed heavily reproduced by both corporations and individuals in today's adventure world, adventurers simultaneously have the capacity to strategically resist these ideologies (see Foucault (1997) for more discussion of strategic agency).

As we suggested earlier in this chapter, the strong corporate presence in adventure has historically been challenged by some participants who see themselves as part of anti-establishment subcultures, which have their own language, norms, and cultural conventions. Adventure subcultures are often predicated upon the rather elusive yet influential notion of 'authentic participation'. For example, Becky Beal and Lisa Weidman (2003) once suggested that skateboarders have long been associated with being nonconformists; these 'boarders felt socially compelled to develop their own personalized forms of practice, where each 'identified his or her own criteria regarding training procedures, goals, and style' (p. 340). The authors explained how demonstrating these internalized ways of skating 'were central to being accepted as a legitimate member' (p. 340). Skateboarding can thus, in one sense, be considered an expression of one's authentic subcultural lifestyle. This subculture is likely related to other subcultures, such as the punk and hip-hop music scenes (see Brayton, 2005; Butz, 2012). A central aspect of this subcultural lifestyle pertains to the notion of do-it-yourself (or DIY), whereby skateboarders consider themselves to be uniquely 'self-made' in terms of their styles, practices, and identities (Atencio, Beal, & Wilson, 2009). From this perspective, practitioners prefer to make, use, and display their own goods, to demonstrate a high level of individuality.

While the idea of subculture has merit in activities such as skateboarding, it has also been found that adventure practice does not always involve active resistance to corporate involvement. Indeed, skateboarders have long been enmeshed in corporate practices despite their claims to counter-cultural authenticity. Furthermore, DIY practices in skateboarding resonate closely with neo-liberal values of individual self-management, promotion, and even profit (Atencio & Beal, 2011). Seen this way, a DIY ethos echoes with the neo-liberal 'hands off', free-market policies advanced by many Western governments. Gramsci (1999/1971) is helpful here, as his concept of hegemony explains how clever capitalist or ruling forces are able to manufacture consent to ideologies that will benefit them. Foucault (1978) would add that people themselves will eventually reproduce these 'truths' about adventure, with certain effects.

In another example of market forces changing how people adventure, scholar Douglas Booth (1995) highlights how surfers' dreams of eternal hedonism vanished when the surplus available

5

for alternative lifestyles dried up with the economic recession in the early 1970s (p. 205). Booth goes on to explain that, within the overarching context of capitalism and consumerism, the only option for surfers who wanted to surf every day (rather than entering the traditional labour market) was to embrace these new corporatized adventure arrangements. The classic image of the bohemian, non-conformist surfer had indeed lost currency, as the influence of capitalism has given rise to more formalized adventure practices, including corporate sponsorships and events, which reflected professionalism and a mainstream trajectory which is actually embraced by many surfers themselves.

It would appear that to live and breathe an adventure sport on a daily basis, one needs to be either independently wealthy or so supremely talented that corporations are paying for you. Indeed, as an advocate for the economic value of surfing claims in a recent feature story in *Fortune Magazine*, surfing 'has lost the image of being a thing for hippies and stoners, of being kinda ragtag and stupid … Surfing today is the Silicon Valley CEO. It's the brain surgeon. It's the super-athlete …' (Kvinta, 2013, para. 1). If we look back to the heyday of rock climbing in the 1960s and 1970s, we can see how many athletes lived below the poverty line and proudly referred to themselves as 'dirtbags', because they eschewed traditional career paths. While there is still some merit in being a climbing dirtbag (or a river rat, or some other subcultural identity), the rise of neo-liberalism and the decline of social support has made these niche lifestyles much more difficult to sustain over the long term (see Telford & Beames, 2016).

Summing up this contradiction between participants' subcultural resistance and integration of the corporate sector, Stranger (2010) suggests that while 'the commodification of subcultural style is often theorized in terms of a division between "authentic" insider producers and mainstream "appropriators"; between resistance to and incorporation by the dominant culture' (p. 1120). Stranger argues that surfers—and we would extend this to many other adventurers—fluidly interact with the corporate world in complex and inconsistent ways. Here again, the Gramscian (1971) concept of hegemony helps us understand how commodification in surfing 'has occurred without alienating significant numbers of core surfers' (p. 1122).

Likewise, other scholars, such as Edwards and Corte (2010) and Coates, Clayton, and Humberstone (2010), provide further compelling commentary on the influence of mass-market commercialization upon adventure activities such as BMX and snowboarding, respectively. For instance, Edwards and Corte claim that while some people within the core BMX subculture 'criticize corporate involvement and decry its influence, others take a more sanguine view emphasizing direct benefits of commercialization to the subculture as a whole and to individuals' (p. 1135).

The above discussion demonstrates how adventure, even with its niche and perhaps counter-cultural (as well as masculine) roots, has a complex and contradictory relationship with private enterprise. Big business exerts a massive amount of influence on how the masses take up adventure practices, in a Gramscian sense. But individuals themselves also have the power to shape their own adventure worlds, and each other, if we accept Foucault's idea of circulating discourses and power relationships. Furthermore, what is of interest to theorists such as Foucault is how these every-day, evolving social interactions reflect unequal power relation-ships, and thus benefit and marginalize members of the public. Further addressing the nuanced forms that adventure takes in capitalistic times, we will now discuss how corporate involvement, while sometimes considered problematic, might positively con-tribute to adventure communities.

5.6 Adventure Capitalism: Social Inequalities and Activism

Most Marxist scholars working in sports, leisure, and physical activ-ity have, over the years, justifiably presented quite critical views of corporate involvement in adventure sports. On one hand, they argue that the power of commercializing forces has given rise to a highly competitive and non-social welfare climate, whereby individuals in society with greater means can participate much more readily than those lacking power and resources. As Rinehart and Sydnor (2003) report, lifestyle sports are mostly pursued by White, wealthy indi-viduals, and are exclusionary because they require 'funds, leisure time and access to specialized environments in order to participate for any length of time' (p. 10). In terms of adventure, we can already see how this idea manifests in the 'pay to play' model of participa-tion, which may render certain activities potentially more accessible (consider indoor climbing gyms, for example) yet still requires sig-nificant money and resources in order to participate.

The involvement of corporations in the sponsorship and orga-nization of major events raises questions about equitable performer-sponsor relationships. Thorpe (2017) explains how corporations such as Red Bull solely own the copyrights and media assets from their events. This fact challenges us to consider how participants in these events 'are in a labour relationship in which they are (often freely) producing media assets for Red Bull who then proceed to make money from both the media products and, ultimately, the sales of energy drinks' (p. 558). Participating in adventure at the elite, corporate-sponsored level, can be a difficult and short-lived undertaking due to major injuries, shifting market trends and competition from peers (Thorpe, 2014), and athletes have even died in pursuit of their work (Thorpe, 2017, p. 559).

5

The globalized nature of our economic systems also facilitates exploitation. Adventure tourists from wealthier nations exploit the cultures and landscapes in less developed nations, without considering power imbalances and negative impacts (Thorpe, 2014), and there is an increasing trend of adventure corporations becoming transnational in terms of production. Today, even those with local, start-up origins, such as Burton Snowboards from Vermont, have joined Quiksilver, Billabong, and Rip Curl by moving their factories to developing nations, where there are lower manufacturing costs (Thorpe, 2014). Simultaneously, 'their "first world" bases concentrate on product development, design, distribution, marketing and promotional activities' (Stranger, 2010, p. 1121).

Inequalities are ever present in these overseas employment arrangements, where it is the lower-paid workers in developing nations who often manufacture adventure goods in poor conditions. Issues thus remain regarding the vast amounts of capital that are flowing into the bank accounts of multinational corporations that are often based in the Global North, but have their goods produced by low-paid workers in countries such as China, Bangladesh, and Vietnam. In response to these inequalities, some companies in developing nations, like Sherpa Adventure Gear from Nepal, are producing and selling their own adventure clothing and equipment, in an attempt to keep the profits more locally (Overdorf, 2013). Despite laudable initiatives like the Sherpa Corporation, the dichotomy of labour in adventure remains mostly one-sided, in terms of how profit is extracted from developing nations where so many products are made. These issues of labour rights and social justice are revisited in ► Chap. 11, which looks at adventure and sustainability.

While these inequalities created and perpetuated by capitalism are indisputable, by contrast, it has been simultaneously suggested that corporate-sponsored social activism programmes and campaigns increasingly use adventure recreation activities such as 'canoeing, surfing, cycling and rock climbing, as political statements' (Erickson, 2011, p. 478). This type of intervention is characteristic of neo-liberal societies where the private sector, rather than the state, may step forward to address community problems. This allows corporations to re-position themselves in the public eye as playing a positive role in society by funding projects that benefit those in need.

In the USA, much of the Corporate Social Responsibility (CSR) approach to supporting communities stems from the private sector historically playing a large role in supporting social welfare through non-profit and corporate bodies; public institutions are less inclined here to provide spending for the social good (Godfrey, 2009, p. 700). With neo-liberalism, the capital-rich private sector has power to decide how and when to contribute to the welfare of society. This is clearly the case when we see major corporations such as Amazon, Facebook, and Google making strategic donations to causes that they specifically want to support. And it is not just private corporations that are funding social services—this often works at the level of individual private donors too.

Following this view of CSR, Atencio et al. (2018) have described the phenomenon of social enterprise in skateboarding practice. They contend that social activist and non-profit organizations in neo-liberal nations are thriving despite the current trend of limiting state resourcing. Indeed, some social activist groups in California have teamed-up with corporate bodies to leverage resources and expertise, jointly working to raise awareness around social inclusion campaigns and facilities. Public and private bodies thus work together to create new 'urban platforms for capital' that will benefit young and old skateboarders in communities such as Oakland and San Jose. Thorpe (2014) suggests that there are now numerous social activist organizations that rely upon private funders who cohere around activities such as surfing, skiing, and skateboarding.

Moreover, there are now corporations directly challenging the prevailing norms of capitalistic society in order to promote environmental sustainability. Outdoor gear company Patagonia, for instance, has recently announced that it will take legal action over President Trump's decision to shrink two national monuments in Utah, as this will further enable profit-making by energy companies that will work on these public lands (see Maffly, 2017; Pham, 2017). Patagonia (n.d.-b), whose mission statement is '[b]uild the best product, cause no unnecessary harm, use business to inspire and implement solutions to the environmental crisis' (para. 1), has a long history of promoting what Erickson (2011) deems 'green liberalism'—which challenges the idea 'that profits and ecosystems are antithetical'—while promoting ecological regulations to 'deliver a sustainable earth' (p. 480).

In a study of corporate environmentalism in Dutch adventure facilities, Salome, van Bottenburg, and van den Heuvel (2013) take a more sceptical view, concluding that, in some cases, the principal drivers behind these greening and altruistic motivations are ultimately to gain 'competitive advantages and improving market image and reputation' (p. 187). The most interesting cases emerge from where these two drivers (profit and social or environmental values) intersect in mutually productive ways.

❓ Discussion Questions

Even with corporations who are engaged in providing public goods, it is important for us citizens to ask critical questions of the shifting social patterns around us.

1. Why would a 'for profit' organization want to give their surplus money to a community project?
2. Would their reputational stake of authenticity increase? Would they get a tax break?

3. Why are governments not at the forefront of environmentally sustainable practices and social programmes? Should there be more government social responsibility initiatives, rather than CSR ones?
4. In your country, who do you think leads the way in terms of environmentally sustainable practices and social programmes: government, corporations, or the third sector (e.g. charities and social enterprises)?

Having asked these critical questions in the above discussion box, there is evidence that the private sector is becoming more involved in notions of social and environmental responsibility. Indeed, there are even instances where corporations are taking up a more socially responsible stance, even when this might potentially reduce their popularity and profits. We saw this with the Patagonia campaign described above. Also, once a major sponsor of professional rock climbers, Clif Bar, has changed their approach due to fears of them unwittingly escalating voluntary risk-taking which has led to recent high-profile deaths of sponsored athletes who are looking to distinguish themselves (see our chapter on risk) (Branch, 2014). Why would corporations do this? Are they just being altruistic? Or do these public relations moves also benefit their 'bottom line'? It is probably not as straightforward a reason as we may think, and requires us to dig deeper in each case, to understand how profit-making relates to social activism and environmentalism!

Case Study: Where Consumerism, Values, and Enterprise Intersect

One of Patagonia's (n.d.-a) most notable marketing campaigns focused on their commitment to repair used garments, so that their customers could continue to use them. Indeed, their recent approaches to 'Black Friday' have included pushing a seemingly anti-consumer, pro-environmental sentiment by running adverts with the tagline 'Don't buy this jacket' and pledged to donate 100% of profits on the day to environmental charities (see also Meltzer, 2017).

Initially, this seems counter-intuitive, but an understanding of how consumer decisions and loyalty are increasingly value-laden suggests that an ethos of green consumerism (see Soron, 2010) actually serves to strengthen Patagonia's brand identity with their core customers, and ultimately increases revenue in the long term. Indeed, Erickson (2011) suggests that Patagonia has taught a valuable lesson to big corporations, whereby 'environmentalism is a valuable market share, and environmentalism itself becomes a produced commodity' (p. 486).

Chapter Summary

This chapter has attempted to explain key elements pertaining to the complex and contradictory relationship that adventure sports have with capitalism. We demonstrated how capitalist practices, including private sector involvement (for example, corporate and entrepreneurial), significantly mediate adventure participation. It is particularly salient that the neo-liberal ethos, which values self-sufficiency and free-market consumerism, guides much of cultural life in Western societies and thus extends its sphere of influence into the world of adventure.

If we accept this chapter's main argument that capitalist and neo-liberal thinking prevail in our societies, then we must seek to understand how these influences directly impact various types of adventure cultures. We showed how the logics of a free-market identity are increasingly represented in the corporate values of companies such as Red Bull, REI, and GoPro. These corporations, and many others involved in the adventure domain, in turn seek to position themselves as authentic and even counter-cultural, in order to develop higher social value with their core customer base (Beal & Weidman, 2003; Salome, 2010; Stranger, 2010). Furthermore, adventure's expanding corporate presence, and the desire for authenticity, is often related to being highly appealing to today's massive and wealthy international youth market.

We then drew upon the key theoretical concepts of hegemony and discourse, which can be used to examine and account for the ways that individual adventurers are coerced into acting in certain ways that align with the private sector mindset, and which are themselves supported by neo-liberal government policies. We have also shown how adventurers possess greater and lesser degrees of agency to engage with and resist the prevailing corporate forces through highly complex modes of participation. This latter line of thinking is especially fascinating because anti-establishment, creative, and even DIY ideals have traditionally underpinned many adventure activities.

We believe, however, that reducing individual and corporate relationships in the world of adventure practices to a 'mainstream versus subculture' dichotomy is unhelpful and fraught with inconsistencies. Kara-Jane Lombard (2010) advises that 'purely oppositional or resistive readings' are problematic when it comes to understanding 'corporate incorporation' in activities such as skateboarding (p. 475). Furthermore, Erickson (2011) argues that practitioners of lifestyle sports and outdoor recreation do actually represent an authentic 'way of being' that is produced by, and supports, billion-dollar industries, 'despite attempts to stray from mainstream conceptions of leisure and consumption' (p. 482). Thorpe (2014) ultimately suggests that action sport participants enact complex and even contradictory practices associated with transnational consumerism.

5

We have demonstrated that CSR and other forms of social activism emerging from capitalist structures play undeniably major roles within the contemporary adventure landscape. There are numerous social welfare and environmental activities that have been supported by corporate entities, and which often work in conjunction with activists and non-profit groups or through privately owned social media channels (Thorpe, 2017).

There is thus a contradiction that exists today, when seemingly progressive social values are advanced by corporations, even as privatization creates and sustains massive social and economic inequalities (Erickson, 2011, p. 479). It remains to be seen whether these seemingly ethical and altruistic activities impact on the 'social good', or further enhance corporate profit-making and the unequal distribution of capital that Marx and Engels so clearly articulated in 1848.

Key Readings

Erickson, B. (2011). Recreational activism: Politics, nature, and the rise of neo-liberalism. *Leisure Studies, 30*(4), 477–494.

Stranger, M. (2010). Surface and substructure: Beneath surfing's commodified surface. *Sport in Society, 13*(7–8), 117–1134.

Wheaton, B. (2004). Introduction: Mapping the lifestyle sport-scape. In B. Wheaton (Ed.), *Understanding lifestyle sports: Consumption, identity, and difference* (pp. 1–28). London: Routledge.

References

Atencio, M., & Beal, B. (2011). Beautiful losers: The symbolic exhibition and legitimization of outsider masculinity. *Sport in Society, 14*(1), 1–16.

Atencio, M., Beal, B., & Wilson, C. (2009). The distinction of risk: Urban skateboarding, street habitus, and the construction of hierarchical gender relations. *Qualitative Research in Sport, Exercise, and Health, 1*(1), 3–20.

Atencio, M., Beal, B., Wright, E., & McClain, Z. (2018). *Moving boarders: Skateboarding and the changing landscape of urban youth sports.* Fayetteville, AR: University of Arkansas Press.

Beal, B., & Weidman, L. (2003). Authenticity in the skateboarding world. In R. Rinehart & S. Sydnor (Eds.), *To the extreme: Alternative sports inside and out* (pp. 337–352). Albany, NY: State University of New York Press.

Beames, S., & Brown, M. (2017). Disneyization and the provision of leisure experiences. In K. Spracklen, B. Lashua, E. Sharpe, & S. Swain (Eds.), *The Palgrave handbook of leisure theory* (pp. 855–871). Milton Keynes, UK: The Open University and Basingstoke: Palgrave Macmillan.

Beames, S., & Varley, P. (2013). Eat, play, shop: The disneyization of adventure. In S. Taylor, P. Varley, & T. Johnston (Eds.), *Adventure tourism: Meanings, experience and learning* (pp. 77–84). Abingdon, UK: Routledge.

Booth, D. (1995). Ambiguities in pleasure and discipline: The development of competitive surfing. *Journal of Sport History, 22*(3), 189–206.

Bradstreet, K. (2016, July 21). The state of skate 2016 official report: How much international growth will the skate market see? Adventure Sports Network. Retrieved from https://www.grindtv.com/transworld-business/features/state-skate-2016-international-growth/

Branch, J. (2014, November 14). A sponsor steps away from the edge. Retrieved from https://www.nytimes.com/2014/11/16/sports/clif-bar-drops-sponsorship-of-5-climbers-citing-risks-they-take.html

Brayton, S. (2005). 'Black-Lash': Revisiting the 'White Negro' through skateboarding. *Sociology of Sport Journal, 22*, 356–372.

Bruce, S., & Yearley, S. (2006). *The SAGE dictionary of sociology*. London: Sage.

Bryman, A. (2004). *The Disneyization of society*. London: Sage.

Butz, K. (2012). *Grinding California: Culture and corporeality in American skate punk*. Bielefeld, Germany: Transcript.

Callois, R. (1961). *Man, play and games*. Glencoe, IL: The Free Press of Glencoe.

Coates, E., Clayton, B., & Humberstone, B. (2010). A battle for control: Exchanges of power in the subculture of snowboarding. *Sport in Society, 13*(7–8), 1082–1101.

Donnelly, M. (2006). Studying extreme sports: Beyond the core participants. *Journal of Sport and Social Issues, 30*(2), 219–224.

Edwards, B., & Corte, U. (2010). Commercialisation and lifestyle sport: Lessons from twenty years of freestyle BMX in 'ProTown' USA. *Sport in Society, 13*(7/8), 1135–1151.

Erickson, B. (2011). Recreational activism: Politics, nature, and the rise of neo-liberalism. *Leisure Studies, 30*(4), 477–494.

Foucault, M. (1978). *The history of sexuality: An introduction* (vol. 1) (trans: Hurley, R.). New York: Pantheon Books.

Foucault, M. (1997). Technologies of the self. In P. Rabinow (Ed.), *Michel Foucault: Ethics, subjectivity and truth. The essential works of Foucault* (Vol. 1, pp. 223–251). New York: New Press.

Godfrey, P. (2009). Corporate social responsibility in sport: An overview and key issues. *Journal of Sport Management, 23*, 698–716.

Gramsci, A. (1999/1971). *Selections from the prison notebooks of Antonio Gramsci* (trans: Hoare, Q. and Smith, G. N. Eds.). London: Elecbook.

Hamann, T. (2009). Neoliberalism, governmentality, and ethics. *Foucault Studies, 2*(6), 37.

Kane, M., & Zink, R. (2004). Package adventure tours: Markers in serious leisure careers. *Leisure Studies, 23*(4), 329–345.

Kaplan, E. A. (2012, July 5). Riding the waves to freedom: SoCal blacks and the surfing culture. KCET social focus. Retrieved from https://www.kcet.org/socal-focus/riding-the-waves-to-freedom-socal-blacks-and-the-surfing-culture

Kvinta, P. (2013, June 5). Surfonomics 101. Fortune. Retrieved from http://fortune.com/2013/06/05/surfonomics-101/

Lombard, K. (2010). Skate and create/skate and destroy: The commercial and governmental incorporation of skateboarding. *Journal of Media & Cultural Studies, 24*(4), 475–488.

Maffly, B. (2017, December 13). Uranium mill pressed Trump officials for Bears Ears reductions, records show. The Salt Lake Tribune. Retrieved from http://www.sltrib.com/news/2017/12/13/uranium-mill-pressed-trump-officials-for-bears-ears-reductions-records-show/

Maida, J. (2016, July 5). Rising popularity of skateboarding to drive the global skateboarding equipment market through 2020, says Technavio. Business Wire. Retrieved from http://www.businesswire.com/news/home/20160705005261/en/Rising-Popularity-Skateboarding-Drive-Global-Skateboarding-Equipment

Martinez, E. & Garcia, A. (1998). What is Neoliberalism? A Brief Definition for Activists. Retrieved from https://corpwatch.org/article/what-neoliberalism

Marx, K., & Engels, F. (2004/1848). *The communist manifesto*. London: Penguin.

Meltzer, M. (2017, March 7). Patagonia and the north face: Saving the world – One puffer jacket at a time. The Guardian. Retrieved from https://www.theguardian.com/business/2017/mar/07/the-north-face-patagonia-saving-world-one-puffer-jacket-at-a-time

Overdorf, J. (2013, June 1). Nepal: Can Sherpas compete with north face? PRI. Retrieved from https://www.pri.org/stories/2013-06-01/nepal-can-sherpas-compete-north-face

Patagonia. (n.d.-a). *Wornwear.* Retrieved from https://wornwear.patagonia.com/

Patagonia. (n.d.-b). *Patagonia's mission statement.* Retrieved from http://www.patagonia.com/company-info.html

Pham, S. (2017, December 5). Patagonia to sue trump: 'The president stole your land'. CNN. Retrieved from http://money.cnn.com/2017/12/05/news/patagonia-trump-national-monuments-utah/index.html

Poulson, S. (2016). *Why would anyone do that?: Lifestyle sport in the twenty-first century.* New Brunswick, NJ: Rutgers University Press.

Pringle, R. (2005). Masculinities, sport, and power: A critical comparison of Gramscian and Foucauldian inspired theoretical tools. *Journal of Sport and Social Issues, 29*(3), 256–278.

Puchan, H. (2005). Living 'extreme': Adventure sports, media and commercialization. *Journal of Communication Management, 9*(2), 171–178.

Recreational Equipment, Inc. (REI). (2018). Getting started rock climbing. Retrieved from https://www.rei.com/learn/expert-advice/getting-started-rock-climbing.html

Rinehart, R. (1998). Inside of the outside: Pecking orders within alternative sport at ESPN's 1995 "The eXtreme games". *Journal of Sport and Social Issues, 22,* 398–415.

Rinehart, R. (2008). ESPN's X games, contests of opposition, resistance, co-option, and negotiation. In M. Atkinson & K. Young (Eds.), *Tribal play: Subcultural journeys through sport* (pp. 175–196). Bingley, UK: Jai Press.

Rinehart, R., & Sydnor, S. (2003). Proem. In R. Rinehart & S. Sydnor (Eds.), *To the extreme: Alternative sports, inside and out* (pp. 1–17). Albany, NY: State University of New York.

Salome, L. (2010). Constructing authenticity in contemporary consumer culture: The case of lifestyle sports. *European Journal for Sport and Society, 7*(1), 69–87.

Salome, L., van Bottenburg, M., & van den Heuvel, M. (2013). We are as green as possible: Environmental responsibility in commercial artificial settings for lifestyle sports. *Leisure Studies, 32*(2), 173–190.

Smith, A. (2000/1723–1790). *The wealth of nations/Adam Smith.* New York: Modern Library.

Soron, D. (2010). Sustainability, self-identity and the sociology of consumption. *Sustainable Development, 18,* 172–181.

Telford, J., & Beames, S. (2016). Bourdieu and alpine mountaineering: The distinction of high peaks, clean lines and pure style. In B. Humberstone, H. Prince, & K. Henderson (Eds.), *Routledge international handbook of outdoor studies.* Abingdon, UK: Routledge.

The Inertia. (2014, November 19). Sal Masekela on racism in surfing. *YouTube.* Retrieved from https://www.youtube.com/watch?v=5Lu4cMsItUA

Thorpe, H. (2014). *Transnational mobilities in action sport cultures (Migration, diasporas and citizenship).* London: Palgrave Macmillan.

Thorpe, H. (2016). Action sports for youth development: Critical insights for the SDP community. *International Journal of Sport Policy and Politics, 8,* 91–116.

Thorpe, H. (2017). Action sports, social media, and new technologies: Towards a research agenda. *Sage Journals, 5*(5), 554–578.

van Bottenburg, M., & Salome, L. (2010). The indoorisation of outdoor sports: An exploration of the rise of lifestyle sports in artificial settings. *Leisure Studies, 29*(2), 143–160.

Wheaton, B. (Ed.). (2004). *Understanding lifestyle sports: Consumption, identity, and difference.* London: Routledge.

5

Adventure, Technology, and Social Media

© The Author(s) 2019
S. Beames et al., *Adventure and Society*, https://doi.org/10.1007/978-3-319-96062-3_6

Chapter Aims

After reading this chapter, you will be able to:

- Understand how technology influences adventure practices in terms of access, comfort, safety, performance, as well as communication
- Conceptualize how Erving Goffman's 'presentation of self' exemplifies an important aspect of technology use and the sharing of adventure performance
- Understand that global and local elements fluidly interact within transnational adventure, in a process known as 'glocalization'
- Consider how new virtual adventure experiences challenge our views of what is 'simulation' and 'reality'

6.1 The Future Is Here

A plethora of adventure-focused corporations and companies, such as those highlighted in the previous chapter, are now using digital technology to connect with adventurers and their communities (Thorpe, 2017). Simultaneously, these adventure participants are 'consuming, adopting, and adapting such technologies' (p. 557). Indeed, it is remarkable how technology, which underpins advances in social media, is so profoundly integrated into many people's adventure practices (see Woermann, 2012). Today it is not unusual, for example, to have everyday outings filmed using the latest device, for example, when GoPro cameras are mounted on surfboards (Thorpe, 2014, p. 71) and then shared through corporate-hosted platforms such as Facebook or Instagram. The popularity of technological filming devices is confirmed, for example, 'with 100 hours of GoPro video currently being uploaded to YouTube every minute of every day, and sales of action cameras growing nearly 50% annually and projected to hit 9 million in 2018' (Future of, 2015, para. 1).

Today's world arguably reflects a 'constantly connected, always available communications environment' (Thorpe, 2014, p. 74). In this context, it is all about individuals capturing the adventure experience to show others that 'you were there' (see Boyd, 2014). This presumably increases one's social status because a person can be recognized through platforms such as Twitter, Facebook, personal websites, and Instagram (to name just a few), as being a knowledgeable 'insider'.

In this chapter, we explore how adventurers now use technology which has led to new types of social media, in order to capture and present themselves to the world.[1] This practice mirrors soci-

---

1   Cultural commentators have argued that new technological advances, such as Web 2.0, *support* the proliferation of social media platforms; this view implies that technology and social media are not the same thing (Backaitis, 2012). We use this distinction throughout this chapter.

ologist Erving Goffman's idea of authentic performance; these 'presentations of self in everyday life', as he called them in his 1959 book, are recognized and acknowledged by others in particular social groups and used to provide information and cues about acceptable practice in adventure networks. Furthermore, the prevalence of virtual adventure experiences also calls into question the nature of reality itself, as many of today's adventures are now mediated, or even simulated, by technological devices. Later in this chapter, we refer to the work of French philosopher Jean Baudrillard's ideas about *simulation* and *hyperreality* to analyse several of these virtual adventures, which can cover everything from first-person view (FPV) drone flying to cycling excursions that resemble multi-player video games.

It is also fascinating how an increasing number of adventurers now integrate an ever-expanding range of new technologies in order to improve performance and develop skills (Thorpe, 2017). In many cases, experienced and novice adventurers alike can make greater gains in performance by using everything from 'competitive feedback loops' (think of a more sophisticated Fitbit device) to artificially created 'perfect' surf waves (Future of, 2015). These technological advances can provide participants with a vast array of bio-mechanical and physiological information throughout and after their session and are becoming commonplace in the fitness industry, for example, which is increasingly marked by 'the integration of customizable, interactive and, in many cases, mobile technologies' (Millington, 2016, p. 1184). Technological innovations have also reduced the time and hardship involved in travelling to the outdoor adventure site (e.g. the crag or the break), which permits more focused practice time.

Technology can also facilitate entry and comfort when it comes to accessing adventure sites previously considered too dangerous. Now, for instance—and rather alarmingly—excursions into avalanche terrain may be perceived as less hazardous by some less-experienced practitioners because of the perceived nearby 'presence of others' afforded through social media (Isaak, 2013). A recent story from *Outside Magazine* highlights this idea of accessibility, in a piece titled 'The high-tech race to make deadly adventure sports safe for anyone' (Kotler & Wheal, 2017). The article contends that technological advances support safer and easier access into adventure zones than ever before. The authors claim that this has the knock-on effect of allowing newcomers to more quickly learn and with less exposure to risk and danger. Consider the following descriptions of skiing, mountain biking, and kitesurfing from this article below:

» Powder skiing, with its utterly magical sensation of floating down a mountain, used to be the rarefied domain of top athletes. Today, extra-fat skis make that float available to

> anyone who can link two turns together. Mountain bikes, which once offered bone-rattling descents to all but the best riders, now have supple front and rear suspensions, oversize balloon tires, and an ability to roll over the most daunting terrain. Even kitesurfing – best known on the Internet for its 'kitemare' footage of people getting dragged by giant sails across highways – has mellowed. (para. 17)

Continuing with this idea of increasing access, the internet makes it easier for consumers to locate adventure services, even for previously obscure activities such as heli-skiing. Indeed, according to a Bloomberg media report, one new internet booking site, Heli, resembles an 'adventure-themed Airbnb' and aims to make adventure sports more accessible to the masses (Sohn, 2017).

Moreover, there is now widespread access to adventure information through various technological platforms. In many cases, this information can be found in databases and even internet websites that support contemporary adventurers in terms of navigation and weather conditions. For example, one internet story, called 'How have computers changed surfing?' (Collins, 2011), describes how one company, named Surfline, uses computers to provide a range of video streaming services to surfers including surf reports, live video streams, and weather forecasts.

Based on the numerous examples above, it is evident that technology has been a game changer for adventure, in terms of facilitating access, enhancing skills and performances, and sharing information. Later in this chapter, we argue that a range of new human-technology relationships are constantly being formed in the context of contemporary adventure. In the following sections, we explore how technology continues to impact upon adventure access, safety, performance, representations, and experiences. These facets of technology in adventure testify to how the identities and cultures of today's adventure practitioners are complex and constantly evolving. For instance, on one hand, it could be argued that adventurists use technology to construct global identities and communities based on their immersion in adventure activities. Yet, on the other hand, each adventurer will have local connections and ways of being in their immediate technological environment that are undoubtedly important to their own and others' experiences. This concept of *glocalized* practice, combining both global and local elements of technology, will be specifically addressed later in this chapter. We close by considering how virtual adventures raise key questions regarding embodiment within adventure.

6.2 Technological Enhancements in Adventure Practice

We first begin our description of how technology currently enhances adventure by offering a compelling personal example. The first-person commentary below exemplifies how one individual incorporates numerous innovative technologies into her cycling adventures. Sarah Cooper is a cyclist well known for competing in ultra-distance riding competitions across all kinds of terrain in the US, while enduring everything from desert temperature fluctuations to tropical storms (Yeager, 2017). In a personal correspondence with Matthew Atencio on December 28, 2017, she outlined her extensive use of technology:

>> Technology is very important in all of my training and racing ... I use Training Peaks to communicate with my coach, plan workouts, and monitor the effects of training. I use a variety of Garmin devices to track my power, heart rate, and other metrics during training. I also use the GPS capabilities to navigate both during events and during training, and my family uses it to monitor my whereabouts and check on me when I am out training. I use RideWithGPS to plan both training routes and race routes ... I also use state of the art equipment whenever possible, including Ice Friction Technology. It is a special coating for the bike chain and drivetrain components to minimize friction and maximize speed for the power that I put out.

These technological innovations are increasingly accessible even to recreational performers. For example, the mobile app and website Strava is a GPS-based sport activity tracker, with an integrated social network that allows runners and cyclists to log their workouts, spur their friends on, and compete with each other on 'segments' of regularly run or cycled routes. In 2017, a staggering one billion activities were uploaded to Strava, by everyone from elite athletes competing in the Ultra Trail du Mont Blanc or the Tour de France to local park runners (Strava, 2018). Users can participate in challenges with other users on different continents or compete with their local clubmates for the coveted King or Queen of the Mountain title on their favourite trail. The app, however, has also been criticized for revealing previously secret trails (Barber, 2018), and has even been involved in legal claims where cyclists have been accused of riding dangerously in pursuit of segment records (Vanderbilt, 2013).

Regular practitioners in other activities have also significantly benefited from technological advances for several decades.

Skateboarding, for example, became much more popular in the 1970s because of technological innovations pertaining to 'board shape and size, the wheels, the bearings, the trucks, and safety equipment' (Beal, 2013, pp. 11–12). In particular, the advent of urethane wheels, rather than clay ones, provided skateboarders with a smoother ride and the ability to navigate more diverse terrain (Beal, 2013). This re-inventing of the skateboard wheel has been hailed as the 'main innovation responsible for the birth of the skateboard as we know it today' (*Skatemag*, 2012, para. 3). Beal ultimately contends that 'Skateboarding is fundamentally about using technology to transverse human-made environments', and thus it constantly incorporates new types of ramps, wheels, decks, and trucks/axles (p. 91). Surfing also has an extensive history of technological innovation, with the introduction of the stabilizing fin in 1935 being one key advance, as well as refinements in surfboard material and wetsuit construction (Rhodes, 2016; Waldron, 2013).

Alan Ewert and Jim Sibthorp (2014) claim that in the context of 'outdoor' recreational and adventure activities, '[t]echnology plays an increasingly influential and important role', and go on to suggest that '[t]he last 10 years, in particular, have seen a virtual explosion of technological developments in the outdoors, ranging from clothes to equipment such as signalling devices and protective gear' (p. 168). Many of these technological innovations for outdoor adventuring have been made (and sold) by corporations such as The North Face and Patagonia, as mentioned in ▶ Chap. 5. According to a feature story in *The Guardian* newspaper, 'both companies understand that the appeal of endurance sports has something to do with acquiring kit that boasts the most advanced technology. For genuine adventure, their marketing implies, you need top-quality gear' (Meltzer, 2017, para. 6).

Ewert and Sibthorp (2014) additionally highlight five key areas where a range of technologies have impacted upon the outdoor recreation and adventure domain, which we summarize with their accompanying examples below (pp. 168–169):

- access and transportation (snowmobiles and off-road-vehicles),
- comfort (better clothing and equipment such as tents),
- safety (calculating technology such as dive computers and better quality equipment),
- communication (GPS units, personal locator beacons and emergency position indicating radio beacons, satellite telephones, smart phone apps, and increased cellular coverage), and
- information (not word of mouth anymore or using maps or brochures, but the Internet, automated telephone exchange, or guidebooks).

In addition to the five key features of technology in outdoor recreation and adventure addressed above, technology has also led to the creation of new adventure spaces, where practitioners can hone their skills in replicable, artificial settings, as we introduced in the previous chapter on capitalism and adventure. This type of emerging technologically enhanced environment can be observed in venues such as those which provide adventurers with such features as the 'perfect' surf wave. An example of this is the NLand Surf Park in Texas, which purportedly 'makes every surfing dream come true' due to its consistent big barrelling waves (Weimart, n.d., para. 6). Many other similar surfing venues have been established globally over the past few years, and some of these are even in landlocked regions (Hamilton, 2016; Surf Snowdonia, n.d.). However, while an artificial surf wave may have a positive value to some, these kinds of advances in technology may influence adventure practices in ways that are not universally approved. According to one 'purist' surfer featured in a *New York Times* story about the NLand surf park, 'There's something very exciting and fun to share about surfing that might not translate to, "Oh, I was in the wave pool for an hour and I finally nailed it – I did this awesome cutback"' (Cardwell & Higgins, 2016). In the next section, we highlight how the extensive use of technology for modern adventuring has been critiqued.

6.3 Critiques of Technological Enhancements in Adventure

Drawing on work by Cuthbertson, Socha, and Potter (2004), Beames (2017) explains how the use of technology to innovate adventure in the outdoor setting, for instance, can serve as a 'double edged sword' (Cuthbertson et al.'s term). Beames tells us that there are positive ways that technology has been incorporated into outdoor adventure-based education:

> » It is arguable that innovations can be considered positive if they can render activities safer (e.g., nylon ropes); make being outside more comfortable (e.g., Gore-Tex); increase participation for those less interested in the outdoors (e.g., GPS use in digital mapping can be a pedagogical hook); be less ecologically disruptive (e.g., tablets for taking photos instead of handling flora); and be less 'burdensome' and more efficient (e.g., boil-in-bag meals). (p. 3)

And yet, according to Beames (2017), there are also negative outcomes associated with the heightened use of technology in outdoor adventure. First, high-tech equipment may be less repairable in the field, be more expensive, and also breed an illusion of competence of wilderness travel and control over nature. Second, technology can be highly environmentally destructive. Consider what are the '"earth costs" associated with the resource extraction and factory manufacturing of a smart-phone or carbon-fibre mountain bike' (p. 3). Further, it is also possible that advanced technological products may be 'so clever that they constrain the degree to which participants can make choices and be creative' (p. 3). This can happen from devices only offering people one fixed way of using it and in turn reduces the requirement for adventurers to develop their skills and knowledge.

Ewert and Sibthorp (2014) also take up this critical stance, with their commentary reflecting one of the ideas expressed above by Beames, that technology may elicit an illusion of control when it comes to feelings of competence in the outdoors. These authors argue that technology 'does not come without a price', as new adventurers may get 'themselves in situations far more challenging than their skill or knowledge levels can accommodate' because they feel as if they are in a technology-driven 'bubble of safety' (p. 169). Therefore, while technology has provided a range of undoubted benefits, in terms of comfort, safety, increased acces-sibility, improved communication and access to more informa-tion, Ewert and Sibthorp contend that it may contribute to unrealistic expectations and unsafe practices, which may in some cases necessitate rescues and other environmental- and resource-demanding interventions.

Discussions surrounding the positive and negative influences of technology on adventure ultimately need to consider what tech-nology means in terms of 'appropriate' and 'real' adventure prac-tice. Perhaps, adventure practice is being increasingly divided between those with the inclination and means to enhance their adventures through top-of-the-line venues and equipment and those with more simplistic, traditional ways of participating? What does this mean in terms of participants' statuses and what constitutes legitimate forms of adventure practice?

The idea that new technologies redefine adventure activities to a point where these activities fundamentally differ from their original form has been extended by Beames' (2017) critique that technology can also serve to negatively impact adventurers' inter-actions with other humans and the natural world. As such, in some outdoor adventure settings, he tells us, 'direct engagement with place and people is reduced' because of technology (p. 3).

The above discussion raises critical views about the use of technology and the nature of what constitutes legitimate, actual adventure practice. We will return to these viewpoints in our later discussion of virtual adventure, where technology has translated adventure into numerous formats and modes of experience.

? Discussion Questions

1. Think of one of your favourite adventure activities. In what ways has technology changed the way you practise this kind of adventure?
2. What are the pros and cons of these technological advances on your adventures?

6.4 Transnationalism and Glocalization: Constantly Connected and Highly Networked Adventures in Global-Local Environments

Several scholars have been instrumental in revealing the global or transnational scope of today's adventures. Thorpe (2014) suggests that transnationalism—reflecting emerging international exchanges, ties, institutions, and interactions—has been supported by technological advances in domains such as telecommunications (p. 9). Likewise, Thorpe's piece with Ahmad (2015) indicates that internet-based media platforms such as YouTube have significantly expanded the reach of adventure activities. BMX, kitesurfing, skateboarding, surfing, and snowboarding, for instance, are now transnational in scope and nature even though they were once considered the exclusive niche domain of White, wealthier Western youths. Snowboarding is a great example of how 'transnational mass communications and corporate sponsors', as well as associated 'entertainment industries', can enable adventure activities to 'spread around the world at a phenomenal rate, and far faster than many established sports' (Thorpe, 2012, pp. 317–318).

With the global spread of adventure activities, Thorpe and Ahmad (2015) explain how, through emerging technological mechanisms, 'others have adopted and reappropriated these activities in relation to their local physical and social environments' (p. 683). They explain how surfing, for example, is becoming more popular in Iran and Bangladesh. It is also claimed that many Pakistani youth are now taking up skateboarding, while sandboarding is emerging within Saudi Arabia.

The adaptation of adventure activities in non-Western environments, such as those identified by Thorpe and Ahmad (2015), demonstrates the power of technology as it supports the flow and cross-pollination of information through adventure. Examining another adventure activity, parkour, these authors remind us that 'youth have (to varying degrees) gained greater access to global information and opportunities to virtually communicate beyond their local environments', despite remaining exposed to certain local, everyday realities, which may include 'war, poverty and political upheaval' (p. 685). This phenomenon of *glocalization*, whereby global adventure culture is inseparable from local conditions, participants, and interpretations, is a conceptual lens that we can use to understand the local impacts of adventure activities and cultures being spread around the world by social innovations using new technologies. One example that speaks to local adaptation of global adventure culture is the Skirtboarders blog run by female skateboarders in Montreal; according to Steph Mackay and Christine Dallaire (2013), this skate crew uses the internet to foster new social relationships, encourage each other, create their identities, and contest dominant media portrayals of female skateboarders.

6.5 Social Media and Adventure Practice/Presentation

The transnational growth and existence of adventure practice is undoubtedly supported by those actively using new technologies that underpin social media. For instance, a recent article from the *New Yorker* called 'Selling rock climbing in the social-media era' (Malone, 2015) recounts the adventures of Sasha DiGiulian, who is a female professional climber sponsored by Adidas. The article goes on to describe the extent to which DiGiulian's performances are documented and proliferated through numerous social media platforms:

> » in addition to multiple awards and records, her online presence is of particular interest to her sponsor Adidas. DiGiulian has more than a hundred thousand Instagram followers and close to two hundred thousand fans on Facebook. Given that climbing has banked its future on word-of-mouth virality, social media is key. (para. 9)

The huge popularity of other climbers mentioned in this story, such as Kevin Jorgeson and Tommy Caldwell, revolves around the use of social media. Indeed, this duo's ascent of one of the world's most difficult rock climbs, Yosemite's The Dawn Wall, was documented in January 2015 on Facebook and Instagram, and featured 'self-filmed videos that played like reality-show confessionals, while hired photographers and videographers documented their moves up close and on the Valley floor' (Malone, 2015, para. 9).

Writing in 2007, McGillivray and Frew explain how mobile devices permit adventure experiences to be captured and transported in real time to an external network of family, friends, and work colleagues. Seen this way, these shared experiences become digital souvenirs that are 'produced, circulated and enjoyed in the longer term as an ongoing episode of an individual's electronic autobiography' (p. 60). The contemporary adventurer thus has the means to instantly 'capture and share' their experiences with interested others. This becomes particularly fascinating when we consider the very deliberate ways that practitioners present themselves to their audiences, especially with teenagers who are 'learning how to present themselves effectively in order to make gains in distinction' (MacIsaac, Kelly and Gray, 2017, p. 15).

6.6 Capturing and Presenting 'the Self' Through Social Media: The Work of Erving Goffman Applied to Adventure Practice

The 'capture and share' adventure culture which is supported by social media innovations can be more deeply understood through the conceptual ideas of sociologist Erving Goffman, who once theorized what he called the 'Presentation of self in everyday life' (1959). According to Simon Beames and Elizabeth Pike (2008), in their paper describing the scenario of a rock climbing group in England, Goffman (1959) perceives the self to be a product of the dramatic interaction between the actor and their audience, whereby people act in a certain manner to fit the expectations of those in their company. Seen this way, people are both actors and audiences simultaneously. From Goffman's perspective, an actor's identity is confirmed by playing the same part to the same audience on different occasions (p. 4).

Beames and Pike (2008) go on to explain that 'humans have different characteristics of themselves that they reveal to, and conceal from, other people' (p. 6). Using this conceptual framework, the authors illustrate how adventurers such as rock climbers present themselves to others by using 'clothing, gestures, and speech patterns' in ways to establish their position within their social groups (p. 7).

Using Goffman's conceptual language, we can see how adventurers who use social media to capture their unique personae and achievements are constructing a 'front' that is usually accepted and taken seriously by others in a social group. Goffman (1959) highlighted how credibility comes from having a 'confirming consistency' between appearance (what I look like and what claims that I make about myself) and manner (what I actually do). The cultivated expression of one's self through technology, and the subsequent acceptance and reproduction of this self by others in a social group, constitutes what is considered meaningful and real in modern adventure practice.

Goffman's work has much relevance to our discussion about online sharing of adventurous activity, as it gives us additional conceptual language with which we can analyse how people are revealing and concealing elements of their adventures. Successes and failures, high and low mood swings, and struggles and luck may not be reported in equal measure.

We will further discuss Goffman's work in ▶ Chap. 8 when we use this framework to highlight the formation of adventure identities.

6.7 Virtual Adventure Expeditions

Virtual adventure experiences can differ from other asynchronous 'capture and share' adventure activities. In some cases, this type of technologically enhanced activity enables participants to share experiences in real time, even when they are located elsewhere. In this section, Goffman's notion that reality is fluidly mediated by humans' interactions with each other (Beames & Pike, 2008) is useful to keep in mind; at the same time, we expand upon this view by suggesting that virtual adventure experiences call into question the nature of reality itself. For example, are these types of adventure experiences actually real or are they just simulations of reality? What does this mean for those participating in virtual adventures, in terms of their embodied experiences, identities, and claims to credibility?

According to Sarah Cooper, the ultra-long-distance cyclist featured earlier in this chapter, virtual riding programmes such as Zwift are important. Cooper explains how technological advances enable her to ride indoors with fellow cyclists even more than she would outdoors, by 'using the connectivity feature to meet friends that live in other states and countries for virtual training rides' (personal communication with M. Atencio, December 28, 2017). While these virtual rides may not embody the characteristics of adventure that were highlighted in ▶ Chap. 1, they serve an instrumental purpose through enhancing training for future adventures and maintaining social relationships.

A step further away from the above kind of virtual ride would be following others' exploits through a live blog, such as those provided by some mountaineering companies (see, e.g. RMI Guides, n.d.). Scholars Ida Berger and Itay Greenspan (2008) analysed a Mount Everest Base Camp mountaineering blog that was simultaneously used by actual climbers as well as blog readers. This latter group included the 'supporters, colleagues, friends, and other readers who participated "virtually" in the expedition through the blog itself from the comfort of their living rooms or offices' (p. 97). The authors went on to explain how the blog readers followed the blog updates 'anxiously, expectantly, and proudly—feeling sometimes that they too were climbing, hiking, and participating in the Everest adventure, however vicariously' (p. 97).

This idea of 'living an adventure' that someone else is having in perilous conditions in a faraway place—from the comfort of one's living room—is becoming increasingly normalized. This phenomenon leads us to a discussion about how adventurers can have direct agency and power over the outcomes of activities through games, or by proxy, through robots and drones.

6.8 Adventures at Arm's Length

An emerging kind of adventure where participants are not directly exposed to physical hazards or the possibility of discomfort or harm is on the rise. One example is drone flying, which has gained tremendous popularity in a short time. The Drone Sports Association and the Drone Racing League have recently arrived on the scene, and according to one article, 'both have attracted sponsors, signed broadcasting deals with ESPN and hosted championship events paying big prize money' (Carson, 2017, para. 10). Further reflecting the transnational scope of adventure, new practitioners from Asian countries such as South Korea and China are becoming heavily involved in the drone adventure scene (Ji-Eun, 2016).

Testifying to the adventure component of these virtual experiences, one recent video clip features a drone participant called the 'Drone Queen'. The queen, Zoe Stumbaugh, claims that '[y]ou get to be Superman, you know. Put on the goggles, and you get to fly. Have an out-of-body experience. Become one with the machine. You get to go where you wanna go' (VICE Canada, 2017, 0:06). The next case study delves further into these type of adventure experiences and reinforces the idea that drone racing is becoming popular across the world and, notably, with young women.

The preponderance of virtual adventures, covering everything from mountaineering to drone flying, raises questions about whether these activities are actually real or just simulations. In this regard, French philosopher Jean Baudrillard (1983) has considered how widespread media platforms have created new forms of representation that actually simulate reality. Baudrillard referred to this type of represented experience as *simulacra*, where media representations simulate reality to the point that they 'become reality' for millions of people around the world. This idea of simulated hyperreality, we believe, can be directly used to investigate the emerging virtual technology practices in adventure.

From this hyperreality perspective, could it be that virtual adventure experiences actually constitute reality as they are broadcast, blogged, or live-streamed to growing audiences? Thorpe (2017) reveals how many people experience adventure in these ways, whereby 'the viewer can imagine what it must "feel" like'

6

(p. 566). New technologies underpinning different types of cameras, in particular, enable viewers to experience adventures such as 'skateparks, city streets, mountain bike trails, rivers, oceans, and mountains', and perhaps allow these viewers 'to be transported into the body of the participant for deeply affective and affecting audience experiences that they might never otherwise be able to access' (p. 566). But, in some cases, could it be that directly experienced adventure activities 'in the field', so to speak, are so fundamentally embodied and phenomenologically experienced by actual practitioners, 'that they cannot be truly experienced through simulations'? (Smith & Riley, 2008). In a similar vein, Poulson's (2016) study of mountain bikers and triathletes claims that '[m]ost often, the realness and authenticity assigned to adventure sport races is closely associated with the physical demands made on the participants', which means that the embodied experience of effort, fatigue, or weather can be seen as a critical factor of adventure practice.

Following on from this discussion, one could arguably categorize adventure based on the divergent states of embodiment that are enabled through technological innovations. Perhaps a multiplayer virtual cycling training programme fundamentally differs from a ride along on a drone adventure, due to the massively unequal physical demands. Mike Dulin, a competitive weekend cyclist who also rides to work every day, indeed claims that 'true analog engagement' felt through 'the physical contact of lever to pavement' can never be replicated or surpassed by virtual technology (Personal communication with M. Atencio, February 10, 2018). Under this same logic, the mountain climber updating a blog while climbing Mount Everest would experience more adventure than the blog reader's wonderment and excitement even if felt in real time, while reading at a café in a Singaporean shopping mall.

With regard to this debate over real or simulated adventure participation, Beal and Smith (2010) provide further food for thought. They first explain that late capitalism has created new technological conditions whereby major surfing events, such as the world-renowned Mavericks, now heavily rely upon online media representations; this resonates with Thorpe's (2017) claim that other similar events, like those hosted by Red Bull and the X Games, are 'increasingly being designed and choreographed for online audiences' (p. 557), who want to feel like they are part of the action.

Beal and Smith (2010) go on to suggest that mediated adventure experiences facilitated through live streams and event websites reflect predictable, efficient, and standardized practices that are reminiscent of sociologist George Ritzer's ideas around *McDonaldization* (see ▶ Chaps. 2 and 10). The authors argue that this type of adventure contradicts the traditional adventure impulses that attract most participants in the first place. Adventure activities like surfing, according to Beal and Smith, are predicated by flexibility, risk, uncertainty, and originality. Thus, while new technologies support online platforms that are used to package adventure activities for increased virtual consumption and participation, this practice may come into tension with the original principles of adventure.

Overall, this is a difficult issue to resolve completely. Still, it is undeniable that technological advances have created new physical, virtual, and digital platforms and spaces that must be accounted for in today's adventure domain (Thorpe, 2017). This section's ideas challenge us to question the nature and experience of these virtual adventures on a case-by-case basis, and to try to make sense of them in view of more traditional adventure formats and participants.

❓ Discussion Questions

Search online for a few adventure celebrities who use 'capture and share' or virtual platforms.

1. What kinds of adventuring 'selves' or personae do they present in either of these platforms?
2. And how do these technologically moderated selves engender financial gain and/or cultural popularity?

Case Study: Drone Adventure Racing

According to one drone adventure enthusiast and event organizer, Colleen Swafford, flying drones, especially with FPV (using goggles) allows the pilot to feel as though they are flying. It allows them to venture to places they might never be able to go normally, and certainly never see from the aerial perspective the drone gives you. Pilots travel all over the world in order to fly at some of the most beautiful locations. And they do not just fly where it is easy to get to. They are willing to hike and bike for miles in order to find that perfect place.

>> I've gone for 'ride-alongs' using a second set of goggles, and it's pretty amazing! You really feel like you're flying. The pilots I know, and whose videos I watch, love to take risks while flying. Flying out over the ocean, diving down cliffs and tall buildings, flying with race cars, flying around moving trains, even flying at illegal/semi-legal locations! I get a bit of a rush on a ride-along, but the pilots themselves get a huge rush! They really get in the zone, kind of a flow state. After an intense flight or a close race, their hands shake and their hearts start pounding, and they can sometimes even get a little nauseous. The drone becomes an extension of them. With the addition of a camera (in addition to the FPV flying camera) like a GoPro, pilots can capture stunning footage of these hard to reach locations. (personal communication with M. Atencio, December 23, 2018)

From this enthusiastic recounting of such intense virtual experiences, we can see how drone flying provides a physical and emotional sense of adventure, both in terms of the adventurous trek to locations and the type of stimulating or even flow experiences (see ► Chap. 3 for more discussion of flow) that are being provided in real time by new GoPro camera technology. This case study serves to 'stretch' the original assumptions we discussed in ► Chap. 1, about what constitutes an adventure.

6

Chapter Summary

In this chapter, we have illustrated a range of technological advances being used in adventure, with great impact. This usage of new technology has, in particular, fostered improvements in performance, both in terms of achievement and safety. At the same time, there have been critiques levelled at the many types of technological interventions supporting contemporary adventure. Dissenting voices have highlighted how technology can provide a false sense of security and competence, and that it can estrange people from the natural environment and even from each other.

In terms of the increasingly social media-driven 'capture and share' culture in adventure, we outlined how Goffman's (1959) sociological work is helpful for understanding how individuals present their adventurous selves to others. From this perspective, a person's 'self' is the product of their interactions with various audiences—all of which, at some level, Goffman regarded as 'performances'. Using this concept, we suggested that individuals use social media platforms in order to present themselves to others in ways that give them cultural kudos and recognition as authentic participants. This idea resonates with the concept of symbolic capital, whereby certain presentations of the self are given symbolic value in certain social networks (Bourdieu, 1984). From these positions, certain 'actors' have the power to influence adventure cultures and their followers. For instance, Rebecca Olive's (2015) study in Byron Bay, Australia, reveals how Instagram enables female surfers to display intimate connections with surf spots from which they previously felt excluded from. 'Gramming' thus provides these women with a sense of legitimacy in these surf spaces and media that was hitherto unavailable to them. At the same time, we wonder what specific personal attributes are being privileged through various social media platforms, and thus can be seen as routes to gaining power? As Thorpe (2017) notes, female surfers may 'self-subjectify' themselves, despite their own personal values, in order to please sponsors and gain popularity through hyper-sexualized portrayals of themselves.

This chapter also demonstrated how technology plays a major role in fostering global adventure practice. We can see this in global participants and tourists, as well as through the simultaneous cross-fertilization of styles, practices, and identities. Young people, in particular, are central to this transnational context of adventure, in terms of how their styles and practices influence adventurers, and also in terms of how they promote products and are seen as avid consumers. Then there are various types of corporate production and promotion that underpin modern adventures. Thorpe (2012) reminds us to consider the dispersal of transnational values, images, information, and objects (including people) that directly impact upon local people, practices, and belief systems.

Finally, we demonstrated how virtual reality experiences, such as those offered through drone racing, cycling, and mountaineering, call into question the nature of adventure reality itself. An increasing number of participants in these virtual cultures experience adventure through live streams, multiplayer gaming platforms, and internet websites. These practices pose challenging questions about adventure and potential new categories and characterizations. To what degree do these virtual experiences count as actual adventure? How important is it for adventures to involve being exposed to arduous, risky, and even dangerous environmental conditions, which have the capacity to elicit responses of pain and emotional suffering? However one looks at these questions, it is clear that the presence of virtual technology has transformed, and continues to transform, adventure activities and their cultures in today's expanding transnational scene.

Key Reading

Berger, I., & Greenspan, I. (2008). High (on) technology: Producing tourist identities through technologized adventure. *Journal of Sport and Tourism, 13*(2), 89–114.

References

Backaitis, V. (2012, June 29). Think social media is technology? You may want to think again. *CMS Wire*. Retrieved from https://www.cmswire.com/cms/social-business/think-social-media-is-technology-you-may-want-to-think-again-016352.php

Barber, J. (2018). *The Strava effect on mountain biking.* Retrieved from: https://www.singletracks.com/blog/gps/the-strava-effect-on-mountain-biking/

Baudrillard, J. (1983). *Simulations.* New York: Semiotext(e).

Beal, B. (2013). *Skateboarding: The ultimate guide.* Santa Barbara, CA: Greenwood.

Beal, B., & Smith, M. (2010). Mavericks: Big wave surfing and the making of 'nothing' from 'something. *Sport and Society, 13*(7-8), 1102–1116.

Beames, S. (2017). Innovation and outdoor education. *Journal of Outdoor and Environmental Education, 20*(1), 2–6.

Beames, S., & Pike, E. (2008). Goffman goes rock climbing: Using creative fiction to explore the presentation of self in outdoor education. *Australian Journal of Outdoor Education, 12*(2), 3–11.

Berger, I., & Greenspan, I. (2008). High (on) technology: Producing tourist identities through technologized adventure. *Journal of Sport and Tourism, 13*(2), 89–114.

Bourdieu, P. (1979/1984). *Distinction* (trans: Nice, R.). Cambridge, MA: Harvard University Press.

Boyd, D. (2014). *It's complicated: The social lives of networked teens.* New Haven, CT: Yale University Press.

Cardwell, D., & Higgins, M. (2016, September 2). Surf's up, and the ocean is nowhere in sight. *The New York Times.* Retrieved from https://www. nytimes.com/2016/09/03/business/energy-environment/surfs-up-and-the-ocean-is-nowhere-in-sight.html

Carson, E. (2017, March 31). Drone racing gets off the ground. *Cnet.* Retrieved from https://www.cnet.com/news/drone-racing-league-fpv-goggles-espn-sports-hobby-gets-off-ground/

Collins, S. (2011, February 23). How have computers changed surfing? *Surfline.* Retrieved from http://www.surfline.com/surf-science/history-of-surf-forecasting-and-computer-technology-computers-change-surfing%2D%2D-forecaster-blog_52892/

Cuthbertson, B., Socha, T., & Potter, T. (2004). The double-edged sword: Critical reflections on traditional and modern technology in outdoor education. *Journal of Adventure Education and Outdoor Learning, 4*(2), 133–144.

Ewert, A., & Sibthorp, J. (2014). *Outdoor adventure education: Foundations, theory, and research.* Champaign, IL: Human Kinetics.

Future of. (2015). Extreme of adventure sports. *Future of.* Retrieved from http://futureof.org/sports-2015/extreme-adventure-sports/

Goffman, E. (1959). *The presentation of self in everyday life.* New York, NY: Anchor.

Hamilton, J. (2016, August 30). Surfers and scientists team up to create the 'perfect wave'. *National Public Radio.* Retrieved from http://www.npr. org/2016/08/30/490545030/surfers-and-scientists-team-up-to-create-the-perfect-wave

Isaak, G. (2013). Decision-making and social media: The Millennial generation's persistent weak layer. *The Avalanche Review, 32*(2), 24–25.

Ji-Eun, S. (2016, July 11). [Venture Abroad] Korea is late to UAV game, while China has the 'Apple of drones'. *Korea JoonAng Daily.* Retrieved from http://koreajoongangdaily.joins.com/news/article/article.aspx?aid=3021 092&cloc=joongangdaily%7Chome%7Cnewslist1

Kotler, S., & Wheal, J. (2017, February 21). The high-tech race to make deadly adventure sports safe for anyone. *Outside.* Retrieved from https://www. outsideonline.com/2158371/high-tech-race-deadly-adventure-sports-safe-everyone

MacIsaac, S., Kelly, J., & Gray, S. (2017). She has like 4000 followers!': The celebrification of self within school social networks. *Journal of Youth Studies.* https://doi.org/10.1080/13676261.2017.1420764

MacKay, S., & Dallaire, C. (2013). Skateboarding women: Building collective identity in cyberspace. *Journal of Sport and Social Issues, 30*(2), 173–196.

Malone, C. (2015, March 30). Selling rock climbing in the social-media era. *The New Yorker.* Retrieved from https://www.newyorker.com/news/sporting-scene/selling-rock-climbing-in-the-social-media-era

Meltzer, M. (2017). Patagonia and The North Face: Saving the world – one puffer jacket at a time. *The Guardian.* Retrieved from https://www.theguardian. com/business/2017/mar/07/the-north-face-patagonia-saving-world-one-puffer-jacket-at-a-time

Millington, B. (2016). Fit for prosumption: Interactivity and the second fitness boom. *Media, Culture & Society, 38*(8), 1184–1200.

Olive, R. (2015). Reframing surfing: Physical culture in online spaces. *Media International Australia, Incorporating Culture and Policy, 155,* 99–107. Retrieved from: https://www.researchgate.net/publication/279804347_Reframing_Surfing_Physical_Culture_in_Online_Spaces

Poulson, S. (2016). *Why would anyone do that? Lifestyle sport in the twenty-first century.* New Brunswick, NJ: Rutgers University Press.

Rhodes, M. (2016, February 25). The fascinating evolution of the surfboard. *Wired.* Retrieved from https://www.wired.com/2016/02/fascinating-evolution-surfboard/

RMI Guides. (n.d.). *RMI Expeditions Blog*. Retrieved from https://www.rmiguides.com/blog/

Skatemag. (2012, February 12). The evolution of skateboard wheels. *Skateboarding Magazine*. Retrieved from: http://www.skateboardingmagazine.com/the-evolution-of-skateboard-wheels/

Smith, P., & Riley, A. (2008). *Cultural theory: An introduction*. Oxford, UK: Wiley-Blackwell.

Sohn, T. (2017, October 30). Can technology bring adventure sports like heli-skiing to the masses? *Bloomberg*. Retrieved from https://www.bloomberg.com/news/articles/2017-10-30/can-technology-bring-adventure-sports-like-heli-skiing-to-the-masses

Strava. (2018). *2017 in stats*. Retrieved from https://blog.strava.com/2017-in-stats/

Surf Snowdonia. (n.d.). *Homepage*. Retrieved from https://www.surfsnowdonia.com

Thorpe, H. (2012). Transnational mobilities in snowboarding culture: Travel, tourism and lifestyle migration. *Mobilities, 7*(2), 317–345.

Thorpe, H. (2014). *Transnational mobilities in action sport cultures (migration, diasporas and citizenship)*. London: Palgrave Macmillan.

Thorpe, H. (2017). Action sports, social media, and new technologies: Towards a research agenda. *Communication and Sport, 5*(5), 554–578.

Thorpe, H., & Ahmad, N. (2015). Youth, action sports and political agency in the Middle East: Lessons from a grassroots parkour group in Gaza. *International Review for the Sociology of Sport, 50*, 678–704.

Vanderbilt, T. (2013). How Strava is changing the way we ride. Retrieved from: https://www.outsideonline.com/1912501/how-strava-changing-way-we-ride

VICE Canada. (2017, September 8). Racing drones with the 'Drone Queen'. *Facebook*. Retrieved from https://www.facebook.com/vicecanada/videos/1665726383447918/

Waldron, R. (2013, July 3). Are new technologies compromising the integrity of the ride? Surfer. Retrieved from https://www.surfer.com/blogs/opinion/make-sure-it%E2%80%99s-still-surfing/

Weimert, K. (n.d.). Rip wave after wave at NLand surf park. *Fitt Austin*. Retrieved from https://fitt.co/austin/nland-surf-austin/

Woermann, N. (2012). On the slope is on the screen: Prosumption, social media practices, and scopic systems in the freeskiing subculture. *American Behavioral Scientist, 56*(4), 618–640.

Yeager, S. (2017, August 10). Learn to get next-level tough from RAAM winner Sarah Cooper. *Bicycling*. Retrieved from https://www.bicycling.com/training/raam/learn-to-get-next-level-tough-from-raam-winner-sarah-cooper/slide/4

Adventure and Equalities

© The Author(s) 2019
S. Beames et al., *Adventure and Society*, https://doi.org/10.1007/978-3-319-96062-3_7

Chapter Aims

﹣ After reading this chapter, you will be able to:
﹣ Use conceptual language to explain how practices can both exclude and include certain members of society
﹣ Identify some of the individual, institutional, and societal barriers to inclusive opportunities in adventure
﹣ Explain the role that adventure cultures play in both reinforcing and removing barriers to participation
﹣ Identify strategies which can help to make access to adventurous experiences more equitable

7.1 White, Non-disabled Men

Social and environmental justice issues are increasingly important in the fields of outdoor studies (Humberstone, 2016; Warren, Roberts, Breunig, & Alvarez, 2014) and lifestyle sport (Wheaton, 2004) which inform our study of adventure. Even casual onlookers of adventure cultures can identify a lack of diversity and under-representation of women, people of colour,[1] people with disabilities, and older people. This chapter considers how the spaces, practices, and cultures associated with adventure are not yet equally accessible, as well as looking at how and why individuals, communities, and society can work to correct this.

In considering (and working to tackle) the inequalities we see in adventure, it is important for us as authors to acknowledge our privileged positions in relation to both academic and adventure cultures. Roberts (2009) states that 'leisure scholars need to examine their participation in institutions that have a history of perpetuating Whiteness as a function of power and privilege' (p. 506). We authors are three men who work in academia, have had adventure-filled childhoods, and who are actively engaged in a workplace that was designed by people like us, primarily for people who were more or less like us. Shifting discourses about sex, gender, race, ethnicity, physical and mental ability, age, and religion make it imperative that we consider the 'equalities' filters that we bring to a book written for all, by a few from a dominant social group. We continue to learn as we read, write, teach, and debate and encourage you to do the same.

As we have detailed in ▶ Chaps. 1 and 5, the development of adventure as a concept can be seen as historically rooted in exploratory colonialism and the desire to accrue capital

---

1   We use the term 'people of colour' when discussing the shared disadvantaged position of non-White groups, as a means of identifying common experiences of exclusion. Where we use the term Black, we are referring specifically to people of the African diaspora and their collective experiences of oppression through history, while acknowledging the ethnic diversity within this community.

(Nehrlich, 1987)—social practices which were, and arguably still are, led and dominated by White men at the cost of others. Although we have also identified clear countercultural elements within adventure, these masculine, 'ableist'[2] approaches have led to a dominant social paradigm which has limited the diversity of people taking part in adventurous activities.

7.2 Key Terms and Concepts

In order for us to have excellent discussions in and from this chapter, we need to make sure that we are using some key terms correctly.

Equality is about treating everybody the same way. This can be a noble idea, in principle, but it is not always ideal. For example, if a government wanted everyone to go mountain biking, it could give everyone a mountain bike. This would involve each citizen being treated the same. However, it is not necessarily *equitable* as some people might already have a mountain bike (or two) and not need another one. Equity is about everyone getting what they need. As we will see, however, sometimes getting what you need is still not enough to guarantee access to exclusive adventure communities.

Discrimination occurs when you are treated less favourably than another person in a similar situation, and this treatment cannot be objectively and reasonably justified.[3] Discrimination takes place on three levels: individual, institutional, and societal (Adams, Bell, & Griffin, 2007). *Individual discrimination* refers to the attitudes and actions of humans on each other. Examples of this might be an employer making unwanted sexual comments at the workplace or being extra-protective of one's belongings in a locker room when someone 'other' is present. *Institutional discrimination* involves laws and policies. Examples of this include the lack of maternity leave for same-sex couples or hosting social events in inaccessible places. Finally, *societal* (aka cultural) *discrimination* has to do with dominant social values and norms being pressed on all members of society. One such social value could be that families are *supposed* to be heterosexual. Another could be the right-wing view that everyone is capable of economic success if they just try hard enough.

Very importantly, alongside these three levels of discrimination there are two ways in which discrimination is enacted. The first and most obvious is *direct discrimination*, where people are

---

2   Able-ist refers to discrimination against people with disabilities.
3   ▶ http://www.equalityhumanrights.com/human-rights/what-are-human-rights/human-rights-in-british-law/protection-from-discrimination/

overtly treated less favourably. A policy of not employing stand-up paddleboard instructors with red hair would be direct discrimination! *Indirect discrimination* involves applying a rule 'equally', but which creates conditions that puts some people at a disadvantage. A blanket policy that 'all employees must work on Sundays' may seem fair, yet marginalize those who cannot work on Sundays on religious grounds. Similarly, a social event open to all, but which is being hosted on the top floor of an organization that has historically excluded people of colour and women and cannot be reached by a wheelchair user because there is no elevator, has indirectly discriminated against three groups of people even though their intentions may have been genuinely well meaning.

While there have been significant improvements in some areas of adventure practice, from recreational to professional and institutional contexts, inequity still exists in society and some adventurous experiences are not equally accessible regardless of wider social change and the slowly increasing financial means of under-represented groups (Corlett, 2017). This chapter will consider three very broad groups of people who are under-represented in adventure, seek to outline the constraints that lead to this, and suggest how *you* can work to make a difference. We will focus primarily on issues relating to gender, race and ethnicity, and ability. This is not to say that we are ignoring other issues (e.g. religion, sexuality and age), but rather aim to highlight how many of the reasons that can account for the under-representation of these large social groups can be used to understand the plight of other marginalized groups.

7.3 Who Is Being Silenced?

Before thinking about how specific characteristics might limit people's ability or motivation to participate in adventurous experiences, we want to acknowledge that exclusion often does not stem from one isolated kind of oppression. People can experience oppression on the basis of their race, sexuality, and ability, for example, at the same time: this is called *intersectionality* (Hancock, 2015). Intersectionality describes how individuals' identities are not formed by exclusive characteristics, but from overlapping ones, which can lead to complex, individualized experiences of oppression caused by multiple unequal power relations (Collins, 2015). This perspective was put forward by Black feminist activists (Crenshaw, 1989) and 'third wave'[4] feminists as a critique of existing feminist thought, which was seen to overemphasize the role of

---

4   It is generally agreed that there have been three waves of feminism—the third of which recognizes the wide diversity in women's experience and thus the intersectionality of oppression.

gender in oppression without fully acknowledging the impact of other identities such as race, ability, class, and sexual orientation, where the sum experience (the intersectionality) could be more powerful than the individual parts. While there is a regularly cited risk of oversimplifying and misapplying the concept of intersectionality, it is useful for us as we begin to consider how exclusion (and therefore inclusion) operates within adventure. We will now examine gender, race, and ability, and the ways in which they influence, and are influenced by, adventure practices, which themselves are located within broader society.

7.4 **Gender and Adventure**

As half of the world's population, women form the largest excluded group in adventure, and a significantly under-represented pool of potential leaders, consumers, athletes, and cultural contributors. Worldwide, women live with constraints in many spheres of social life. For example, while the gaps between health outcomes and educational attainment have closed significantly over the last ten years, even in the Global North there are still marked differences between the sexes in terms of economic and political participation (World Economic Forum, 2015). In the UK, the average full-time wage is 9.4% lower for women than men, and 18.1% lower when also looking at part-time employment (Office for National Statistics, 2016), while in the US it is estimated that women earn up to 21% less than men when looking at all employees (US Congress Joint Economic Committee, 2016). The main reasons for this are that a higher proportion of women work part-time and in lower paid jobs, most often because they take time out to have and care for children.

Acknowledging the influence that structural factors like unequal pay and career progression have on women's abilities to participate in outdoor adventure has led to a significant amount of research into gender and outdoor education contexts since the 1990s (see Gray, 2016 and Gray & Mitten, 2018). More recently, there has also been an increasing interest in trans people's experiences. Trans people do not identify with their biological sex and thus do not fit within the male/female binary that is called *heteronormativity*. This research on gender and outdoor adventure covers topics such as identity (Boniface, 2006), leadership approaches (Saunders & Sharp, 2002), employment (Allin & West, 2013), skill development (Warren & Loeffler, 2006), and 'hegemonic masculinities' (Humberstone, 2000). Much of this research considers interpersonal and intrapersonal constraints to participation. A constraint is anything that serves to limit how, or to what extent, someone does something; its fluidity makes it a more useful term than 'barrier', which implies fixed, universal roadblocks which have to be overcome rather than negotiated or adapted to. *Interpersonal* constraints are things which involve other people, like family responsibilities and time commitments, or the absence of a peer group, while *intrapersonal* constraints are internalized ideas about the self which make it harder for a person to take part, such as how competent you think you are, anxiety about activities, or what you think is expected of you by certain people. While, as we outlined at the start of the chapter, these constraints do not only affect people because of their gender, and while women are increasingly overcoming barriers to participation in adventure recreation (Little, 2002)—thanks in part to initiatives led by national sport policies—there is no doubt that many women continue to experience challenges that their male counterparts do not.

For Karen Warren (2016), much of the discrimination against women is rooted in the oppressive effects of gender roles and gender socialization. In sociology, a *role* is a cluster of expected and recognized behaviours associated with someone's position in society, which we understand by watching how other people in these positions behave. For example, students might expect their professors to behave in certain ways and have specific obligations based on their understanding of that role. These ways of behaving might differ from those associated with the same professors' other roles as 'mothers', 'daughters', or 'colleagues'.

While 'sex' is a biological characteristic, *gender identity, gender expression*, and *sexual orientation* are dynamic individual and cultural constructs. This means they exist because of, and relative to, the societies in which they are located and experienced. We should also emphasize that all four of these terms are independent of each other, and manifest on continuums rather than as 'either/or' binaries. This means that all individuals sit somewhere on sliding scales of male-ness and female-ness (biological sex); man-ness and woman-ness (gender identity); femininity and masculinity (gender expression); and attraction to men and women (sexual orientation). We might move around on these scales on a day-to-day basis, or more frequently, depending on whom we are interacting with.

We learn much of how to dress, act, and communicate through the process of *socialization*, which Coakley (2003) defines as 'an active process of learning and social development, which occurs as we interact with one another and become acquainted with the social world in which we live' (p. 98). Depending on your theoretical perspective, this can occur in different ways and serve different social functions. For Warren (1996) and other feminist thinkers, the socialization associated with women's varied roles contributes to obligations, responsibilities, and ways of acting which limit their ability to participate in certain activities, even when 'on paper' there is nothing stopping them. She states that:

> » The primary factor that advances the myth of accessibility is a woman's social conditioning. When deciding between the needs of her loved ones and her own desire for adventure, an outdoor trip seems frivolous and trivial compared to a child who might need her. Making the choice to take for herself when she is trained to always give to others creates an internal conflict. (Warren, 1996, pp. 11–12)

In addition to *primary socialization* which takes place around the home in early childhood, social roles, and the norms associated with them are reinforced through experience of broader social contexts, such as school or work or local culture, in what can be characterized as *secondary socialization*. Although there has been some progress in recent years, we can see clear examples of this in how media and advertising represent women in adventure. Take, for example, the mainstream media's response to the death of climber Alison Hargreaves on K2 in 1995 (see Frohlick, 2006). While lauded for her solo ascent of Everest without bottled oxygen earlier in the year, her similar, and ultimately fatal, ascent of K2 was criticized by the media. Much of the criticism in the main-stream press portrayed Hargreaves as choosing to put her role as a climber before her role as a mother through undertaking such a dangerous climb, in what was presented as a selfish act. Paul Gilchrist (2007) explains this in relation to the political climate at the time, stating that Hargreaves' 'actions were displayed as an affront to the prescriptive ideal of the family in Conservative Britain, an institution seen as morally laudable and civilly respon-sible' (p. 399). The Hargreaves case is an illustrative example of how dominant socio-political beliefs can shape the ways in which adventure practices are viewed by the masses. Consider media reports about male mountaineers who are fathers and who die while climbing. How many of them focus primarily on their neglected paternal obligations, rather than their achievements in the mountains?

We can also observe the influence of gender role socialization in advertising. McNiel, Harris, and Fondren (2012) analysed all of the advertisements in two years of the American magazines *Backpacker* and *Outside*, in order to examine how women were depicted. While *Outside* has since published a dedicated issue focusing on women in the outdoors, with all-female contributors (*Outside Magazine*, 2017), this study still helps us to understand the power of representation in popular media. The analysis found that, although women made up 46% of the people shown in the advertisements, they were generally shown in contexts which implied that they participated in adventurous activities on a lower technical level than men and that they required leadership and guidance in the outdoors (usually by men). Women's participation in the outdoors was also often depicted as a way to escape from domestic obligations, or an extension of these into adventurous settings (e.g. cooking or making camp), whereas men were more often depicted as engaged in dynamic, less camp-based activities. McNiel and colleagues' final finding was that the smaller number of advertisements which did show women in more committed and adventurous contexts implied that these women were somehow 'special', but also sought to emphasize feminizing features of their character, whereas similar advertisements featuring male athletes focused solely on their accomplishments.

This final finding about these 'special' female adventurers is directly connected with a point made by Warren more than 20 years ago about one of the central challenges of increasing participation—not just for women, but for all under-represented groups. Warren (1996) explains the widely held assumption that those women who have managed to get past the restrictive gender roles and structural challenges are positive role models, who will in time influence the processes of socialization for all girls. This assumption has been labelled the 'myth of the superwoman' and is especially prevalent in professional outdoor leadership contexts, where people perceive highly competent female leaders as unique and an exception to the rule (Warren, 1996). The distance between women starting out in activities and the 'superstars' is perceived as too great ('I could never be like her'), and so the highly competent female instructors are not as effective role models as they otherwise might be: indeed, they are regarded as being successful in spite of their femininity, rather than because of it. This occurs in a context which has historically valued 'masculine' qualities over and above those identified as characteristic of feminist outdoor leadership (Warren, 2016), and where women tend to underestimate what they are able to do (Warren & Loeffler, 2006) and fall victim to 'blind spots' in professional settings which limit the visibility of their achievements (Gray, 2016).

Acknowledging that there might be more masculine and feminine ways of *doing* adventure is the starting point for what can be termed *gender-sensitive* approaches, which are proposed by some as one way of enhancing the value of more feminine forms of leadership and adventure experiences. These approaches emerged out of women-only training courses and expeditions, which were designed to create supportive environments for women. In these early courses, greater emphasis was placed on safety (both emotional and physical), individualized goal setting, valuing diversity, intrinsically motivated journeying (not as a means to an end), collective decision-making, and flexibility (Mitten, 1996). What is important to recognize here is that, while questioning and challenging the masculine status quo and using generalizations as a way to proactively reach out to under-represented groups is good, not all women learn in the same way. With hindsight, we could argue that the leadership approaches used in early single gender trips may have equally suited some men, who might also have felt uncomfortable in 'mainstream' settings. Hopefully, you should be beginning to see that an informed understanding of the bigger social issues at play is most useful when combined with an understanding of limiting factors at an individual level.

Recent work by Holly Thorpe and Rebecca Olive (2016) highlights how, while some female action sport athletes may have a high level of media coverage, they are usually young, White, slim, and heterosexual. The authors' point here is that there are lots of older women of other ethnic backgrounds, with different gender identities and varying abilities who are out there, but remain largely invisible.

We cannot hope to do full justice to the topic of adventure and gender in this section, but we have introduced concepts associated with gender and outlined some of the structural and cultural challenges that women in particular face when participating in adventurous activities. Gender role socialization, limited media representation and hegemonic male-dominated professional/industry settings all make it harder for women to achieve equitable experiences in adventurous settings (Humberstone, 2000). Supportive, gender-specific activities are one way of making things easier, but the value of diverse people involved in diverse ways of *being* adventurous needs to extend into the wider field and be visible in media and organizations.

7.5 Race and Ethnicity

Many of the structural, symbolic, and social forces that we have identified as limiting female participation in adventure also work to exclude other groups. Socialization, representation, and prejudice based on assumptions about social roles can also affect people of all genders who do not fit the image of adventurers that has been put forward and perpetuated by those in positions of power. When taken together, race and ethnicity continue to be one of the central characteristics that affect an individual's experiences of society, and have been observed as determining factors in terms of engaging in adventure and outdoor life more generally (Roberts, 2016). In this section, while we will mainly draw on examples from North American and European contexts, we encourage you to think about how the principles and issues might apply to communities you have been, or are, part of.

The concept of 'race' is based on the historic misconception that there are significant biological differences between groups of human beings, which led to some groups of people being treated differently according to their skin colour and other distinguishing features. Although it is now firmly established that there is no scientific basis for this distinction, the fact that people have historically experienced and continue to experience discrimination based on 'racial' characteristics makes what is called *racism* hard to ignore. Pilkington (2003) asserts that the flawed understanding of race is 'distinctly modern' and based on incorrectly held assumptions:

» a limited number of fixed and discrete races can be distinguished on the basis of clear physical and differences between people; these races are not only physically different but also different in terms of their intellectual capacities and cultural achievements; as a result they form a hierarchy whereby some are inherently superior to others. (pp. 6–7)

All of these distinctions have been proven as baseless by science, but remain stubbornly persistent in some cultures. Historic examples of racial inequality are most obvious in places like the US and South Africa, where racial segregation and inequality was institutionalized and laid down in law within living memory. These nationwide interventions demonstrate how race is a social construct, while providing examples of racially dualist frameworks (White/Black), which were prevalent until the late twentieth century.

In contrast to this discourse on race, most social scientists and policy makers (particularly in the UK) now tend to use the term *ethnicity* when discussing groups with shared cultural heritage within a society. Giddens and Sutton (2017) define ethnicity as 'a source of identity whose basis lies in society and culture' (p. 665), which implies that membership is based on the belief of shared common culture and connection to a certain identity, rather than any external marker such as skin colour. This is a much more useful way of understanding the nuances of multicultural identity in particular, as it acknowledges that ethnic identities are multifaceted and fluid through time and across contexts; indeed, new ethnic identities are emerging from changing social circumstances, and are validated by how people identify with them rather than solely by external, objective indicators (Cornell & Hartmann, 2007).

Irrespective of the words we use to understand it, the lack of ethnic diversity on ski hills, mountain bike trails, and surf breaks around the world is testament to oppressive experiences of racialized geographies and everyday racism. Historically, researchers tried to explain this either in terms of marginality or ethnicity. The marginality hypothesis highlights how dominant groups have access to more disposable income and thus more choice in their leisure activities—both of which further reinforce the marginalization of other groups. Conversely, the ethnicity hypothesis suggests that it is ethnic groups' distinct cultures and values that result in fairly fixed subcultural leisure practices (e.g. 'Black people don't like to ski'). However, both of these approaches have been shown to be flawed, as they are based on the assumption that what the dominant group does for fun is what everyone should aspire to do for fun. In other words, the more money or fewer ethnic ties you have (i.e. the closer to Whiteness you are), the more likely you are to participate in dominant forms of leisure (Floyd, 1998). As we deepen our understanding of the importance of individual experience in society, we come to recognize the necessity for new approaches to understanding leisure identities, which must acknowledge the complexity of multicultural identities and focus on community voice (Roberts, 2016). In places like Australia, New Zealand, and North America, there are historic examples of ethnic community voices being silenced. In such colonized landscapes, the knowledge structures and ways of being in the outdoors belonging to colonizing ethnic groups have subjugated Indigenous connections to the land (Brookes, 2002; Lowan, 2009). The colonizers have largely dictated how people are 'supposed' to play on the land and in the water.

In the US, where people who identify as Black have the lowest participation rate in outdoor sport and recreation (National Park Service, 2011; Outdoor Foundation, 2017), everyday racism, and prejudice based on stereotype can be observed (Haile, 2017). Many of the environments where adventure sports take place, particularly wilderness areas, are 'sites where African Americans experience insecurity, exclusion and fear born out of historical precedent, collective memory and contemporary concerns' (Finney, 2014, p. 28). Reflecting on her experiences at a rural writing retreat, the African-American writer Evelyn White (1996) articulates this as:

» a sense of absolute doom about what might befall me in the backwoods. My genetic memory of ancestors hunted down and preyed upon in rural settings counters my fervent hopes of finding peace in the wilderness. Instead of the solace and comfort I seek, I imagine myself in the country as my forebears were – exposed, vulnerable, and unprotected – a target of cruelty and hate. (p. 376)

This *collective memory* is powerful: while White herself has not seen a lynching first-hand, the environments in which these summary executions took place have cultural connotations that are reinforced through shared experiences of events still within living memory. This is also informed by the additional acknowledgement of a shared ethnic heritage where slavery forced engagement with natural spaces.

Ethnicity has a flipside, too, of course, and can be a source of privilege for White people, in particular. Even if the beneficiaries do not set out to create or exploit an advantage over others, their unconscious privilege may compound other cultural groups' experiences of exclusion. Peggy McIntosh (1989) calls this the 'invisible knapsack' of White privilege, which is full of 'special provisions, maps, passports, codebooks, visas, clothes, tools and blank checks' (p. 11), and thus affords White people benefits they are not necessarily aware of. This discussion links back to our earlier mention of the crucial difference between equality and equity; just because there are *equal* opportunities for a group of people, does not mean that there are *equitable* experiences for each individual—especially when those opportunities are controlled by people who may be oblivious to their position of relative privilege.

Case Study: Mainstream and Social Media Representation

How we consume media has changed dramatically since the studies that looked at the representation of women and Black people in print advertisements in the 1980s and 1990s.[5] Clever computer algorithms and internet cookies have conspired to ensure that we are subjected to curated streams of images and news articles that seem to know all about our taste in goods and services—many of which will be based on our gender, ethnicity and age. The positive side to these new modes of communicating is the way they provide a voice for groups who have historically had little control over how they were represented in the media; anyone with access to Instagram can develop a platform for resisting oppression.

Take Brothers of Climbing, for example, which started out as individual climbers in Brooklyn looking out at the gym for others like themselves. The organization has grown to be a public and positive force for increasing inclusion in the sport. Brothers of Climbing uses social media to build diverse climbing communities by organizing events like Color the Crag (n.d.).

Representation is also being shaped by corporate organizations, such as Getty Images. The company's Lean In collection, which is co-curated with the women's empowerment nonprofit organization, has already added 14,000 contemporary images of powerful women and girls in work, leisure and family settings into the world's largest stock photo resource. In 2007, Getty's most downloaded photograph associated with the search term 'woman' showed a half-naked woman lying in bed, looking at the camera; in 2017 it is a wide shot of a solo woman hiking high up in Banff National Park (Cain Miller, 2017).

---

5   McNiel et al. (2012) and Martin (2004).

Skiing in the US, which has been critiqued in terms of its' 'Whiteness' (Coleman, 1996; Harrison, 2013), offers a fascinating example of the cultural influences of ethnicity on exclusion/inclusion. Skiing is rooted in a European cultural heritage and aesthetic that feels very comfortable to many White people; on paper there is, of course, nothing stopping someone from a different ethnic group who can afford skis, lessons and a lift ticket from getting involved. However, even in the face of concerted efforts from organizations like the National Brotherhood of Skiers, which promotes and facilitates skiing for people of colour, skiing remains primarily a sport for White people. *Intergenerationality* is a key characteristic of skiing, as families tend to participate together, with each generation often teaching the next, which in turn makes it harder for new entrants to the field to start as adults. Imagine how you would feel trying a new sport for the first time and being aware that everyone else around you looked different from you, and was aware of the apparent 'inconsistency' between your ethnicity and the public space you were in.

We have shown in this section that, at present, there are big differences in how, and to what degree, people from different ethnic backgrounds participate in adventurous experiences. This can be explained in different ways and is compounded by cultural constraints, such as a lack of role models and limited visibility of diversity in adventure media, as well as people's broader experiences of everyday racism and White privilege. However, newer, more democratic means of communication are showing signs of diversifying the ethnicities found on waves, couloirs, and trails.

❓ Discussion Questions

Using either a print edition of your favourite adventure magazine, a blog that you read regularly, or your social media feed, look closely and critically at the images that you see presented and answer the following questions:

1. *Who* do you see?
2. *What* are they doing?
3. What do the activities suggest about the people engaged in them?
4. What does this suggest about the 'others' who are not in the images?

7.6 Adventurers with Disabilities

» Disability is part of the human condition. Almost everyone will be temporarily or permanently impaired at some point in life, and those who survive to old age will experience increasing difficulties in functioning. (World Health Organisation, 2011, p. 3)

7

How we understand disability has changed over time, which means that how disability, society and adventure interact is also changing. In this section, we will provide you with some key ways of understanding disability and examples of how inclusive approaches can facilitate increased involvement of people with disabilities in adventurous experiences.

In modern history, disabilities were seen as problems which doctors should try to fix, a perspective that can be summed up as 'society is fine; it's the individual who has something wrong with them'. Rather than their impairment being seen as a difference or limitation, those with disabilities are not seen as 'normal' people who are capable of functioning in society. This is normally called the *medical model* of disability, and represents a way of under-standing disability as a deficit, which is seen to devalue people with disabilities' experiences (Pfeiffer, 2002).

This contrasts with the *social model* of disability (Oliver, 1996), which emerged out of the disability rights movements of the latter part of the twentieth century, where people with disabilities argued for legal rights to tackle discrimination based on their impair-ments. A social model of disability asserts that it is not impair-ment which disables people, but society.

For an example of the social model of disability, if a deaf per-son wants to learn how to sail, but the training centre running the course does not provide a sign language interpreter to help the instructors communicate with her, it is not her deafness (the impairment) which stops her from learning to sail, but the fact that the instructor cannot communicate on her terms. Seen this way, society has not met her needs to allow for an equitable experience. This can also be understood in terms of economic agency: if workplaces do not accommodate disabled workers, then those people are disempowered and less able to realize their potential to the same degree as non-disabled workers. Disabilities can be reduced or removed by society's individuals and institu-tions being more open and accommodating to people's diverse requirements.

A third way of understanding disability is the *functional model* that informs the World Health Organisation's (WHO) policy, and is perhaps more useful for the dynamic, often natural settings where adventure activities take place. This model uses a 'bio-psycho-social' approach (WHO, 2011, p. 4), which focuses on how impair-ments, personal factors, environments, and activities interact to produce degrees of disability. Take, for example, two wheelchair users trying out a sit-ski for the first time: one was an expert skier before being injured in car accident, while the other has used a wheelchair since childhood and is getting on the slopes for the first time. In this form of skiing, the skier does not need to use their legs, and both skiers are able to easily transfer into the sit-ski and go for their first run, while being supported by an instructor who helps them to balance. In terms of impairment, and the 'social' facilitation of the situation by the instruction and support staff, many disabling factors have been avoided, but do you think the two skiers will have the same experience? How might having an understanding of how the chairlifts work, how body weight aids turning, and memories of pre-injury skiing affect each skier's experience?

The difference between the two skiers' experiences is where a functional approach acknowledges and responds to personal and psychological factors, such as motivation, self-esteem, and preferred communication styles, and encourages us to try to understand people as individuals. This applies equally whether you are coaching a young athlete or showing a new student around your college. It really has nothing to do with disability; it is about being able to ask sensitively, 'What do you need in order to be able to do this activity?', listening to the answer, and looking for creative solutions together.

These solutions often require innovation or adaptation, and developments in technology and the increased visibility of more diverse participants through social media are opening up adventure sports to more and more people. Think about the effects of recent developments in battery technology on electric mountain bikes and wheelchairs, or the visibility of paraclimbing[6] through the world championships and films like Arc'teryx's *Gimp Monkeys*, which documented the first all-disabled ascent of El Cap in Yosemite. In recent years, the increasing visibility of some people with disabilities in adventure sport has also been driven by the higher numbers of wounded, injured, or sick soldiers returning from Iraq and Afghanistan who are looking for new ways to find adventure in their lives.

Some of the examples we have presented here involve people who were already involved in adventurous activities before a change in circumstance affected their capacity to participate—often due to a physical disability. The greatest inequality in adventure is for those people with disabilities who do not get the chance to take part at all. Impairments take a range of forms—from cognitive impairments associated with learning disabilities to the symptoms of chronic illness—and are often complex. Because meeting the needs of these people is therefore more complicated, they often do not get the same opportunities as their non-disabled peers. This might be because of financial constraints, family perceptions about what is and is not possible, lack of visibility of other people like them in the media, and health and safety concerns from schools or carers.

---

6   Paraclimbing is a term used for rock-climbing specifically by and for people with disabilities. In competition, athletes compete in categories based on their impairments, as in other para sports.

In attempts to make sport in general more inclusive, researchers and coaches have developed various models and approaches to encourage inclusion in physical activities, which can be applied to adventure sports. These span from full inclusion, where anyone can take part, through parallel provision, where alternative activities might be provided for some people, to separate or specialist provision and dedicated disability sports (Black & Stevenson, 2011; Crosbie, 2016). Here again is the difference between equality and equity: some people need more or different support than others to take part in, and get the same benefits from, adventure experiences.

Chapter Summary

In this chapter, we set out to provide an overview of some of the inequalities present in contemporary adventure and equip you with the language and key concepts to understand what might cause and perpetuate them. When looking at the big picture, there are some central challenges and opportunities that apply to all of the groups we have covered. These are highlighted in the box below, so that you can consider the ways in which the adventures you are involved in are inclusive and equitable.

Key points to keep in mind:

- What unconscious filters do we bring to our adventures?
- What are the different ways that people can 'do' adventure?
- How might our individual behaviours and institutional policies indirectly or unconsciously discriminate against others?
- How can you increase the visibility of under-represented groups in your world?
- Ultimately, inclusivity can be facilitated by asking the question, 'How I can help you participate?', listening carefully to the answer, and then together negotiating a solution.

Visibility and representation of diversity is a key theme in all of the strands that we have looked at in this chapter. Not having realistic role models to connect with at all stages of participation makes it much harder to progress, and adds another layer of constraints which those in positions of privilege may be unaware of. In the UK, recent campaigns like Sport England's #ThisGirlCan, which used advertisements, social media, and real-life examples to show a diverse range of women participating in lots of different sports, are working to support broader inclusion policies at a national level, such as the Equality Standard in Sport (Equality in Sport, 2017).

Critically examining our own attitudes and actions (and non-actions) is crucially important when attempting to relate to other people's experiences of exclusion. Exploring the factors that have enabled us to do, and stopped us from doing, the things we want to are good first steps towards understanding other people's experiences. If we can begin to unpack our own knapsacks of privilege (McIntosh, 1989), we can better identify how that privilege might affect other people's adventure practices.

You might also have noticed how important it is to use the right language during these discussions. For example, you will see that we have always used the term 'people with disabilities' rather than 'disabled people' in this chapter. This might seem like a small difference, but in some ways it is a shorthand for bigger ideas: it ensures that you always think of the person first, and are thus more likely to consider how that person *can* do something, rather than assuming that they cannot.

Language is also about listening: listening to how people identify themselves rather than making assumptions; not being afraid to ask questions sensitively and then listen to the answers; and making an effort to enable voices which have historically been silenced to be heard. This person-centred approach to inclusion is equally as important as the big ideas from the social sciences and national campaigns.

You may have noticed that this chapter has one additional element than the other chapters in the book: it comes with a moral imperative. Where most chapters use some theory to illustrate how adventure and society influence each other, this chapter, on adventure and equalities, implores readers to use their individual agency to shape adventure practices in ways that make them more equitable for all.

Key Readings

Gray, T., & Mitten, D. (2018). Nourishing terrains: Women's contributions to outdoor learning. In T. Gray & D. Mitten (Eds.), *The Palgrave international handbook of women and outdoor learning* (pp. 3–18). London: Palgrave Macmillan.

Thorpe, H., & Olive, R. (2016). Introduction: Contextualizing women in action sport cultures. In H. Thorpe & R. Olive (Eds.), *Women in action sport cultures* (pp. 1–20). London: Palgrave Macmillan.

References

Adams, M., Bell, L., & Griffin, P. (2007). *Teaching for diversity and social justice*. New York: Routledge.

Allin, L., & West, A. (2013). Feminist theory and outdoor leadership. In E. Pike & S. Beames (Eds.), *Outdoor adventure and social theory* (pp. 113–124). Abingdon, UK: Routledge.

7

Black, K., & Stevenson, P. (2011). *The inclusion spectrum*. Retrieved from http://www.sportdevelopment.info/index.php/browse-all-documents/748-the-inclusion-spectrum

Boniface, M. (2006). The meaning of adventurous activities for 'women in the outdoors'. *Journal of Adventure Education & Outdoor Learning, 6*(1), 9–24.

Brookes, A. (2002). Lost in the Australian bush: Outdoor education as curriculum. *Journal of Curriculum Studies, 34*(4), 405–425.

Cain Miller, C. (2017). From sex object to gritty woman: The evolution of women in stock photos. *New York Times,* 7/9/2017. Retrieved from https://www.nytimes.com/2017/09/07/upshot/from-sex-object-to-gritty-woman-the-evolution-of-women-in-stock-photos.html

Coakley, J. (2003). *Sport in society: Issues and controversies* (8th ed.). New York: McGraw-Hill.

Coleman, A. (1996). The unbearable whiteness of skiing. *Pacific Historical Review, 65,* 583–614.

Collins, P. (2015). Intersectionality's definitional dilemmas. *Palo Alto: Annual Reviews, 41,* 1–20.

Color the Crag. (n.d.). *Homepage*. Retrieved from colorthecrag.com

Corlett, A. (2017). *Diverse outcomes: Living standards by ethnicity*. Resolution Foundation. Retrieved from http://www.resolutionfoundation.org/app/uploads/2017/08/Diverse-outcomes.pdf

Cornell, S., & Hartmann, D. (2007). Ethnicity and race: Making identities in a changing world. In *Sociology for a new century* (2nd ed.). London: Pine Forge Press.

Crenshaw, K. (1989). Demarginalizing the intersection of race and sex: A black feminist critique of antidiscrimination doctrine, feminist theory and antiracist politics. *University of Chicago Legal Forum, 1*(8), 139–167 Retrieved from http://chicagounbound.uchicago.edu/uclf/vol1989/iss1/8

Crosbie, J. (2016). Disability and the outdoors: Some considerations for inclusion. In B. Humberstone, H. Prince, & K. Henderson (Eds.), *Routledge international handbook of outdoor studies* (pp. 378–387). Abingdon, UK: Routledge.

Equality in Sport. (2017). *The equality standard: A framework for sport*. Retrieved from http://equalityinsport.org/

Finney, C. (2014). *Black faces, white spaces*. Chapel Hill, NC: University of North Carolina Press.

Floyd, M. (1998). Getting beyond marginality and ethnicity: the challenge for race and ethnic studies in leisure research. *J Leis Res. 30*(1):3–22.

Frohlick, S. (2006). 'Wanting the children and wanting K2': The incommensurability of motherhood and mountaineering in Britain and North America in the late twentieth century. *Gender, Place & Culture, 13*(5), 477–490.

Giddens, A., & Sutton, P. (2017). *Sociology*. Cambridge, UK: Polity Press.

Gilchrist, P. (2007). Motherhood, ambition and risk': Mediating the sporting hero/ine in conservative Britain. *Media, Culture & Society, 29*(3), 395–414.

Gray, T. (2016). The F word in outdoor education. *Journal of Outdoor & Environmental Education, 19*(2), 25–41.

Gray, T., & Mitten, D. (Eds.). (2018). *The Palgrave international handbook of women and outdoor learning*. London: Palgrave.

Haile, R. (2017). Going it alone. *Outside Magazine,* May 2017. Retrieved from https://www.outsideonline.com/2170266/solo-hiking-appalachian-trail-queer-black-woman

Hancock, A. (2015). *Intersectionality*. Oxford: Oxford University Press.

Harrison, A. (2013). Black skiing, everyday racism, and the racial spatiality of whiteness. *Journal of Sport & Social Issues, 37*(4), 315–339.

Humberstone, B. (2000). The 'outdoor industry' as social and educational phenomena: Gender and outdoor adventure/education. *Journal of Adventure Education and Outdoor Learning, 1*(1), 21–36.

Humberstone, B. (2016). Social and environmental justice in outdoor studies. In B. Humberstone, H. Prince, & K. Henderson (Eds.), *Routledge international handbook of outdoor studies* (pp. 335–339). Abingdon, UK: Routledge.

Little, D. (2002). Women and adventure recreation: Reconstructing leisure constraints and adventure experiences to negotiate continuing participation. *Journal of Leisure Research, 34*(2), 157–177.

Lowan, G. (2009). Exploring place from an aboriginal perspective: Considerations for outdoor and environmental education. *Canadian Journal of Environmental Education, 14*(1), 42–58.

Martin, D. (2004). Apartheid in the great outdoors: American advertising and the reproduction of a racialized outdoor leisure identity. *Journal of Leisure Research, 36*(4), 513–535.

McIntosh, P. (1989). White privilege: Unpacking the invisible knapsack. *Peace and Freedom Magazine*, July/August, 10–12.

McNiel, J., Harris, D., & Fondren, K. (2012). Women and the wild: Gender socialization in wilderness recreation advertising. *Gender Issues, 29*(1), 39–55.

Mitten, D. (1996). A philosophical basis for a women's outdoor adventure program. In K. Warren (Ed.), *Women's voices in experiential education* (pp. 78–84). Boulder, CO: Association for Experiential Education.

National Park Service. (2011). *National Park Service comprehensive survey of the American public. Racial and ethnic diversity of national park system visitors and non-visitors.* Fort Collins, CO: US Department of the Interior. Retrieved from https://www.nature.nps.gov/socialscience/docs/CompSurvey2008_2009RaceEthnicity.pdf

Nerlich, M. (1987). Ideology of adventure: studies in modern consciousness, 1100–1750. Vols. 1 and 2. Minneapolis: University of Minnesota Press.

Office of National Statistics. (2016). *Annual survey of hours and earnings: 2016 provisional results.* Retrieved from https://www.ons.gov.uk/employmentandlabourmarket/peopleinwork/earningsandworkinghours/bulletins/annualsurveyofhoursandearnings/2016provisionalresults

Oliver, M. (1996). *Understanding disability: From theory to practice.* London: Macmillan.

Outdoor Foundation. (2017). *Outdoor participation report.* Retrieved from https://outdoorindustry.org/wp-content/uploads/2017/05/2017-Outdoor-Recreation-Participation-Report_FINAL.pdf

Outside Magazine (2017, May). *The New Icons: The future of adventure is female.* Retrieved from https://www.outsideonline.com/2168656/new-icons

Pfeiffer, D. (2002). The philosophical foundations of disability studies. *Disability Studies Quarterly, 22*(2), 3–23.

Pilkington, A. (2003). *Racial disadvantage and ethnic diversity in the UK.* London: Palgrave Macmillan.

Roberts, N. (2009). Crossing the color line with a different perspective on whiteness and (anti)racism: A response to Mary McDonald. *Journal of Leisure Research, 41*(4), 495–509.

Roberts, N. (2016). Race, ethnicity and outdoor studies: Trends, challenges and forward momentum. In B. Humberstone, H. Prince, & K. Henderson (Eds.), *Routledge international handbook of outdoor studies* (pp. 445–456). Abingdon, UK: Routledge.

Saunders, N., & Sharp, B. (2002). Outdoor leadership: The last male domain? *European Journal of Physical Education, 7*(2), 85–94.

US Congress Joint Economic Committee. (2016). *Gender pay inequality. Consequences for women, families and the economy.* Retrieved from https://www.jec.senate.gov/public/_cache/files/0779dc2f-4a4e-4386-b847-9ae919735acc/gender-pay-inequality%2D%2D%2Dus-congress-joint-economic-committee.pdf

Warren, K. (1996). *Women's voices in experiential education.* Boulder, CO: Association for Experiential Education.

Warren, K. (2016). Gender in outdoor studies. In B. Humberstone, H. Prince, & K. Henderson (Eds.), *Routledge international handbook of outdoor studies* (pp. 360–368). Abingdon, UK: Routledge.

Warren, K., & Loeffler, T. (2006). Factors that influence women's technical skill development in outdoor adventure. *Journal of Adventure Education & Outdoor Learning, 6*(2), 107–119.

Warren, K., Roberts, N., Breunig, M., & Alvarez, M. (2014). Social justice in outdoor experiential education: A state of knowledge review. *The Journal of Experimental Education, 37*(1), 89–103.

Wheaton, B. (2004). *Understanding lifestyle sports: Consumption, identity, and difference.* London: Routledge.

White, E. (1996). Black women and the wilderness. In T. Jordan & J. Hepworth (Eds.), *The stories that shape us: Contemporary women write about the west.* New York: W.W. Norton & Co.

World Economic Forum. (2015). *The global gender gap report 2015.* Retrieved from http://www3.weforum.org/docs/GGGR2015/cover.pdf

World Health Organisation. (2011). *World report on disability.* Retrieved from http://www.who.int/disabilities/world_report/2011/report.pdf

7

Adventure and Identity

© The Author(s) 2019
S. Beames et al., *Adventure and Society*, https://doi.org/10.1007/978-3-319-96062-3_8

8

Chapter Aims

After reading this chapter, you will be able to:

- Understand six key theoretical elements of identity that are relevant to adventure practice
- Explain how adventure identities are largely constructed through social presentation and interaction
- Understand that individuals have multiple identities and how these are 'fluid' in nature
- Describe how the media influences the ways in which adventurers think and behave
- Articulate how adventures can facilitate the transformation of identity

This chapter on identity is particularly fascinating to us because it has strong links to themes highlighted in other chapters, such as everyday adventure, risk, capitalism, technology, and social media. Indeed, if you read those chapters again with your identity theory knowledge in hand, you may gain yet a deeper understanding of how those concepts shape how we think about ourselves.

First, in this chapter, we discuss six key elements of identity. We then go a little further and continue our discussion on the theoretical concepts of Erving Goffman's 'presentation of self' that were introduced in ▶ Chap. 6. The third section discusses how adventurous identities are constructed and maintained on a daily basis. Fourth, we look at the influence of the media on adventure identity practices. Finally, we examine how adventure can even facilitate a wholesale transformation of a person's identity and potentially lead to the creation of multiple, fluid identities. This last idea resonates with the notion of subject formation through dominant social processes and beliefs, which we examined in ▶ Chap. 5 with the help of Antonio Gramsci and Michel Foucault.

8.1 Who Are You?

The term 'identity' has a rather vague meaning, and it is often assumed that everyone knows what we mean when we use this term. For example, a person might say that being a teacher, parent, or an environmental activist is a strong part of their identity. We can make some assumptions about what that person means, yet it is still difficult to succinctly define what we mean by this usage of the word 'identity'.

Early discussions on identity revolved principally around the 'legal association of a name with a particular person' (Fearon, 1999, p. 8), such as the corresponding data on our passport information page. Burke and Stets (2009) further tell us that an 'identity is a set of meanings that define who one is when one is an occupant of a particular role in society, a member of a particular group, or claims particular characteristics that identify him or her as a unique person' (p. 3). Indeed, it has been noted that people have only been discussing identities in the way we are now since the 1950s, when the psychologist Erik Erikson used the term to describe 'one's feelings about one's self, character, goals, and origins' (Fearon, 1999, p. 10). Moreover, drawing on interactionist social theory, Pike and Weinstock (2013) explain how humans attribute meanings to everything they interact with: physical objects, abstract concepts, and other people, to name three big categories. These interactions enable individuals to construct identities, which in turn govern what people think and do.

The introductory discussion above has provided a brief glimpse of how identity formation has been characterized over recent years. Looking ahead, we lay the foundations for our discussions on identity and adventure through a more specific conversation, and we have identified six specific concepts that will assist with understanding identity theory more clearly. These concepts position identity as being social, personal, multiple, while being stable yet malleable. At the same time, we demonstrate how identity relates to specific symbols and language, and to presenting a certain appearance.

▪ Social

The first concept that we highlight is *social identity*. Later on, we discuss how this idea can be understood through the notion of 'subjectivities' more specifically. Writing in 1979, Tajfel and Turner detailed how it is natural for humans to put themselves and each other into categories, in order to make sense of their social environments. Scholar James Fearon (1999) explains how our identities stem from being part of various social categories, such as American, lesbian, sister, feminist, Catholic, or cellist. Humans generally take on the identity/ies of the group/groups to which they claim membership (Tajfel & Turner, 1979). This aspect of identity is relatively straightforward to understand, as much of it refers to 'a set of persons marked by a label and distinguished by rules deciding membership and (alleged) characteristic features or attributes' (Fearon, 1999, p. 11). Social identities can also refer directly to other forms of social context, including the past (e.g. I used to be a hiker), present (e.g. I am a university student), and future (e.g. I will become a father).

▪ Personal

Personal identity refers to a set of 'attributes, beliefs, desires, or principles of action' that a person considers important (Fearon, 1999, p. 11). Furthermore, philosopher Charles Taylor (1992) explains how one's identity enables one to decide 'what is good, or valuable, or what ought to be done, or what I endorse or oppose' (p. 27). Seen this way, this second concept of identity—personal identity—is often regarded as having a deeper, more enduring nature than one's social identity. Indeed, some elements of our personal identities may remain unchangeable (such as height, eye colour, shoe size) and may not be something one wants to make public (such as one's religious beliefs or sexual orientation).

Fearon (1999) further brings our attention to an especially interesting element of this personal identity, which he refers to as attributes or achievements in which people take special pride. These might include one's rank in the armed forces or being able to land the hardest snowboarding trick on a half-pipe. Crucially, should these attributes or achievements be diminished, there would be a loss of self-respect and self-esteem. This understanding highlights how identity can be a huge motivator for one's actions and can elicit powerful emotions (Fearon, 1999, p. 24).

Wren (2002) has explained how the once-dominant psychological explanations of identity regarded personality traits as being very stable and fixed, whereas nowadays the focus of much identity research often pays attention to the socio-cultural forces that influence who we think we are and who others think we are. However, you'll see from these two sub-sections on personal and social identity that there actually is a degree of overlap between one's social and personal identities; these are both powerful aspects of identity and it can be very difficult to entirely distinguish between the two. For example, completing a difficult rock climb may be both personally meaningful and socially rewarding. We'll further discuss this intertwining of the personal and social as the chapter progresses.

■ Multiple Selves

As we saw above, one's social identity is constituted by the various groups within which they participate. Inherent in this statement about social identity is the assertion that we all have multiple and flexible selves, rather than just an unchanging 'core' self. This is because 'the self emerges in social interaction within the context of a complex differentiated society' and because 'people occupy different positions in society' (Burke & Stets, 2009, p. 10). So, as we noted above, it is possible to simultaneously identify as an American, lesbian, sister, feminist, Catholic, and cellist, with each of these identity elements being enacted or emphasized in different ways. Similarly, Atencio and Wright (2009) show how young women can identify themselves in diverse, strategic ways, and traverse between different racial and ethnic identity categories, depending on their social contexts. The authors here refer to

Michel Foucault's (2000) concept of *subjectivity-formation*, to suggest that people can actively negotiate, and even challenge, prevailing social contexts and norms to create more desirable ways of being.

Similarly, a useful concept to be mindful of when discussing this notion of multiple, socially generated identities is the *prominence hierarchy* of identities (McCall & Simmons, 1978). This hierarchy arguably enables people to position their various identities on a scale of relative importance. For example, we might place being a Muslim on a higher level of importance than, say, being a garden shed owner. Kristin Walseth's (2006) study in Norway indeed reveals that young women from immigrant backgrounds selectively emphasized certain nationalist, cultural, ethnic, and religious identity categories over others, and in different ways from each other. Where a particular identity is placed on the prominence hierarchy arguably depends on three principal factors. The first, support, refers to the amount of support from within themselves and from others that an identity is given. The second has to do with the amount of commitment one feels to a given identity—the degree to which a person is invested in being a certain kind of person in society. Finally, there are rewards, and these can be both intrinsic and extrinsic. Intrinsic rewards are the internal feelings of gratification and pleasure, whereas extrinsic rewards come in the form of money, items of value, and prestige. There are links here to the motivations for engaging in adventure activities that we explored in ▶ Chap. 4, but also a crucial connection to our central point in this chapter: adventure activities are influential sites of identity design, construction, and maintenance.

As we discuss these first three concepts of identity it is very important to note that identity encompasses not just how we view ourselves, but how others view us as well. In other words, our identity may be considered 'core' and consistent, yet it could also be argued that multiple, hierarchical identities develop through social engagements and roles. Within adventure activities, there can be multiple and even competing identities found within each of them, which means that there is not just one way of identifying as a surfer, skater, climber, or bike rider.

■ Symbols, Gestures, and Language

Other key aspects that underpin our identity/ies are symbolic, expressive, and linguistic in nature. In this regard, Burke and Stets (2009) state that '[a]ll organisms learn to respond to cues in their environment' (p. 10). We know that a 'thumbs up' sign means 'everything is OK' and that a ski run with a tape running across the top of it has been deemed unsafe by the hill operator. Signs and symbols thus often elicit responses that are similar to those evoked from earlier stimuli (Burke & Stets, 2009). What is crucial to note here, too, is that the meanings behind the thumbs up and the tape placed across the ski run do not reside in the hand or the tape: they are rooted in the responses that our social groups have given to these objects. Seen this way, specific social groups will have their own meanings that they have attributed to particular symbols—each of which will 'evoke the same meaning responses in different individuals' (p. 11).

The ways in which these meanings are circulated and taken up in social networks in turn influence particular group identities that can be quite strong. For example, it has been suggested that skateboarders respond to certain symbolic meanings and signs found in skate videos, according to Emily Chivers-Yochim (2010):

> » Although skate videos are produced by the skateboarding industry as promotional materials for their products, they are widely regarded by skateboarders as 'authentic,' and their representation of individual skateboarders' various identities signifies this authenticity for the audience. In fact, the videos are so firmly regarded as a 'true' element of skateboarding culture that many amateur skateboarders produce their own short versions of skate videos (approximately 3 to 10 minutes long) as representations of their 'unique' identities. (p. 140)

Symbols and gestures are important to identity formation, but words are arguably very crucial too. This is because they are highly versatile and enable us to communicate in very nuanced ways about complex ideas (Burke & Stets, 2009). In qualitative research studies, for example, identities are often expressed through interviewing, when participants use words to explain their lives and experiences. Also, in another sense, feminist scholars such as Judith Butler (1997) contend that words like 'male' and 'female' are loaded, in terms of how they carry certain identity meanings. Similarly, we 'assume and perform' gender identities through our speech acts.

When these ideas are taken together, we can see how most aspects of our lives have a certain symbolic quality, as the meanings about identities are derived from society's symbols, gestures, and language. These socially circulated meanings thus directly support certain types of identities found in adventure realms.

■ Appearance

Along with the above ways that we signal meanings to others, in order to create identities, appearance is another feature that closely overlaps here. How we decide to dress and act, whether intentionally or not, signals to others information about how we perceive ourselves and how we wish to be perceived (Goffman, 1959). With few exceptions, if you are walking down the street and encounter someone who looks and acts like a BMX biker or mountaineer, it stands to reason that they see themselves as such and want you to see themselves that way as well, for particular reasons.

Drawing on Stone's (1962) ideas on appearance, Burke and Stets (2009) summarize that '[b]y dressing a certain way, one announces to oneself and to the audience the identity that is being enacted such as one's age, gender, occupation, and so forth' (p. 38). While we agree with most of this, we would add that people may also use their appearance to deliberately constrain others' capacity to categorize them into a particular arbitrary or stereotypical role (e.g. male or female, Black or White). Appearance, then, can also be employed to resist and challenge rigid, dominant stereotypes and social categories. Wearing clothing 'normally' worn by the opposite sex is, according to Judith Butler (1990), an example of dressing to disrupt dominant gender-based identity categories.

■ Stable yet Malleable

Our final concept regarding identity is really a tension between two opposing ideas. As we have alluded to earlier, in one way, identity can be seen as something stable, while in another sense, it can be seen as something malleable. Both ends of this artificial stable/malleable spectrum are legitimate, so it is important to have a deeper grounding in some theory that will help us make sense of this sometimes hazy middle ground.

Feeling that one deeply knows oneself is important, as it helps us perceive, make sense of, and negotiate social situations. Oyserman et al. (2012) employ the phrase 'feeling that one knows oneself' (p. 69), as this 'assumption of stability' helps them go about their daily business with a certain evenness. Without the stability that comes from a certain amount of feeling that we (and others) know ourselves, it is arguable that many basic human interactions would be rendered chaotic. Our uncertain, rapidly changing, late-modern world makes maintaining a stable identity more difficult than ever.

This relatively stable self does not, however, exist independently, in some kind of vacuum. At some point, it is confronted and influenced by external factors. This is further complicated, as we have seen, by occupying different roles in various social groups. In sum, there exists a tension between having a somewhat stable self that has been moulded over the years, and feelings and actions that are heavily influenced by other people, and their symbols, gestures, language, and appearances (Burke & Stets, 2009; Goffman, 1959; Oyserman et al., 2012). Thus, the self is at once 'a stable yet malleable mental construct' (Oyserman et al., 2012, p. 70).

This irreconcilable tension points towards a central tenet that underlies this chapter: at some level, our identities are malleable, as context will always play a role in influencing how we feel about ourselves and how we behave. Oyserman et al. (2012) remind us that identities are situated, pragmatic, and attuned to the affordances and constraints of the immediate context. Identity construction is thus a fluid, ongoing process, as we alluded to earlier in our discussion of multi-faceted identity formation. It is a combination of personal identity and what has been variously called social, cultural, and group identity, that is continually being reconstructed (Wren, 2002).

The above discussion on these six concepts of identity (social, personal, multiple, symbols, appearance, stable yet malleable) is important because they provide us with a toolkit to more deeply explain how we feel about ourselves and present ourselves to our 'publics'. This toolkit is an essential part of understanding how humans undertake identity work. We now revisit and extend our examination of Goffman's work on the 'presentation of self' (which was introduced two chapters ago). We saw in ▶ Chap. 6 that adventurers use technology and social media to capture their daring feats and choose carefully selected excerpts to share with others.

8.2 A Little More Theory: Goffman's Presentation of Self

The year 1959 saw the mainstream publication of a remarkably novel approach to understanding human interaction. As we saw in ▶ Chap. 6, Erving Goffman's book, entitled *The presentation of self in everyday life*, employed language of the stage to outline his conceptual framework, which he called *dramaturgy*. Drawing on work by seminal interactionist theorists, such as George Herbert Mead, Herbert Blumer, and Charles Horton Cooley, Goffman explained how 'the self' is borne out of interaction between actors and their audience, and identities are effectively 'cemented' by playing the same role to the same audience, over and over. This interactionist view also helps us accept this overlap between social and personal identities that we discussed above. Indeed, Wren (2002) tells us that identities are not fixed and determinate, but are ongoing narratives.

Goffman (1959) highlights that whenever humans enter any social situation, they instinctively seek information about the others who are there. Because all of this information is never readily available, people use 'cues, tests, hints, expressive gestures, status symbols' (p. 249) to determine what is going on in a particular scene. Following this line of thinking, we are all, Goffman argued, constantly engaged in 'impression management', where we offer and withhold certain pieces of information about ourselves. In most cases, people will attempt to manage their impression in such a way that they will 'appear in as favourable a light as possible' (Donnelly, 2002, p. 95).

Integral to impression management is the *expressive equipment* that is 'intentionally or unwittingly employed' (Goffman, 1959, p. 22). This is done by presenting a *front* that involves clothing, gestures, and speech patterns. You will note the similarity between this line of thinking and ideas around symbols, gestures, and language that we discussed in the first section, above. Beames and Pike (2008) draw on the Presentation of Self framework to highlight how, in an outdoor education course that features rock climbing, 'participants' attitudes and actions shape their social contexts while being shaped by them' (p. 10). What makes Goffman's work so helpful is the tenet that people are constantly (and often unconsciously or unwittingly) curating their behaviours in relation to the anticipated responses from their audiences.

❓ Discussion Questions

1. Consider one adventure sport in which you participate. What kinds of expressive equipment do participants use to communicate with each other and with 'outsiders'? This 'equipment' might include clothing, exclusive language, symbols, brands, gestures, and overall comportment (e.g. acting disinterested, hyped up, or risk-taking).
2. What elements about your participation in this adventure sport do you emphasize or de-emphasize? These elements might include your emotions, equipment, skill, and knowledge.

8.3 The Negotiation and Construction of Identity

One of the central claims that can be made in the lifestyle and adventure sports literature is that participants negotiate and construct their identities through their various forms of involvement with specific adventure practices (Wheaton, 2004; Wheaton & Beal, 2003). For many adventurers, their sport becomes the central organizing feature of their lives and their identities are developed through relations with the people, places, and normalized practices found in their sport contexts (Light, 2006). Drawing on Lave and Wenger's (1991) concept of *situated learning*, Light explains how the formation of identity involves people's 'bodies, senses, emotions, and thoughts' (p. 170) engaging with the above influences in order to learn 'the skills, knowledge, and culture of their social environment' (p. 170).

As we have seen from the above discussion of adventurers' participation in social contexts, being able to be labelled as a

8

member of a certain community of practitioners or believers is centrally important to identity (Fearon, 1999). In the contexts of windsurfing and skateboarding, for example, showing a strong commitment to one's community is a highly valued signal of identity (Wheaton & Beal, 2003). Indeed, Kay and Laberge's (2002) research on adventure racing even highlights that, for some competitors, maintaining a social identity as an adventure racer was more important than participating in the race itself.

What can be especially difficult is when multiple social identities, or subjectivities as some social theorists call these, intersect in the same arena. Susan Frohlick (2006) explains how female professional alpinists who are mothers must simultaneously manage being a parent while being a full-time athlete in a pastime that can be very dangerous. This was made plain when British climber Alison Hargreaves died on K2 in 1995. As noted in the previous chapter, Hargreaves was vilified in the press for being a poor mother because she 'selfishly' chose to take part in high-risk activities. Four men died in the same storm and no comments were made about the families they left behind. This is a good example of what Wheaton (2004) and others refer to as people's identities, or subjectivities, being 'contested' over during outdoor adventure sports participation; in one sense, Hargreaves could not escape her identity as a mother, while her fellow male mountaineers were 'freed from fatherhood' (Frohlick, 2006, p. 488). At the same time, however, Hargreaves challenged social stereotypes of what it meant to be a woman and a mother and thus contested conventional identity categories of mother, gender, and climber. Likewise, Humberstone (2011) provides another relevant example of 'Kitty', a windsurfer in her mid-60s, whose subjectivity also showed 'what is possible for an older woman and what she might find enjoyable' (p. 166) in ways that challenged dominant perceptions of age, gender, and ability. This same type of analysis was found in Spowart, Burrows, and Shaw's (2010) study of a surfing mothers group; they developed identities (or 'subjectivities') that challenged prevailing societal beliefs regarding traditional motherhood and what it means to be a surfer.

This struggle over how different adventure identities are valued, contested, and even resisted, is often referred to as *identity politics*. Identity politics is a term that refers to ideas about how 'some social groups are relatively privileged, while others are oppressed and marginalized' (Pike & Weinstock, 2013, p. 127). As we saw in ▸ Chap. 7 on equalities, while some adventure sports may offer opportunities for historically disadvantaged populations, there remain—as we have suggested throughout this book— many kinds of adventure practices that continue to feature predominantly White, male, middle-class, and non-disabled bodies (see Wheaton, 2004). This type of social inequality, whereby certain identities are given priority over others, raises pertinent questions that have been addressed by adventure and lifestyle sport scholars using Bourdieu's 'forms of capital' theoretical framework.

Drawing on Bourdieu's (1986) work on the diverse forms of capital, Fletcher (2008) outlines how, although some adventure sports athletes may be capable of accessing economic capital (i.e. money), they choose not to, as the cultural capital needed to cement one's identity as an authentic practitioner has more to do with the kind of knowledge, skills, and preferences one has. In other words, there is a prominent line of thinking in adventure circles that 'money can't buy status'. This kind of capital lies in contrast to the symbolic capital we discussed in ▸ Chap. 4 on risk, where adventurers gain prestige and recognition from others through performing daring acts with a cool head, rather than from how much economic capital they have accrued.

Furthermore, writing about climbing and mountaineering, Telford and Beames (2016) explain how the image of the 'dirtbag' climber living out of a van on an extremely limited income conjures up strong images of what it means to be an authentic climber. They go on to argue that, under the gaze of the climbing community (who effectively determine what is culturally desirable in their world), it would not be possible to be 'live the climbing dream' if one drove a Mercedes and stayed at fancy hotels every night. When viewed this way, some ways of adventuring are regarded by their specific communities of practice as more authentic than others.

Bourdieu (1979/1984, 1986) is helpful here, as he explains how each field is a site of social struggle, where different forms of capital have different 'currencies'. In one sense, we know that some adventure sports demand high levels of economic capital simply to take part at a basic level (e.g. the cultural 'field' of heli-skiing). However, in some adventure subcultures, even though someone might be financially rich, they might choose to live a very low-cost existence, as that aligned with the ethos of the cultural field of rock climbing, for example. Both of our examples (heli-skiing and climbing) show how the preferred forms of capital within those communities serve to sustain the social identities of its members.

Wheaton (2010) explains how social identities are developed through 'recognizable styles, bodily dispositions, expressions and attitudes' (p. 1059), which become integrated into entire lifestyles. Similarly, Kay and Laberge (2002), in their work on adventure racing, describe how adventure communities create an accepted social consensus on language, rituals, myths, and core values that 'real' practitioners accept and perpetuate. These adventure communities—which are increasingly transnational—may actually be a more powerful source of social identity than nationality (Thorpe, 2012). As we saw in ▸ Chap. 5 on capitalism, corporations, and brands often attempt to align themselves with core values espoused by these communities.

8.4 Identity and the Media

Media, in their many forms, also have very considerable influences on our identities. Traditional sources, such as newspapers and magazines, give us news about events that have taken place and the main agents involved. 'New media', such as Facebook, Twitter, Instagram, and Snapchat, has made identity study in the new millennium highly compelling (see MacIsaac, Kelly & Gray, 2017). This is principally because there now exist countless opportunities for individuals to announce to the world what they think, what they have done (or are in the middle of doing!), and what they look like, as we discussed in ► Chap. 6 regarding the use of technology and social media.

Many of you reading this will have sat on a couch in the evening and checked the Instagram feeds of friends who have done something adventurous, such as snowboarding down a gully earlier in the day, and posted some kind of evidence of this feat. Similarly, many of you know what it is like to demonstrate to your social media 'followers' what you have been up to and how you feel about things. This notion of sharing exploits with 'online others' (see McGillivary & Frew, 2007) is what Wheaton and Beal (2003) refer to as the production and consumption of culture, through which our identities are consequently 'defined, constructed, contested, and reconstituted' (p. 156).

This idea of identities being reconstituted, reconstructed, and contested through the media adds an additional layer of complexity to our identity discussion. Referring to our treatment of adventure and capitalism in ► Chap. 5, it is clear that corporations wield high levels of influence in ways that identities are created, reimagined, and sustained. This influence exists on multiple planes. For example, corporate influences may, through clever marketing, prompt us to buy certain products more readily than we might have otherwise. Perhaps on a deeper and more interesting level, all forms of media provide signals of what and who are cool or 'in'. These cues from the media thus serve to determine how some individuals or groups have high social currency, which in turn leads to the exclusion of certain groups of people; historically, this has rendered some adventure activities or spaces particularly male and/or White (see Wheaton & Beal, 2003). For instance, with regard to the able-bodied White male category, some surf and skate magazines present a very narrow view of 'hyper-masculinity' that serves to constrain the different ways that members of these adventure cultures should think, behave, and identify (Atencio, Beal & Wilson, 2009; Spowart et al., 2010). Then, in the world of mountaineering films, Frohlick (2005) has argued that the 'male adventure subject' is presented as the norm, through identities such as the 'world explorer, elite athlete and extreme adventurer'; these typologies of White masculinity serve to push 'women and non-white men to the periphery of the adventure imaginary' (p. 175). These questions and issues regarding inclusive and exclusive identities are examined more specifically in ▶ Chap. 7.

Returning to our discussion on how media consumption influences identities, Wheaton and Beal (2003) found that it was intermediate practitioners (specifically skaters) who were the most likely to buy magazines, as this would permit them to gather 'required' information about the cultural practices in their leisure activity. Wheaton and Beal refer to Elliot and Wattanasuwan's (1998) argument that 'advertising literacy' is a crucial way that consumers of magazines (and any other kind of media) form their identities. Seen this way, practitioners of specific kinds of activities can possess a collective understanding of what these advertisements mean (Wheaton & Beal, p. 172). A more recent piece from Gilchrist and Wheaton (2013) illustrates how social networking sites and digital media technologies greatly influence the reproduction of identities in adventure activities such as parkour, mountaineering, and surfing.

Therefore, drawing on Goffman's (1959) work on the presentation of self once again, we can see how shared online spaces like YouTube, Facebook, and Instagram, as well as more conventional sources such as magazine articles and advertisements, together work as powerful influences on the choices we make regarding our 'expressive equipment'. These expressions of ourselves are a central part of how we construct our identity.

It is important to note that impression management doesn't have to be solely expressed through appearance, such as the clothing we wear; it can also be observed in the one's physical comportment during the most banal activities, such as walking. Picture a skater walking along and meeting with another skater. Irrespective of the clothes they are wearing and the fact that they are carrying skateboards, they will have a different way of holding themselves than, say, two business people who meet each other outside their high-rise office building. Overall, it is undeniable that the way we act (and identify) is heavily influenced by the social circles in which we operate and the media we consume.

8.5 Transforming Identity Through Adventure

Thus far, some of our discussions have focused upon relatively stable accounts of identity construction, where climbers, surfers, or skaters, for example, are constantly moulding and re-moulding their identities through the consumption of media, participation in adventurous activities, and the projection of certain images of themselves to their publics.

We now turn our attention to the ways adventure practices may quite markedly facilitate the transformation of a person's identity. Pike and Weinstock (2013) write about ageing 'wild swimmers', who have begun swimming in lakes, rivers, and oceans all over the world in their later years. This shift in identity from, say, employed office manager (the identity being left behind in retirement) to competitive wild swimmer (the identity being constructed in retirement) involves changing the social groups with which one identifies.

In the above example, the office manager may have chosen to retire and take up wild swimming. There may be instances, however, where injury or illness forces an unwanted shift in identity. Adventure is one means through which unforeseen shifts in identity can be re-directed. The case study below illustrates this kind of deliberate re-shaping of identity.

Case Study: Walking with the Wounded

Consider soldiers who have lost a limb in a conflict zone: in an instant, they went from being a proud and useful member of a mission to a victim who is infirm, unable to do their job, and who requires a high level of medical care. They experienced a rapid and unexpected change in their identities.

Walking with the Wounded was founded in 2010 to help injured service men and women regain their independence and integrate back into society. Although Walking with the Wounded's mission is largely based around employment, it runs high-profile expeditions to increase its media reach, and thereby raise money and awareness. These expeditions to Mt. Everest, the North Pole, the South Pole, and so on provide examples of how service personnel, who had their identities damaged along with their bodies, were able to re-construct the ways they and others viewed themselves by undertaking extraordinarily demanding physical and mental challenges (see Walking with the Wounded, n.d.).

Undertaking an adventurous expedition effectively permitted these former soldiers to re-invent themselves and move from identifying as a person with a disability to also being someone who has walked, for example, to the South Pole.

There are countless other examples of people who have taken on adventure identities later in life. John O'Brien was a professional soccer player who, after retirement, turned his attention to surfing. For O'Brien, it was not only about going surfing everyday (and sometimes twice a day) and going on extended surf trips: he plays 'fantasy surfer' with friends and watches professional surf competitions. Crucially, at this life stage, O'Brien said that he now 'felt like a surfer', as surfing was a 'top priority' (Personal communication with M. Atencio, October 14, 2017).

Transforming identity can take months and years, under different circumstances, as the above example of the war vets and ex-professional soccer player indicates. This change can also happen very quickly, in some circumstances. For instance, Ferguson and Veer (2015) explain how bungy jumping involves overcoming deep fear, and argue that bungy operators are effectively selling the glory that will come from participants overcoming their fears and seeing themselves as heroes because of this. Our example becomes even more intriguing when we consider that adventure activities like bungy jumping are so highly regulated and controlled that the risk of harming oneself is incredibly low (Bentley, Page, Meyer, Chalmers & Laird, 2001; Fletcher, 2010; Martinkova & Parry, 2017). Nevertheless, the practice of bungy jumping can be regarded as a means to take on the additional identity of a fearless, death-defying thrill-seeker—as well as that of a hero (Kane, 2013). These examples of using adventure to transform one's identity often draw on notions of 'difficulty, suffering, resilience', where the self-reliant individual travels to 'places, takes risks and stands out' (Bell, 2017, p. 11).

Chapter Summary

This chapter began by introducing some key concepts of identity theory. One of the most important points made is that identity is highly social and is deeply influenced by those we interact with and those we see in magazines and online. Since we are all part of more than one social group (e.g. at school, on the river, at home), we all have multiple identities that manifest according to certain contexts and situations. Members of every social group, to some degree, possess core or shared values, which reveal themselves in displayed attitudes and actions. Simultaneously, however, scholars such as Atencio et al. (2009) and Humberstone (2011) have used the concept of subjectivities to argue that adventurers can actively contest and re-interpret dominant social values and practices, in quite strategic and beneficial ways. This means that participants in the same activity may have quite divergent identities or subjectivities—all of which are constituted differently by power structures, social inequalities, and economic conditions (Wheaton, 2015). According to Wheaton, as adventure cultures continue to emerge, studies investigating identity politics should aim to 'expose the complex and contradictory articulations of race, gender, sexuality, class, nationhood, dis/ability' (p. 638) that underpin contemporary adventure practice.

We devoted a special section to the Presentation of Self theoretical framework, which was masterminded by Erving Goffman (1959). Goffman's framework is important because it gives us the conceptual language to discuss the fronts people display, using expressive equipment. For Goffman, maintaining fronts that are at risk of being 'disrupted', by failing to land a trick on a BMX bike, for example, is a central aspect of his impression management framework.

We also continued discussions about capitalism (from ▶ Chap. 5) and media and technology (from ▶ Chap. 6), as collectively they have a powerful influence on how we think about our lives and gain a sense of self. These sources also play an integral 'two-way' role in actively responding to perceived trends, while shaping what practitioners consume, in terms of desired brands, online content, and, more generally, 'ways of being'.

From Wheaton's (2013) work, we know about adventure practitioners' needs with regard to maintaining certain preferred identities that are associated with particular social groups. Groups distinguish themselves by adopting 'a range of symbolic markers, extending from the specialist equipment used and clothing worn, to musical taste and the vehicles driven' (p. 32). Seen this way, the twenty-first-century adventurer is often someone who desires to stand apart from 'regular folk' by having membership in a unique, valorized social network. For many theorists, the ongoing interest in identity politics in adventure contexts is to expose existing disproportionate power and inequalities (Wheaton, 2010). It is up to practitioners, as well as institutions and programmes that purport to support these individuals, to challenge unjust social arrangements that we encounter on the rocks, rivers, oceans, trails, and slopes.

Key Readings

Goffman, E. (1959). *The presentation of self in everyday life*. New York: Anchor.
Wheaton, B. (2004). *Understanding lifestyle sports: Consumption, identity and difference*. New York: Routledge.
Wheaton, B., & Beal, B. (2003). Keeping it real. *International Review for the Sociology of Sport, 38*(3), 155–176.

References

Atencio, M., Beal, B., & Wilson, C. (2009). The distinction of risk: Urban skateboarding, street habitus, and the construction of hierarchical gender relations. *Qualitative Research in Sport, Exercise, and Health, 1*(1), 3–20.
Atencio, M., & Wright, J. (2009). Ballet it's too whitey': Discursive hierarchies of high school dance spaces and the constitution of embodied feminine subjectivities. *Gender and Education, 21*(1), 31–46.
Beames, S., & Pike, E. (2008). Goffman goes rock climbing: Using creative fiction to explore the presentation of self in outdoor education. *Australian Journal of Outdoor Education, 12*(2), 3–11.
Bell, M. (2017). The romance of risk: Adventure's incorporation in risk society. *Journal of Adventure Education and Outdoor Learning*. https://doi.org/10.1080/14729679.2016.1263802

Bentley, T., Page, S., Meyer, D., Chalmers, D., & Laird, I. (2001). How safe is adventure tourism in New Zealand? An exploratory analysis. *Applied Ergonomics, 32*(4), 327–338.

Bourdieu, P. (1979/1984). *Distinction* (trans: Nice, R.). Cambridge, MA: Harvard University Press.

Bourdieu, P. (1986). The forms of capital. In J. Richardson (Ed.), *Handbook of theory and research for the sociology of education* (pp. 241–258). New York: Greenwood.

Burke, P., & Stets, J. (2009). *Identity theory*. New York: Oxford University Press.

Butler, J. (1990). *Gender trouble*. New York: Routledge.

Butler, J. (1997). *Excitable speech: A politics of the performance*. New York: Routledge.

Chivers-Yochim, E. (2010). *Skate life: Re-imagining white masculinity*. Ann Arbor, MI: University of Michigan Press.

Donnelly, P. (2002). George Herbert Mead and an interpretive sociology of sport. In J. Maguire & K. Young (Eds.), *Theory, sport & society* (pp. 83–104). Oxford: Elsevier.

Elliott, R., & Wattanasuwan, K. (1998). Brands as a symbolic resource for the construction of identity. *International Journal of Advertising, 17*, 131–144.

Fearon, J. (1999). *What is identity (as we now use the word)?* Unpublished manuscript. Stanford, CA: Stanford University Department of Political Science.

Ferguson, S., & Veer, E. (2015). 3-2-1 bungy: A typology of performance styles. *Annals of Tourism Research, 55*, 61–76.

Fletcher, R. (2008). Living on the edge: The appeal of risk sports for the professional middle class. *Sociology of Sport Journal, 25*(3), 1–23.

Fletcher, R. (2010). The emperor's new adventure: Public secrecy and the paradox of adventure tourism. *Journal of Contemporary Ethnography, 39*(1), 6–33.

Foucault, M. (2000). The ethics of the concern for self as a practice of freedom. In P. Rabinow (Ed.), *Ethics: Subjectivity and truth: The essential works of Foucault 1954–1984* (Vol. 1, pp. 281–301). London: Penguin.

Frohlick, S. (2005). 'That playfulness of white masculinity': Mediating masculinities and adventure at mountain film festivals. *Tourist Studies, 5*(2), 175–193.

Frohlick, S. (2006). Wanting the children and wanting K2: The incommensurability of motherhood and mountaineering in Britain and North America in the late twentieth century. *Gender, Place and Culture, 13*(5), 477–490.

Gilchrist, P., & Wheaton, B. (2013). New media technologies in lifestyle sport. In B. Hutchins & D. Rowe (Eds.), *Digital media sport: Technology and power in the network society* (pp. 169–185). New York: Routledge.

Goffman, E. (1959). *The presentation of self in everyday life*. New York: Anchor.

Humberstone, B. (2011). Engagements with nature: Ageing and windsurfing. In B. Watson & J. Harpin (Eds.), *Identities, cultures and voices in leisure and sport* (pp. 159–169). Eastbourne, UK: Leisure Studies Association.

Kane, M. (2013). New Zealand's transformed adventure: From hero myth to accessible tourism experience. *Leisure Studies, 32*(2), 133–151.

Kay, J., & Laberge, S. (2002). The 'new' corporate habitus in adventure racing. *International Review for the Sociology of Sport, 37*(1), 17–36.

Lave, J., & Wenger, E. (1991). *Situated learning: Legitimate peripheral participation*. Cambridge: Cambridge University Press.

Light, R. (2006). Situated learning in an Australian surf club. *Sport, Education and Society, 11*(2), 155–172.

MacIsaac, S., Kelly, J., & Gray, S. (2017). She has like 4000 followers!': The celebrification of self within school social networks. *Journal of Youth Studies*. https://doi.org/10.1080/13676261.2017.1420764

Martínková, I., & Parry, J. (2017). Safe danger: On the experience of challenge, adventure and risk in education. *Sport, Ethics and Philosophy, 11*(1), 75–91.

McCall, G., & Simmons, J. (1978). *Identities and interactions.* New York: Free Press.

McGillivray, D., & Frew, M. (2007). Capturing adventure: Trading experiences in the symbolic economy. *Annals of Leisure Research, 10*(1), 54–78.

Oyserman, D., Elmore, K., & Smith, G. (2012). Self, self-concept, and identity. In M. Leary & J. Tangney (Eds.), *Handbook of self and identity* (2nd ed., pp. 69–104). New York: Guilford Press.

Pike, E., & Weinstock, J. (2013). Identity politics in the outdoor adventure environment. In E. Pike & S. Beames (Eds.), *Outdoor adventure and social theory* (pp. 125–134). Abingdon, UK: Routledge.

Spowart, L., Burrows, L., & Shaw, S. (2010). 'I just eat, sleep and dream of surfing': When surfing meets motherhood. *Sport in Society, 13,* 7–8.

Stone, G. (1962). Appearance of self. In A. Rose (Ed.), *Human behavior and social processes* (pp. 86–118). Boston: Houghton Mifflin.

Tajfel, H., & Turner, J. (1979). An integrative theory of intergroup conflict. In W. Austin & S. Worchel (Eds.), *The social psychology of intergroup relations* (pp. 33–37). Monterey, CA: Brooks/Cole.

Taylor, C. (1992). *Sources of the self: The making of the modern identity.* Boston: Harvard University Press.

Telford, J., & Beames, S. (2016). Bourdieu and alpine mountaineering: The distinction of high peaks, clean lines, and pure style. In B. Humberstone, H. Prince, & K. Henderson (Eds.), *Routledge international handbook of outdoor studies* (pp. 482–490). Abingdon, UK: Routledge.

Thorpe, H. (2012). Transnational mobilities in snowboarding culture: Travel, tourism and lifestyle migration. *Mobilities, 7*(2), 317–345.

Walking with the Wounded. (n.d.). *South Pole expedition.* Retrieved from https://walkingwiththewounded.org.uk/Home/About/62

Walseth, K. (2006). Young Muslim women and sport: The impact of identity work. *Leisure Studies, 25,* 75–94.

Wheaton, B. (Ed.). (2004). *Understanding lifestyle sports: Consumption, identity and difference.* London: Routledge.

Wheaton, B. (2010). Introducing the consumption and representation of lifestyle sports. The representation and consumption of lifestyle sport. *Sport in Society, 13*(7/8), 1057–1081.

Wheaton, B. (2013). *The cultural politics of lifestyle sports.* Abingdon, UK: Routledge.

Wheaton, B. (2015). Assessing the sociology of sport: On action sport and the politics of identity. *International Review for the Sociology of Sport, 50*(4–5), 634–639.

Wheaton, B., & Beal, B. (2003). Keeping it real. *International Review for the Sociology of Sport, 38*(3), 155–176.

Wren, T. (2002). Cultural identity and personal identity: Philosophical reflections on the identity discourse of social psychology. In A. Musschenga, A. van Haaften, B. Speicker, & M. Slors (Eds.), *Personal and moral identity* (pp. 231–258). Dordrecht, The Netherlands: Kluwer.

Adventure and Personal and Social Development

S. Beames et al., *Adventure and Society*, https://doi.org/10.1007/978-3-319-96062-3_9

Chapter Aims
— After reading this chapter, you will be able to:
— Articulate the historical roots of programmes that use adventure to elicit personal and social development (PSD) within their participants
— Understand the philosophical foundations of character education, and its relation to programmes with similar labels
— Explain key conceptual features of programmes that use adventure as a tool for personal growth
— Understand the distinction between adventure therapy and other forms of adventure-based PSD

By this stage, it should be clear that adventures are not isolated experiences that exist independently of society's influences. We have shown how adventures can mean different things to different people, perform a range of social functions, and be deeply intertwined with cultures and economies. As with all forms of experience, they can inform learning and development, and adventures have long been used to achieve certain personally and socially desirable outcomes, to various degrees of success. In this chapter, we look at some of the ways that adventure has been formally used in education and development programmes throughout the modern period and highlight some of the challenges and opportunities associated with these.

From some perspectives, education is never a neutral process (Freire, 1970), and the same thinking can be applied to 'adventure programming', which is the term Priest and Gass (2005, p. 23) use to refer to instances where adventure is deliberately used to achieve certain outcomes. Their four types of adventure programming (recreational, educational, developmental, and therapeutic) and the intersections between them will be useful to bear in mind when thinking of how to apply the content covered in this chapter. We will focus most of our attention on adventure education programmes.

❓ Discussion Questions
Reflecting on an educational or developmental adventure programme that you are familiar with, ask yourself:
— Who decided the outcomes of this programme?
— What activities, teaching methods, and locations were used to achieve these outcomes?

9.1 The 'Character Factory' and Its Empire Building Roots

Direct experience and challenge have always been part of the learning and development of young people, as components of indigenous education, through the work of classical philosophers like Plato and Aristotle (Stonehouse, Allison, & Carr, 2011), and on to modern and contemporary pedagogies. The development of 'character', defined for our purposes as the 'interlocked set of personal values and virtues which normally guide conduct' (Arthur, Deakin Crick, Samuel, Wilson, & McGettrick, 2006, p. 3), can be seen as one of the central aims of education in general. When reduced to its core, education is the way in which communities develop shared values with their members. In this section, we examine how character training and adventure became inextricably linked and the influence that this has had on the field of adventure-based education.

Learning through direct experience has always been central to becoming a good citizen and, thanks to the influence of educational philosophers like John Dewey (1938/1963), has also become a core component of how we understand adventurous learning (Beames & Brown, 2016; Mortlock, 1984; Roberts, 2012). The work of classical Greek philosophers is often held up as the philosophical bedrock that supports outdoor adventure education programmes (Stonehouse et al., 2011). From Plato, we get the need for holistic education of both body and mind, which we will see exemplified below in the influence of the progressive educator Kurt Hahn, while Aristotle's writing on cultivating moral virtue and 'character ethics' has had a significant influence on a range of educators, particularly those working in outdoor and adventurous contexts (Stonehouse, 2010, p. 17).

In terms of what we now think of as adventure programming, Loynes (2007) states that, 'the roots of informal education outdoors are based in a moral panic of the late Victorian era' (p. 119), when evangelical and radical social reformers sought to tackle the problems they saw in a generation of young people who had been exposed to rapid social change. Various early forms of youth work, such as the Young Men's and Women's Christian Associations (YMCA and YWCA), drew on physical activity, access to the countryside, and spiritual or moral guidance to tackle idleness and urban deprivation—and often did this from a specific religious position (Smith, 2013). The perceived 'crisis of manhood [sic]' during the time led to an increased emphasis on militarism and cultural responses which looked to historic English independent school approaches of physicality, moral education, and religious observation, which have since been characterized as 'muscular Christianity' (Hall, 1994)—all of which inform early developments that are of interest to us here.

In the UK, these shifting patterns of education included organizations such as the Boys' Brigade, which was formed in 1883 and used military drill and other activities to engage communities of young people who were disengaged from the church. Parallel 'character education' movements were emerging in the US in the form of the YMCA and the more secular 4-H clubs (head, heart, hands, and health), which originally aimed to enhance the provision of agricultural education and develop the rural workforce (4-H, 2018). While they did not historically use methods that were explicitly 'adventurous', these early examples of youth work show how reformers believed that socially desirable attributes could be achieved in a more accelerated way through out-of-classroom experiences, and both 4-H and the Boys Brigade now include adventurous activities in their programming.

The international Scouting movement is probably the most successful example of how these early interventions developed in line with social need (as perceived by those in positions of authority), and played a significant role in the adventure education field throughout the twentieth century. Inspired by the success of the Boys' Brigade and Ernest Thompson Seton's early woodcraft initiatives in the US (see Smith, 2011), Robert Baden-Powell, the leading figure of the Scouting movement, organized his first camp for boys at Brownsea Island in 1907 and published *Scouting for Boys* in 1908. This inspired large numbers of young men and mainly male adults to come together to put his ideas into practice and, by 1910, the Scouting movement had 100,000 members, with one million by 1922 (Rosenthal, 1986). While Baden-Powell liked to play up the spontaneity of this growth, Scouting's success was the result of a well-managed campaign, and clearly appealed to broader societal concerns about the declining military power of Great Britain and the perceived deviance of urban youth (Rosenthal, 1986). In addition to elements of woodcraft and the practical skills of observation and survival gleaned from his military service, *Scouting for Boys* promoted a specific form of citizenship manifest in the responsibility of young people to 'do good' and what is expected of them by those in authority (Smith, 2011). Indeed, Springhall (1971) writes that, '[i]f duty, honour and patriotism were the emotional moulds within which British Imperial attitudes set, they also provided the mottoes for the new youth movements' (p. 127).

The manifestation of dominant attitudes at the time in youth work extended to gender roles, with Mills (2011) highlighting that 'the "model" Scouting citizen was also distinctly male' (p. 541). In Mills' account, which analyses the evolution of girls' involvement in Scouting from a feminist geopolitics perspective, early self-organized girls Scout troops reflected a growing social tension: the girls genuinely wanted to embody ideals which were not necessarily 'for them', and had to do so in unsanctioned spaces and forms. Applying for membership using their initials or brothers' names, organizing informal patrols, and wearing home-made uniforms, allowed girls to circumvent official controls to some degree, until the first mass rally of Scouts at Crystal Palace (near London) in 1909, which a small number of girl Scouts attended. Following a more public realization (and some condemnation) of these girls' actions, a 'sister' organization was conceived: the Girl Guides. While also named after a military unit and focused on imperial duty, '[t]he ideal Guiding citizen and their citizenship training focused on a Girl Guide's future role as a woman, wife and mother to create a future womanhood fit to support and help the men of the nation' (Mills, 2011, p. 546).

It is clear from the rapid development of the Scouting movement that its principles resonated with public feeling at the time. The provision of physical activity and clear moral direction for young men were seen as ways to address various social problems, and ensure that the young men of the British Empire were more prepared for warfare than they had been during the Second Boer War, in which Baden-Powell had made his name and in which the British military were found to be lacking. The surge of pacifism following the First World War (particularly in the working classes) required the Scouts to play down the military elements of the early years somewhat. But, on the whole, the paternalistic militarism and independent school values central to the Scouting movement came to inform mainstream education, as educators began increasingly to use the outdoors and adventurous activities for various purposes after the Second World War, in particular (Cook, 1999; McCulloch, 1991).

In the UK, the 1944 Education Act, and the recommendations of the Norwood Committee on how to implement it, has been identified as one of the most influential factors on the development of adventure education, as it led to obligations on local authorities to provide productive youth leisure and residential activities for the masses. This 'taste of public school life ... associated with outdoor activities, residential experiences, character building, widening the horizons of children and improving their health' (Cook, 1999, p.166), was seen as the culmination of multiple factors that were identified through the war. These included the health benefits experienced by children who were evacuated to the countryside from heavily bombed urban areas and the need to have young men prepared for military-related service. Up to this point, most of the energy was focused on programmes for younger men that were developed by older men. While the mainstreaming of adventurous activities in education during the post-war period undoubtedly enabled more girls and young women to experience adventurous activities, there is evidence that there were clear gendered distinctions that lingered well into the following decades (Cook, 1999).

Along with developments in the state sector, the first half of the twentieth century also saw progressive educators changing the way boys (and at this stage it was just boys) from the upper classes were taught in the hope of affecting top-down change. The most influential of these was Kurt Hahn, who was involved in founding several independent schools, Outward Bound (OB), and what came to be known as The Duke of Edinburgh's Award.[1] Hahn began his formal involvement in education in 1920, when he was involved in the founding of Salem School, which had the chief aim of developing 'moral and civic virtue', and was informed by Platonic educational ideals (James, 1990, p. 7). Marina Ewald was also instrumental in planning the school's curriculum, led extended expeditions, and was a long-term collaborator of Hahn's (Veevers & Allison, 2011).

Hahn identified six principal 'declines of modern youth': fitness, skill and care, self-discipline, initiative and enterprise, memory and imagination, and compassion (James, 1990, p. 7). He proposed that these could be tackled through a holistic education that featured fitness training, expeditionary learning, project-based craft work, and community service to develop well-rounded individuals. This approach found its fullest expression in Gordonstoun School in the north-east of Scotland, established in 1934, but informed and influenced multiple sectors, from military leadership training through to what we now think of as personal development and 'management' training.

Hahn's educational convictions were largely based on the idea that good habits make good citizens, and that young people might understandably need some encouragement to form these habits. Hahn famously said, 'It is the sin of the soul to force young people into opinions - indoctrination is of the devil - but it is culpable neglect not to impel young people into experience' (1965, p. 3).

The types of experience that Hahn called for were those which he thought could provide the 'moral equivalent of war', which philosopher William James (1910) had argued was necessary for social stability and effective learning. Hahn's approaches looked for peacetime opportunities to elicit the same sense of common purpose that James claimed was elicited through war. At Gordonstoun, he championed student-run coastguard, fire, and mountain rescue services. Speaking of how such Samaritan service 'can satisfy the thirst for action in an honourable way' (1959, p. 6), Hahn argued for the effectiveness of this way of engaging young people:

» There are three ways of trying to capture the young; one is to preach at them - I'm afraid that is a hook without a work; the second is to coerce them like the Fascists and the Communists do and to tell them 'You must volunteer'; that is of the devil; the third is an appeal which never fails, 'You are needed'. (p. 6)

This overriding ethos then moved into what has become known as The Duke of Edinburgh's Award scheme—a widely used extracurricular award that requires commitment to the four strands of

---

1   For a comprehensive account of Hahn's life and work, see Veevers and Allison (2011).

volunteering, physical activity, skills development, and expeditioning. This idea of actively forming habits which result in positive or virtuous behaviours is an important one to consider as we begin to think about what causes the perceived benefits of adventure experiences, and how people go about creating them. As we will see, its application in contemporary practice has not gone uncriticized (Brookes, 2003a, 2003b).

Hahn's resistance to Nazism became critical in the run up to, and during, the Second World War, as the distinction between individualized character development in young people (e.g. Gordonstoun) and mass or collective approaches (e.g. the Hitler youth) became more marked and influenced broader educational policy (Loynes, 2007). For Hahn, social change was affected at an individual level, through acting virtuously and leading by example, compared to the emphasis on being a 'brick in the wall' of the empire manifest in Scouting. The impact of this perspective was partly due to the involvement of key figures from politics, industry, and education in the founding of OB, which is arguably one of the most influential organizations in the field of adventure and personal growth.

The first OB school was opened in 1941, and the purpose, approach, and development in those early years can tell us a lot about that time, and the roots of contemporary practice. Based in the harbour village of Aberdovey, Wales, the school offered four-week residential training courses for young men; it drew on Hahn's experiences at Gordonstoun, and co-founder Lawrence Holt's experience of sail-training through his involvement with his family shipping business and the HMS Conway, which was a nineteenth-century frigate used to prepare young sailors for leadership roles (Freeman, 2011). Holt was adamant that the number of merchant sailors dying during the ongoing Battle of the Atlantic could be reduced if they had more experience of sailing small boats, which he felt developed 'a sense of wind and weather, a reliance on their own resources – physical, nervous and technical' (Hogan, 1968, p. 27). The key components of Hahn's school-based approaches (physical activity, service and project work) were delivered at Aberdovey and implemented by the School's first Warden, James Hogan. The focus on developing leadership and collaborative skills in young people who were already in work (or, in the early days, preparing for war) became central to the OB approach over the following two decades. Holt's statement that 'the training at Aberdovey must be less a training *for* the sea than a training *through* the sea, and benefit all walks of life' (Hahn, 1957, p.444a, as cited in Veevers & Allison, 2011, p. 55) sums up the relatively egalitarian foundations of OB, and the idea that purposeful, practical, and physical education was as necessary as the acquisition of knowledge.

By 1964 there were six schools in the UK, including one which provided courses for young women (although it took 18 years), and over 55,000 young people had undertaken OB training (Freeman, 2011, p. 26). Most of these trainees were sent by their employers, who hoped that the four-week course would develop those effective habits and 'good character', which they could then apply to their work and training in industry. Increasingly, the language at OB shifted away from terms like 'character education' towards individualized notions of 'personal development' and 'self-discovery', which are still at the heart of its programmes.

The influence of these changes is especially clear in the OB schools which were established in the US, the first of which opened in Colorado in 1962, but catered only to men. Millikan (2006) notes that the emerging wave of character development at this time was distinct from earlier muscular Christian approaches. For OB, character was 'something that must be unleashed from within the individual as opposed to imposed from the outside [by society]' (p.847). This emphasis on *self-actualization*—a state which is defined as 'the motive to realize one's latent potential, understand oneself, and establish oneself as a whole person' (Colman, 2015, p.678)—reflects a wider shift in outdoor and adventure education, which we can also identify in more contemporary approaches to character education.

Muscular Christian approaches were rooted in the early enlightenment perspective that 'human nature was not necessarily inclined toward the good' (Roberts, 2012, p.30). Indeed, from the late seventeenth century and early eighteenth century, the dominant intellectual view was that, if 'left to their own devices, instincts, and impulses, individuals were not really to be trusted at all' (p. 30). This philosophical and cultural view was opposed by the Romantics towards the end of the eighteenth century, who took the position that society corrupted the inherently good 'natural' self, and that the only way to truly know something was through *empirical* evidence, gained through direct experience and experimentation. The idealistic work of romantic philosophers like Jean Jacques Rousseau introduced an alternative conception of childhood. In his novel *Emile, or, On Education*, Rousseau (1762/1979) posited that children are innately innocent, and proposed a highly individualized education that was based entirely on direct experiences and interaction. Rousseau influenced both educational thinking and how many people saw the natural environment (Roberts, 2012). The influence of this strand of philosophy, which positioned 'wild' environments as full of potential for largely self-directed learning through subjective experience, informed the development of alternative forms of education. These emerging alternatives spanned a range of contexts, from adventure education through to the work of the visionary nineteenth-century educator Charlotte Mason, whose emphasis on children's exploration, reflection, and observation in natural environments and outdoor living was passed on to generations of teachers and governesses and remains influential, particularly in contemporary home education (Mason, 1905).

An example of these educational developments, in terms of adventurous experiences, comes from Colin Mortlock (1984). Mortlock was one of contemporary adventure education's earliest academics and claimed that adventure allowed learners respite from the 'anxieties of modern existence' (p. 19), and facilitated an expression of the natural self. Mortlock advocated a move away from the deficiency model outlined above, which used organized adventurous activities as a way to suppress identities and behaviours that threatened the power structure and efficiency of Britain in the early twentieth century (Loynes, 2007).

9.2 Character Development and Its Synonyms

The title and subject of this chapter is 'Adventure and Personal Growth', but it could well have had several other names, such as 'Adventure and Character Building', 'Adventure and Developing Resilience', 'Adventure and Developing Personality Traits', 'Adventure and Developing Grit', 'Adventure and Fostering Self-esteem', 'Adventure and Moral Development', or 'Adventure and Intra- and Inter-personal Growth'—to name only a few. While there may be subtle differences between these labels, for our general purposes at this moment, we will loosely put them in the same amorphous pot that features combinations of personal, social, moral, and emotional development.

It is arguable that all educators, whether they do so deliberately or not, are in the business of character education. Since its founding in 2012, the UK's Jubilee Centre for Character and Virtue has done a huge amount of work in an effort to clarify what is character education and how it might be delivered and measured. They claim that the concise aim of character education is to develop the capacity to 'choose the right course of action in difficult situations' (Jubilee Centre, 2017, p. 2), and that this is acquired through experience.

The Character Education Framework developed by the Jubilee Centre notes that, at its roots, character refers to one's dispositions that inform moral emotions and how we act (2017). Character education comprises 'educational activities that help young people develop positive personal strengths called virtues' (p. 2). Now, this seems straightforward enough so far, but this business of character education, or what some call 'personal and social development' (or PSD for short), is full of problems. Back in 1982, Richard Pring highlighted several, four of which we find especially pertinent today.

The first problem with PSD is *conceptual*. People find it difficult to agree on what PSD, PSE, character education, and the various other labels actually mean in universally accepted terms. Second, it is impossible for the educator's role to be neutral, as whatever content is being delivered will be done so through means reflecting some kind of *political* agenda. The third of Pring's (1982) problems is *pedagogical*: even if conceptual and political elements of the PSD initiative had complete agreement, the matter of how moral excellence is taught is fraught with controversy. Finally, there is the *empirical* challenge of trying to measure the degree to which a person may have been personally and socially developed by a given programme.

Pring's (1982) concerns might seem rather pessimistic with respect to the prospects of helping a young person to acquire virtues. Still, these dated critiques can be a good place to start when designing programmes with aims. Certainly, just because PSD may be harder to define, teach, and measure than history or math does not mean that it should not be attempted. Indeed, seeing character education as yet another thing that teachers and instructors have to do on top of what they are already doing is the wrong way to view this. As Lickona argues in the Foreword to Arthur, Kristjánsson, Walker, Sanderse, and Jones, 2015 report on character education in UK schools, '[c]haracter education isn't something else on educator's plates; it is the plate' (p. 4).

Irrespective of what label is used, there are arguably two principal assumptions located within the overall notion of programmes purporting to develop personal growth in their participants. The first assumption is that there is a deficit to be addressed. Participants must need to build their characters because, as it stands, their characters are not adequately formed. The second assumption is that formal schooling, home life, and whatever happens between the two are individually or collectively not doing a good enough of job of developing people's characters. As we saw in the first section of this chapter, adventure programmes have been held aloft since the late 1800s as alternative locations for PSD initiatives. What is fascinating to us is how this notion of what Brookes (2003a) labels 'neo-Hahnian' programme has endured for more than a century. These programmes are predicated on two assumptions:

» 1. Personal traits (such as honesty, trust, loyalty, compassion, care for nature, or, for that matter, ruthlessness) can be developed in an individual in one situation (the adventure programme) and
2. These traits will persist when that individual is in other, different situations (often the workplace, or everyday life). (Brookes, 2003a, p. 51)

Brookes goes on to highlight a crucial contradiction within the above premises, where participants' personality traits (which have been slowly cementing for years) can be so malleable as to be changed by a relatively short outdoor adventure programme, and then expected to endure once the person has returned to their original social pattern, in a way which does not acknowledge the influence of situational factors.

If outdoor adventure programmes have a role to play in developing character and people's intra- (within) and inter- (between) personal skills, there are many factors to consider. When it comes to fostering the acquisition of these traits within students, the Jubilee Centre (2017) advises that character can be both 'caught' and 'taught'. It is caught largely through role modelling, and it is taught by providing 'opportunities for children to exercise the virtues in practice as well as encourage a rich discourse of virtue language, understanding and reasoning' (p. 8).

Aristotelian virtue scholars are quite certain that helping students develop *phronesis*, or practical wisdom, is central to 'developing the good': first one must have the intellectual virtue of thinking well; then one must have the moral virtue to act based on one's reasoning (Stonehouse, 2010). For Aristotle—the philosophical starting point for many debates around character and moral education—character is not something episodic; rather, it is formed over a lifetime (Aristotle, 2000; Stonehouse, 2010). Phronesis is regarded as a sort of 'over-arching meta virtue', as it demands 'considered deliberation, well founded judgement and the vigorous enactment of decisions' (Jubilee, 2017, p. 4).

Case Study: The Canoe Expedition as 'Moral Laboratory'[2]

In order to get a better understanding of what phronesis—or practical wisdom—can look like in an adventure-based PSD programme, we will use the example of a multi-day, wilderness canoe trip for young people.

If one wanted to develop militaristic notions of leadership and followership, there might be pre-determined places to camp, standard methods of portaging canoes, set rules for setting-up tents, and certain ways of cooking dinner. If the principal aim of the trip was to develop participants' ability to make moral decisions, it would be crucial for them to be faced with 'an abundance of opportunities for moral practice' (Stonehouse, 2010, p. 20) within a community.

Phronesis is developed through the practice of deliberation with others—both peers and those who are practically wise—and then making decisions based on this process. From a character development perspective, adventure programmes that provide a multitude of opportunities for participants to make choices and, crucially, reflect back on them will be better able to foster enduring practical wisdom. A canoe trip in this vein would include plenty of deliberation about suitable distances to be travelled, how portaging loads were organized, and fair ways of distributing domestic duties around camp.

It would be impossible to say that a person became virtuous through participating in a canoe trip, but it could be arguable that they had plenty of practice in becoming an excellent 'reasoner'. To be clear, developing phronesis is not about learning what is the right thing to do in a given set of circumstances, as one might glean from a manual; it is about developing a rigorous approach to moral decision-making that can be used in all aspects of social life.

A question for us to ponder is the degree to which adventure-based programmes might be more or less better placed to help young people live more thoughtfully and decisively than other forms of education.

---

2 Stonehouse (2010) claims that expeditions can be considered 'a moral laboratory that invites ethical examination' (p. 21).

Thinking about Aristotelian virtue ethics a little more critically than we did at the start of this chapter has two implications for adventure-based PSD programmes. First, a one-off programme is unlikely to transform a person's character, personality, self-esteem, self-confidence, or resilience. These kinds of deep, personal changes usually come about over long periods of time—months, years, and decades, rather than days. Second, adventures need to provide participants with numerous opportunities to make intellectual decisions and take morally driven actions. The same implications can apply to educational programmes of all kinds, but as we saw in the early part of the chapter, for more than a century, many proponents of adventure education have regarded intensely physical, emotional, and psychological outdoor programmes as being especially well placed to elicit PSD within their participants (Hopkins & Putnam, 1993; Priest & Gass, 2005).

It should be noted that this search for a virtuous path through life is at the heart of many religions and philosophies—it is often called 'the Middle Way' in Buddhism—but Western forms of education and PSD have drawn almost exclusively on classical philosophy to make sense of it.

9.3 The Formalization of Adventure Programmes for PSD

While we now have a more solid understanding of what we mean by character education and how we might develop it, it is arguably only since the late 1970s that practitioners and researchers (mostly working in the UK, the US, Australia and New Zealand) have sought to understand and contextualize the processes at play in adventure education and apply them more effectively (e.g. Drasdo, 1972; Mortlock, 1973, 1984). Up until this point, as Hopkins and Putnam (1993) state, 'in a rather typically pragmatic British way, benefits were assumed to flow from such experience and few attempts were made to assess and explain the effects systematically' (p. 55).

One of the earliest attempts to understand adventure education experiences was put forward by Walsh and Golins in 1976, in what they called the OB Process Model. As they saw it, there were seven steps to the process: learners had to be motivated and prepared, before being placed into specific physical and social environments that contrasted with their everyday lives (that is, in a group with ten other people, in the mountains). Once in these environments, they were set problem-solving tasks which caused them to experience a state of 'adaptive dissonance', where they had to respond to feeling challenged and uncomfortable by applying their skills or knowledge in a way that 'reorganizes the meaning and direction of [the] learner's experience' (Walsh & Golins, 1976, p. 17) so that they could go on to apply their learning in later life.

For years, this way of conceptualizing learning through adventurous experiences informed theory and practice and did so across the globe (Sibthorp, 2003). In order to understand the impacts of this widespread conceptualization, let us return to that term 'adventure programming'. The word 'programming' can mean different things, such as scheduling a selection of events or shows, writing instructions for a computer to carry out, or planning a suite of activities or actions to achieve a goal. You might notice that all of these share a similar starting assumption: that someone can plan (or input) specific elements and expect a fixed outcome. When applied to adventure-based PSD programmes, the implication is that instructors can put learners into certain situations and expect them to respond in predictable ways, and then go on to apply that learning in very different situations. This set of assumptions has been critiqued by Ringer (1999) and Loynes (2002) as being akin to an 'algorithmic paradigm', which can be linked to a rationalized, McDonaldized, and production-line approach to adventurous learning (Loynes, 1998).

The Walsh and Golins (1976) model and the countless derivations of it arguably represent the dominant approach to PSD through adventure. This dominance endures despite the fact that purported outcomes—especially how participants transfer and apply their lessons learned 'in the woods' back to their everyday life—continue to be elusive and hard to measure. Early attempts to empirically understand the processes and outcomes emerged as recently as the early 2000s (e.g. McKenzie, 2000; Sibthorp, 2003) and critiques of anthropocentric, egoistic, and culturally decontextualized adventure experiences have gained increasing traction (e.g. Brookes, 2003a, 2003b; Beames & Brown, 2016; Loynes, 2002; Wattchow & Brown, 2011). Tolich (2012) provides a particularly insightful autoethnographic account of the complexity of subjective adventure education experiences. In recounting how starkly his and another student's experiences on an OB New Zealand course contrasted, he highlights the ways in which the same programme may be experienced completely differently by its participants.

❓ Discussion Questions

1. What do you think are the most important elements of personal growth through adventure?
2. Can you pin down the most influential elements of an adventurous experience that you have had? Was it the environment, the instructor, your peers, or something else?
3. If it was a group experience, how do you think your experiences differed from others' in the group?

9.4 Adventure Therapy

The 1980s saw the more formal emergence of another branch of the personal growth through adventure tree. Although therapeutic applications of adventure have been traced to some summer camps in the early twentieth century (see Davis-Berman & Berman, 1994), more formalized programmes and supporting literature really only emerged in the late 1970s. For example, the Dartmouth Medical School and Hurricane Island Outward Bound School's Mental Health Project was developed in 1975 with the express aim of working with people with a history of poor mental health (Gass, Gillis, & Russell, 2012). Seminal books soon followed, with titles such as *The conscious use of metaphor in Outward Bound* (Bacon, 1983); *Islands of healing: A guide to adventure based counseling* (Schoel, Radcliffe, & Prouty, 1988); *Adventure therapy: Therapeutic applications of adventure programming* (Gass, 1993); *Wilderness therapy for women: The power of adventure* (Cole, Erdman, & Rothblum, 1994); and *Wilderness therapy: Foundations, theory and research* (Davis-Berman & Berman, 1994), which together formed an early base of literature that was simultaneously being developed by empirical studies (Gillis & Thomsen, 1997) and professional dialogue (Itin, 1998).

Adventure therapy has been sharply defined as '[t]he prescriptive use of adventure experiences provided by mental health professionals, often conducted in natural settings that kinaesthetically engage clients on cognitive, affective, and behavioural levels' (Gass et al., 2012, p. 1). This definition is helpful as it highlights some boundaries between what adventure therapy is and is not. The first noteworthy point here is that this involves 'mental health professionals'. This in turn raises a key distinction between therapeutic applications of adventure and adventure therapy. In short, anyone can run a programme that has therapeutic aims and practices, but only a trained and qualified professional can do therapy. Herein lies a key difference between PSD or character development adventure programmes and adventure therapy programmes.

Another noteworthy, but more subtle, definitional point is that adventure therapy is 'often conducted in natural settings', where a primary emphasis is put on the subjective experience of adventure. While they are more likely to take place outdoors, adventure therapy activities may include indoor experiences. What is of central importance is that the programme features the elements of adventure that we articulated in ► Chap. 1. Adventure therapies may have some theoretical and practical overlaps with therapeutic approaches that aim to increase mental health through time spent in green spaces (see, e.g. Jordan, 2015). However, these therapeutic approaches may not be characterized by features of adventure.

Despite this nuanced outline of what can, and what cannot, be considered adventure therapy, what is crucial to remember is that any therapy programme will involve some kind of healing. Adventure therapy programmes aim to help people address problems that are causing them distress by helping them gain insights into some aspect of self-limiting behaviour, and supporting them as they aim to function more effectively in their daily lives (Richards, 2016, p. 252). Such programmes can be classified as primary therapy (or uni-modal), when it is the principal intervention used to treat a problem, or as adjunctive therapy (or multi-modal), which is employed in conjunction with other therapies (Crisp, 1998; Gillis et al., 1991).

There are a number of frameworks highlighting key elements of adventure therapy programmes (e.g. Gass & Gillis, 1995; Gass et al., 2012). From these, we can extract some general themes that are common to many adventure therapy programmes. The first is that the environment is novel, in that it contrasts with participants' typical daily lives. Second, the challenges presented within the programme require participants to physically take action to overcome; it is not enough for solutions to be intellectually considered. Third, these novel environments and challenges provide contexts for therapists to actively facilitate processes that aim to lead individuals towards developing a greater understanding of themselves. Established techniques from the fields of psychology and psychotherapy provide participants with tools that can help people more effectively manage the challenges they face in day-to-day life (Gillis & Gass, 2004; Richards, 2016). Of course, these programme elements are facilitated by qualified practitioners. Despite literature outlining the 'good' these programmes can do, there have been critiques of some adventure therapy programmes, both from feminist perspectives (Mitten, 1994) and in relation to participant safety and abuse (Government Accountability Office, 2007). The latter could be seen to have contributed to a recent push for accreditation and sharing of good practice and research, which can be identified, for example, in the work of the Outdoor Behavioural Healthcare Council (OBHC) and the associated research centre (OBHC, 2014).

As a final note on this very brief overview of adventure therapy, it is important to recognize that programmes will differ based on cultural attitudes to counselling, landscapes, and national health care services. The journey from the early days of practices in the US that were labelled as 'adventure therapy', to the last 20 years of international research and practice, demonstrates an increased understanding of the diversity and heritage in this rich field. Throughout this, debates about definitions, approaches to practice, and professional agendas clearly reflect the variety of international perspectives which have developed over time (Bandoroff & Newes, 2005; Carpenter, Norton, & Pryor, 2015; Itin, 1998; Mitten & Itin, 2009; Richards & Smith, 2003; Richards, Harper, & Carpenter, 2011).

9

Chapter Summary

In this chapter, we have taken a critical look at how adventure has historically been used to develop certain socially desirable attributes in individuals, and how this has informed more recent developments and discourses, particularly in relation to character development and PSD and therapeutic approaches.

Looking back through the gradual emergence and formalization of the adventure education sector reveals five key themes that have shown remarkable endurance over the years. First, most programmes feature novel environments (e.g. remote river) and activities (e.g. how to steer a canoe and cook over a camp stove). Together, the unfamiliar elements elicit feelings of emotional disequilibrium and excitement. Second, the programme involves an experienced instructor or two and a group of (usually) similar others—many of whom may initially be strangers (which also adds to the excitement). Third, the nature of the programme, where no participants are experts, allows for people to experiment with new ways of thinking, feeling, and acting. Fourth, there are very tangible consequences—such as cold, joy, satisfaction, hunger, or pain—for participants' actions (or non-actions). Finally, all such programmes are united by their goal of giving participants the tools to better function in society, both in terms of their relationships with themselves and their relationships with others.

All kinds of programmes exist to develop people personally, socially, emotionally, and morally. Historically, many of these programmes have privileged the development of some forms of character more than others, and excluded some people who either did not fit within these moulds or did not have equal access to opportunities to participate. Everyone involved in planning and delivering programmes with these aims needs to critically consider what is unique about their initiatives and how to create an educational and development enterprise where the intended outcomes for participants are inherently very difficult to elicit, measure, and sustain over time.

Key Reading

Brookes, A. (2003). A critique of neo-Hahnian outdoor education theory. Part one: Challenges to the concept of 'character building'. *Journal of Adventure Education and Outdoor Learning, 3*(1), 49–62.

References

4-H (2018). *4-H History*. Retrieved from https://4-h.org/about/history/

Aristotle. (2000). *Nicomachean ethics* (trans: Crisp, R.). Cambridge: Cambridge University Press.

Arthur, J., Deakin Crick, R., Samuel, E., Wilson, K., & McGettrick, B. (2006). Character education: The formation of virtues and dispositions in 16–19 year olds with particular reference to the religious and spiritual. Christ Church Canterbury University.

Arthur, J., Kristjánsson, K., Walker, D., Sanderse, W., & Jones, C. (2015). *Character education in UK schools*. Birmingham, UK: University of Birmingham Retrieved from http://www.jubileecentre.ac.uk/userfiles/jubileecentre/pdf/Research%20Reports/Character_Education_in_UK_Schools.pdf

Bacon, S. (1983). *The conscious use of metaphor in outward bound*. Denver, CO: Colorado Outward Bound School.

Baden-Powell, R. S. (1908). *Scouting for boys*. London: Horace Cox.

Bandoroff, S., & Newes, S. (Eds.), (2005). Coming of age: The evolving field of adventure therapy. *Proceedings of the Third International Adventure Therapy Conference, Vancouver Island, Canada*. Boulder, CO: Association for Experiential Education.

Beames, S., & Brown, M. (2016). *Adventurous learning: A pedagogy for a changing world*. New York: Routledge.

Brookes, A. (2003a). A critique of neo-Hahnian outdoor education theory. Part one: Challenges to the concept of 'character building'. *Journal of Adventure Education and Outdoor Learning, 3*(1), 49–62.

Brookes, A. (2003b). A critique of neo-Hahnian outdoor education theory. Part two: 'The fundamental attribution error' in contemporary outdoor education discourse. *Journal of Adventure Education and Outdoor Learning, 3*(2), 119–132.

Carpenter, C., Norton, C., & Pryor, A. (2015). Adventure therapy around the globe: International perspectives and diverse approaches. Health, wellness and society. *Proceedings of 5th and the 6th International Adventure Therapy Conference*. Champaign, IL: Common Ground.

Cole, E., Erdman, E., & Rothblum, E. (1994). *Wilderness therapy for women: The power of adventure*. New York: Haworth Press.

Colman, A. (2015). *A dictionary of psychology*. Oxford, UK: Oxford University Press.

Cook, L. (1999). The 1944 Education Act and outdoor education: From policy to practice. *History of Education, 28*(20), 157–172.

Crisp, S. (1998). International models of best practice in wilderness and adventure therapy. In C. Itin (Ed.), *Exploring the boundaries of adventure therapy: International perspectives* (pp. 56–74). Boulder, CO: Association for Experiential Education.

Davis-Berman, J., & Berman, D. (1994). *Wilderness therapy: Foundations, theory and research*. Dubuque, IA: Kendall Hunt.

Dewey, J. (1938/1963). *Experience and education*. New York: Collier.

Drasdo, H. (1972). *Education and the mountain centres*. Tyddyn Gabriel, Wales: Frank Davies.

Freeman, M. (2011). From 'character training' to 'personal growth': The early history of outward bound: 1941–1965. *History of Education, 40*(1), 21–43.

Freire, P. (1970). *Pedagogy of the oppressed*. New York: Seabury Press.

Gass, M. (1993). *Adventure therapy: Therapeutic applications of adventure programming*. Dubuque, IA: Kendall Hunt.

Gass, M., & Gillis, H. (1995). Constructing solutions in adventure therapy. *The Journal of Experimental Education, 1*(2), 63–69.

Gass, M., Gillis, H., & Russell, K. (2012). *Adventure therapy: Theory, research, and practice*. New York: Routledge.

Gillis, H., & Gass, M. (2004). Adventure therapy with groups. In J. DeLucia-Waack, D. Gerrity, C. Kalodner, & M. Riva (Eds.), *Handbook of group counseling and psychotherapy* (pp. 593–605). New York: Norton-Sage.

Gillis, H., Gass, M., Bandoroff, S., Rudolph, S., Clapp, C., & Nadler, R. (1991). *Family Adventure Questionnaire: Results and discussion*. Paper presented at the International Association for Experiential Education, Lake Junaluska, NC.

Gillis, H., & Thomsen, D. (1997). Research update of adventure therapy (1992–1995): *Challenge activities and ropes courses, wilderness expeditions, and residential camping programs*. Paper presented at the Coalition for Education in the Outdoors, Martinsville, IN.

Government Accountability Office. (2007). Residential treatment programs: concerns regarding abuse and death in certain programs for troubled youth (GAO Publication no. 08-146T). Washington DC: U.S. Government Printing Office.

Hahn, K. (1957). Outward bound. In G. Bereday & J. Lauwerys (Eds.), *The year book of education 1957* (pp. 436–462). New York: Yonkers-on-Hudson.

Hahn, K. (1959). Address at the forty-eighth annual dinner of old Centralians: An address on the failure of educational systems and the essential elements of the Outward Bound experience, including expeditionary learning and Samaritan service. *The Central: The Journal of Old Centralians, 119*, 3–8 Retrieved from http://www.kurthahn.org/wp-content/uploads/2017/02/2017-oldcentral.pdf

Hahn, K. (1965). *Outward Bound*. Address at the annual meeting of the Outward Bound Trust. London: Outward Bound Trust. Retrieved from http://www.kurthahn.org/wp-content/uploads/2016/04/gate.pdf

Hall, D. (Ed.). (1994). *Muscular Christianity: Embodying the Victorian age*. Cambridge, UK: Cambridge University Press.

Hogan, J. (1968). *Impelled into experiences: The story of the Outward Bound schools*. Wakefield, UK: Educational Productions.

Itin, C. (1998). Exploring the boundaries of adventure therapy: International perspectives. *Proceedings of the first International Adventure Therapy Conference*. Boulder, CO: Association for Experiential Education.

Hopkins, D., & Putnam, R. (1993). *Personal growth through adventure*. London: D. Fulton.

James, T. (1990). Kurt Hahn and the aims of education. *The Journal of Experimental Education, 13*(1), 6–13.

James, W. (1910). The moral equivalent of war. *McClure's magazine, 35*(4), 463–469.

Jordan, M. (2015). *Nature and therapy understanding counselling and psychotherapy in outdoor spaces*. New York: Routledge.

Jubilee Centre. (2017). *A framework for character education in schools*. The Jubilee Centre for character and virtues. Retrieved from http://www.jubileecentre.ac.uk/userfiles/jubileecentre/pdf/character-education/Framework%20for%20Character%20Education.pdf

Loynes, C. (1998). Adventure in a bun. *The Journal of Experimental Education, 21*(1), 35–39.

Loynes, C. (2002). The generative paradigm. *Journal of Adventure Education and Outdoor Learning, 2*(2), 113–125.

Loynes, C. (2007). Social reform, militarism and other historical influences on the practice of outdoor education in youth work. In P. Becker, K. Braun, & J. Schirp (Eds.), *Abenteuer, erlebnisse und die pädagogik: kulturkritische und modernisierungstheoretische blicke auf die erlebnispädagogik* (pp. 115–133). Leverkusen, Germany: Budrich-Verlag.

Mason, C. (1905). *Home education*. London: Paul, Trench, Trübner.

McCulloch, G. (1991). *Philosophers and kings: Education for leadership in modern England*. Cambridge, UK: Cambridge University Press.

McKenzie, M. D. (2000). How are adventure education program outcomes achieved? A review of the literature. *Australian Journal of Outdoor Education, 5*(1), 19–28.

9

Millikan, M. (2006). The muscular Christian ethos in post-second world war American liberalism: Women in Outward Bound 1962–1975. *The International Journal of the History of Sport, 23*(5), 838–855.

Mills, S. (2011). Scouting for girls? Gender and the scout movement in Britain. *Gender, Place & Culture, 18*(4), 537–556.

Mitten, D. (1994). Ethical considerations in adventure therapy. *Women & Therapy, 15*(3–4), 55–84.

Mitten, D., & Itin, C. (2009). Connecting with the essence. *Proceedings of the Fourth International Adventure Therapy Conference.* Boulder, CO: Association for Experiential Education.

Mortlock, C. (1973). *Adventure education and outdoor pursuits.* Ambleside, UK: Colin Mortlock.

Mortlock, C. (1984). *The adventure alternative.* Milnthorpe, UK: Cicerone.

Outdoor Behavioural Healthcare Council. (2014). *Outdoor behavioural healthcare council.* Retrieved from https://obhcouncil.com

Priest, S., & Gass, M. (2005). *Effective leadership in adventure programming* (2nd ed.). Champaign, IL: Human Kinetics.

Pring, R. (1982). Personal and social development: Some principles for curriculum planning. *Cambridge Journal of Education, 12*(1), 3–14.

Richards, K. (2016). Developing therapeutic practice: Adventure therapy. In B. Humberstone, H. Prince, & K. Henderson (Eds.), *Routledge international handbook of outdoor studies* (pp. 251–259). Abingdon, UK: Routledge.

Richards, K, & Smith, B. (2003). Therapy within adventure. *Proceedings of the Second International Adventure Therapy Conference.* Augsburg, Germany: Zeil.

Richards, K., Harper, N., & Carpenter, C. (Eds.). (2011). Looking at the landscape of adventure therapy: Making links to theory and practice. *Journal of Adventure Education and Outdoor Learning, Special Issue: Outdoor and adventure therapy: International Perspectives, 11*(2), 83–90.

Ringer, M. (1999). The facile–itation of facilitation? Searching for competencies in group workleadership. *Scisco Conscientia, 2*, 1–19.

Roberts, J. (2012). *Beyond learning by doing: Theoretical currents in experiential education.* New York: Routledge.

Rosenthal, M. (1986). *The character factory: Baden-Powell's scouts and the imperatives of empire.* New York: Pantheon.

Rousseau, J. (1762/1979). *Emile, or, On education.* New York: Basic Books.

Schoel, J., Radcliffe, P., & Prouty, D. (1988). *Islands of healing: A guide to adventure based counseling.* Hamilton, MA: Project Adventure.

Sibthorp, J. (2003). An empirical look at Walsh and Golins' adventure education process model: Relationships between antecedent factors, perceptions of characteristics of an adventure education experience, and changes in self-efficacy. *Journal of Leisure Research, 35*(1), 80–106.

Smith, M. (2011). *Robert Baden-Powell as an educational innovator.* Retrieved from: http://infed.org/mobi/robert-baden-powell-as-an-educational-innovator/

Smith, M. (2013) *What is youth work? Exploring the history, theory and practice of youth work.* Retrieved from: www.infed.org/mobi/what-is-youth-work-exploring-the-history-theory-and-practice-of-work-with-young-people/

Springhall, J. (1971). The boy scouts, class and militarism in relation to British youth movements 1908–1930. *International Review of Social History, 16*(2), 125–158.

Stonehouse, P. (2010). Virtue ethics and expeditions. In S. Beames (Ed.), *Understanding educational expeditions* (pp. 17–23). Rotterdam, The Netherlands: Sense.

Stonehouse, P., Allison, P., & Carr, D. (2011). Aristotle, Plato, and Socrates: Ancient Greek perspectives on experiential learning. In T. Smith & C. Knapp (Eds.), *Sourcebook of experiential education: Key thinkers and their contributions* (pp. 18–25). Abingdon, UK: Routledge.

Tolich, M. (2012). My eye-opening midnight swim: An Outward Bound auto-ethnography. *New Zealand Journal of Outdoor Education, 3*(1), 9–23.

Veevers, N., & Allison, P. (2011). *Kurt Hahn: Inspirational, visionary, outdoor and experiential educator.* Rotterdam, The Netherlands: Sense.

Walsh, V., & Golins, G. (1976). *The exploration of the Outward Bound process.* Denver, CO: Colorado Outward Bound School Retrieved from http://wilderdom.com/pdf/Walsh&Golins1976ExplorationOBProcess.pdf

Wattchow, B., & Brown, M. (2011). *A pedagogy of place: Outdoor education for a changing world.* Victoria, Australia: Monash University.

9

Adventure and Tourism

© The Author(s) 2019
S. Beames et al., *Adventure and Society*, https://doi.org/10.1007/978-3-319-96062-3_10

Chapter Aims

— After reading this chapter, you will be able to:

— Describe the key historical factors that contributed to the development of tourism in the Global North

— Define adventure tourism and describe some of the factors that motivate adventure tourists

— Understand and apply the concepts of McDonaldization and Disneyization to adventure tourism and other adventure practices

— Explain how experience, motivation, social factors, and the market interact to produce a wide range of commercial adventure experiences

— Use a range of examples to explain the different ways in which guides and companies facilitate adventure tourism experiences

10

The sun is rising over the lake near Pokhara in Nepal. On the hilltop of Sarangkot, 2000 feet above the city, people are strapping into paraglider harnesses and launching themselves into the clear Himalayan air. Most are visitors to the region who are flying as a passenger with an experienced pilot who skilfully navigates the thermals rising from the valley in order to provide their client with the promised views of three of the world's highest mountains. Throughout the 45-minute flight, a small camera captures the client's excitement and the guide's confident narrative, which will be downloaded when they land outside the paragliding company's office and shop. Here they can drink a mango lassi, buy a branded t-shirt, and start telling their friends about their flight on social media while the video of it is being processed.

None of these clients could have had this experience without paying for the services provided by the pilots, who have spent years developing the skills, purchasing the equipment, and gaining the qualifications necessary to fly commercially. For the client, it is a once-in-a-lifetime experience; the pilot will do it all again tomorrow. This scene encapsulates many of the elements that characterize adventure tourism.

In this chapter, we focus on adventure tourism as a particular form of practice that is closely related to key topics we have already introduced, such as identity, capitalism, and technology. We will consider how adventure tourism has evolved alongside wider social changes; how we may experience adventure differently as paying customers; and examine how various market forces have influenced contemporary forms of adventure tourism.

10.1 The Emergence of Adventure Tourism

Tourism can be defined as the activities undertaken by those who travel to places outside their usual environment for any reason other than employment (United Nations World Tourism

Organization [UNWTO], 2018a). The economic and social activity associated with tourism has been estimated to account for 10% of Gross Domestic Product (GDP), 7% of trade, and 10% of jobs, across the globe (UNWTO, 2018b).

While it is hard to lay down strict boundaries for what constitutes adventure tourism, and many estimates come from trade bodies, the adventure travel market has most recently been valued at 683 billion USD and has grown significantly over the last decade (Adventure Travel Trade Association [ATTA], 2018). We do not have space for a full examination of the development of modern tourism here,[1] and much of the tourism literature is limited by its Eurocentric focus, but we do need to spend some time outlining where our contemporary understandings of the field come from before we can get into the detail of what adventure tourism looks like and means to different people.

Tourism is often about *negation*—seeking out the opposite of our day-to-day lives or a break from our routine experiences; the holiday is the antithesis of work and is often characterized by extraordinary conditions (hence the constant stream of northern Europeans and Canadians flying south for sunshine during their own dark winters). The rapid growth and normalization of adventure tourism activities that now seem so familiar to us, such as white-water rafting, bungy jumping, or guided mountaineering, is testament to the social changes of the last 50 years. As we have considered throughout this volume, demand for adventurous experiences (which, in the context of tourism, people can buy regardless of experience) is partly down to people's desire for elements that are perceived to be missing from their day-to-day existences. As highlighted in ▶ Chap. 1, the predictability of everyday life makes the feeling that one is taking risks particularly appealing, and the outdoor settings, slower pace, and feeling of control or engagement that are associated with some adventure activities contrast with the intensity, urbanism, and speed of late modern lifestyles (Beedie, 2016).

■ **Early Roots**

The very idea of the natural world as a separate place to escape to, or enjoy for recreation purposes, is a distinctly modern one. Prior to the urbanization and prevailing rationalism associated with the industrial revolution in the Global North, nature was part of an 'all-inclusive cosmological order' (MacNaghten & Urry, 1998, p. 10), where humans had very little understanding of their relationship to it, and had very limited power within it. This, along with the fact that all but the most wealthy people spent much of their time working and living outside, meant that the natural world and the risks that went along with it *were* everyday life.

---

1   For more detail, readers might refer to Swarbrooke and Horner (2007), Sharpley (2003), or Inglis (2000), for example.

The following history is obviously skewed towards a European context. This is partly because in newly colonized countries, few were making money from tourism before the nineteenth century, and most travel for pleasure would have been primarily linked to maintaining social and familial connections. While accounts from outside the Global North have been notably absent in the tourism literature until recently (Chang, Teo, & Winter, 2009), there is increasing light being shone on outdoor practices around the world (see Humberstone, Prince, & Henderson, 2016), and a significant heritage of adventurous travel which is relevant to our discussion, but recounted in different disciplines and languages other than English. Southeast Asia, for example, offers wonderfully lyrical histories, from monks retreating to inaccessible mountains, poets heading out on wandering adventures, to writers, such as the prodigious seventeenth-century traveller Xu Xiake. There is a wealth of related material that we encourage you to seek out.

■ The Romantics, Industrialization, and the Victorians

Between the mid-seventeenth century and nineteenth century, most people would not have considered going to wild places, particularly mountains, for pleasure (MacFarlane, 2003). Travel purely for pleasure and learning had always been a preserve of the elite, while other adventurous journeys, such as religious pilgrimages, involved a lot of discomfort and hardship. In Europe, accounts show that tourism was a distinct part of upper-class culture as far back as ancient Greece and the Roman Empire (Lomine, 2005). Indeed, the fifth-century Greek historian Herodotus is often cited as the first travel writer, and well-off Romans could escape to purpose-built spa resorts or visit important cultural 'sights' (Sharpley, 2003). However, the formation of a new, stable upper class in late eighteenth-century Britain meant that a generation of young men (and some women) travelled into continental Europe in search of education, culture, sex, and drink, and crossed the European Alps by various passes *en route* to the great cities of Paris, Rome, Venice, Naples, and Florence.

This 'Grand Tour' which emerged in the 30-year window of relative peace and stability in Europe from 1763 is often cited as the start of tourism as we know it today (Buzard, 1993; Inglis, 2000). The Grand Tour is frequently described as a type of 'finishing school' for upper-class youths, who were usually accompanied by a guide and equipped with books stipulating where to go and what to see. They returned having accrued the cultural capital that came from learning about food, art, wine, and architecture, through direct experience. When war broke out again in 1793, many of these travellers were limited to focusing on domestic journeys, thus channelling their aesthetic and cultural activities into the emerging Romantic movement. These changing social patterns laid the foundations for an emerging kind of tourism that was becoming more accessible to a broader cross section of the population in Europe (Inglis, 2000).

The rapid effects of industrialization and urbanization in the early 1800s led to a counter-cultural movement which saw modern life as unhealthy and opposed the dominance of reductionist scientific thinking that ignored the spiritual and subjective elements of experience. In Europe, these Romantic movements in art, literature, and philosophy looked to 'wild nature' as a salve to the sores caused by urban living, which even then, was hectic, dirty, and stressful. Nature was also seen as a source of creative inspiration and awe. The art and poetry of this period began to showcase the natural landscape as something powerful and unknowable, which should be embraced in its raw, unfettered state. This contrasted starkly with the dominant culture of the time, which presented the natural environment as a neat, sterile, and picturesque backdrop, as well as something that should be understood from a scientific perspective. This emerging creative direction, which captured the strong emotions elicited from natural beauty, was the cultural kindling for the burgeoning tourism industry.

■ **The Roots of Contemporary Tourism**

The technological advances and socio-political shifts of the Victorian era created a market for forms of tourism that appealed to a much wider customer base, which eventually led to the international industry that is such a core element of our globalized society. British workers secured paid holidays and the middle classes grew; railways and bicycles connected them to seaside resorts, Highland towns, and spas—much in the same way that affordable air travel opened up parts of the world to the middle classes in the late twentieth century.

Tourism developed along similar lines in North America, where spa resort towns and the new national parks were opened up to broader markets by an improved steamboat and railway infrastructure (Weiss, 2004). On both continents, entrepreneurs met the emerging tourism demand by working to remove much of the anxiety-inducing uncertainty that accompanied new places and practices by offering packaged excursions and holidays; guides took visitors to the 'must-see' locations and photographers captured the visitors' experiences, which could be shared with others. While at Niagara Falls in the nineteenth century, this might have been captured in the posed photographs of couples in their waterproof capes, now we see international tourists 'checking in' and streaming their experiences live on social media from the end of a selfie stick (see ► Chap. 6 for more on this).

These elements of the tourism industry—packaging socially desirable experiences, developing associated infrastructures, supplying guiding services, and documenting and representing tourist experiences—are central to the rest of this chapter, as they encapsulate the inherent tensions around selling, consuming, and sharing tourist experiences. Motivation to participate in (and share) these experiences can be both intrinsic (e.g. it makes you feel personally fulfilled) and extrinsic (e.g. to accrue forms of capital or consolidate identities through recognition from others). Another way of understanding tourist motivation is from a *functionalist* perspective, which considers how society needs to achieve a stable social order through regulating hedonistic behaviour and maintain a productive workforce (Holden, 2005). There are multiple ways of understanding tourist motivation, just as we have seen in relation to adventure, and it is important to remember that individuals will be simultaneously influenced by a range of factors to varying degrees. Providers consider these motivations as they develop and market their products, and the key components that we are interested in here relate to how 'adventure' can be packaged and sold.

10.2 Consuming Adventure: Definitions and Two Shifts

We can begin our theoretical examination of adventure tourism by recognizing that the experiences provided are about much more than the activity itself. Each consumer comes with a distinct set of motivations, from seeking nature connection, to thrill, to connection with other people (Arnould & Price, 1993; Buckley, 2010; Pomfret & Bramwell, 2016). It is these motivations that the market both creates and seeks to meet.

The academic field of adventure tourism draws primarily from the parallel perspectives of social science and business. In terms of specific literature and research, adventure tourism has only really been investigated as distinct from the related fields of adventure recreation, outdoor education, and other forms of nature-based tourism, since the beginning of the twenty-first century (Buckley, 2006).

In 2006, Buckley provided a clear-cut definition of adventure tourism as 'guided commercial tours where the principal attraction is an outdoor activity that relies on features of the natural terrain, generally requires specialized sporting or similar equipment, and is exciting for the tour clients' (p. 1). The strength of this definition is its emphasis on subjective lived experience. Buckley's (2010) later statement that '[f]rom the perspective of the individual tourist, anything which they personally consider adventurous can be counted as adventure tourism' (p. 7) suggests that the key features of adventure tourism become the commercial aspects, the setting, and the experience of something that is perceived as adventurous by the paying customer. They do not need to be active, or skilful participants, but they do experience the activity directly. We now consider the importance of this direct experience with discussion questions below.

? Discussion Questions

1.   Which of these examples do you think are adventure tourism, and which are adventure recreation or education?
2.   If the answer is not clear, then what extra information would push you either way?
     - A multi-day white-water rafting trip with eight paying customers, two river guides, and a chef.
     - A married couple undertaking the classic Haute Route ski tour in the Alps, staying in catered alpine huts and a hotel at the end. They have their own equipment and one is an experienced ski mountaineer who takes the technical and navigation decisions.
     - A series of high-ropes challenges and zip-lines through a forest, where one follows a prescribed route, and is supported by a member of staff.
     - A long weekend spent skiing, eating, drinking, and shopping at a ski resort with restaurants, shops, gondolas, and instructors.
     - A week of guided scrambling in Grand Teton National Park based out of a mountain lodge.
     - A three-day residential trip for primary school students at a multi-activity centre.
     - A person solo hiking the Pacific Crest Trail over three months

For each example, summarize the distinguishing features that emerged from the 'extra' information you needed to decide which field each example belonged to.

We know that adventure tourism features a wide variety of commercial offerings that are designed to meet the needs of customers with a diverse range of experiences and motivations. Historically, this spectrum has been used to segment adventure tourism activities from 'soft' to 'hard', with the bulk of the market occupying the 'soft' end, which comprises accessible, low- or no-skill activities, such as hiking, bicycle touring, and animal watching (Swarbrooke, Beard, Leckie, & Pomfret, 2003). These are the sort of adventure activities that one can do with no prior experience or specialist equipment, the latter of which may be provided by the company organizing the activity. Towards the 'hard' end of the spectrum, tourist numbers and guide-to-client ratios decrease, as the skill, commitment, and cost increase (Buckley, 2006). Examples of these activities include high-altitude mountaineering, heli mountain-biking, and white-water kayaking.

In the past, the sort of activities on the high skill/experience end were only accessible to those people who had served a long apprenticeship through years of participation in adventure recreation. This involved learning from more experienced practitioners and investing time and money to build a collection of skills and equipment that permitted taking on increasingly difficult challenges, at a deep level of sustained commitment that Bob Stebbins (2007) refers to as 'serious leisure'. A major shift in adventure leisure practices is that the adventure tourism market increasingly facilitates more people operating in the high skill/experience area, because they are managed and coached by a more experienced, knowledgeable, and skilled expert.

We urge caution with the 'hard and soft' language used above, as this may create barriers to participation, regardless of whether the context is commercial or recreational. Instead, we prefer speaking of a spectrum that has low versus high levels of skill, experience, and commitment. Both ends of the spectrum can cost lots of money, but activities at the high skill/experience end may be much more likely to incur higher financial demands and may involve a higher likelihood of being harmed. Whatever kind of adventure we are willing to pay for, it is undeniable that the factors surrounding what people value most and what they are willing to pay have become very complex. The shift towards an 'experience economy' is the other notable feature of contemporary adventure tourism.

With their book, *The Experience Economy*, first published in 1998, Pine & Gilmore popularized the idea of the 'progression of economic value', from commodity to goods, services, experiences, and, most recently, transformation (Pine & Gilmore, 2011). Take coffee, for example. At its cheapest and simplest, we can trade it as an interchangeable *commodity*, in the form of bulk-bought unroasted beans. If we want to use these green beans, we have to invest our own time processing them or pay for a pre-packaged *good* (roasted beans or instant coffee) that is more convenient and saves us time. If we are happy to pay even more for someone else to make us that coffee, then we can make use of the *services* provided by staff in a coffee shop. However, we know that people do not value coffee shops equally: many people are happy to pay much more for a specific type of coffee drinking *experience*, of the sort that you get in your local artisanal coffee house, where the coffee is served in a mug made by a local potter, local art is for sale on the walls, and the wifi signal is strong. Here, the customer is not just consuming the coffee or extracting value from the caffeine boost, but from the whole experience, which is effectively a site where they can play out their identity roles with others (see ► Chap. 8 on identity for more on this).

More recently, the *transformative* potential of the experience economy has been emphasized (Pine & Gilmore, 2011). Indeed, there are increasing examples of yoga holidays and guided treks that focus specifically on somehow developing, healing, or improving individual clients.

While it has been criticized as oversimplistic and for not acknowledging similar frameworks in parallel fields, Pine and Gilmore's (2011) progression of economic value illustrates three key points that are relevant to our consideration of adventure tourism. First, it is clear that, as the late modern economy has developed, consumers have become increasingly 'cash rich and time poor'. Where people might have previously invested time rather than money to create memorable experiences for themselves and others, the highly fragmented nature of our social and work lives means that we are now more likely to pay for the convenience of a pre-defined experience at a time and place which suits us. Second, experiences are inherently direct and multi-sensory, even when the participant has little active control. Consumers want this because it feels 'real', and producers make the most of this through the ways they curate and stage their experience. Third, the demand for direct experience, when and where it is convenient, means that successful providers need to be able to dependably offer memorable experiences when it suits the customer, which creates a paradox for the adventure tourism field. Paul Beedie captures this paradox, by explaining how '"adventure" is defined as uncertainty of outcome, and "tourism" as a systematic organisation of people's leisure time' (2016, p. 473). This points to an extraordinary challenge facing adventure tourist operators, as they need to find ways to provide experiences that are perceived as unique and thrilling, while keeping their clients safe and organizing equipment and transport logistics in a predictable manner.

❓ Discussion Question

Go on the internet and note down five experiences that people have identified as being on their 'bucket list' of things to do before they die. For which of these activities would the 'average' person need a paid guide or expert help with their adventurous pursuits?

10.3 McDonaldization and Disneyization: Providing Safe, Repeatable, Memorable, and Profitable Adventures

The two parallel shifts that have been outlined above, the move from small numbers of people engaged in 'serious leisure' to lots of less-experienced customers looking for adventure, and the shift from a service economy to an experience economy have had significant impacts on the development of adventure tourism. This has led to tensions, and the identification of a paradox

(Beedie, 2016; Holyfield, Jonas, & Zajicek, 2005) or 'public secret' (Fletcher, 2010) around the notions of risk, and arguments that adventure is becoming increasingly commodified (Varley, 2006), McDonaldized (Loynes, 1998, 2013) and Disneyized (Beames & Brown, 2014, 2017).

At the heart of these discussions is the fact that, because adventure tourists do not necessarily have the requisite skills, experience, or equipment to have the adventures they desire, they pay other people to manage these shortcomings. While uncertainty of outcome and risk are defining elements of adventure, the people in the guide role clearly have a vested interest in keeping their customers alive and well, and therefore do everything they can to minimize the *real* risks and keep their clients as safe as possible (2006). This means that the responsibility of managing risk, and for the outcome of the activity, lies predominantly with the guide rather than the customer.

An important theoretical approach to understanding what Martinkova and Parry (Martínková & Parry, 2017) call 'safe danger' in adventure activities draws on the work of the German sociologist Max Weber. Weber argued that the rational, scientific way of seeing the material world was increasingly dominating many aspects of social life. Seen this way, systems, structures, and processes are becoming more and more carefully designed and managed in order to ensure that all aspects of social life operate in ways that maximize efficiencies. This has been considered in relation to various forms of adventure in order to understand how the application of these increasingly rationalizing processes affects the nature of experience (Loynes, 1998, 2013; Varley, 2006, 2012).

In his 1993 book, *The McDonaldization of Society*, the American sociologist George Ritzer identified the fast-food restaurant as a prime example of Weber's concept of rationalization, and argued that key dimensions of McDonald's approach to business can now be seen throughout wider society due to global capitalism's broad reach. The five key aspects are *efficiency* (stripping out all but the essential processes), *calculability* (quantifying the operation wherever possible), *predictability* (reducing the chance of unexpected outcomes), *control* (of both customers' and staff's behaviour), and using *technology in place of human labour* (valuing the dependability of mechanization over 'fallible' humans).

It seems counter-intuitive to apply this thinking to adventure experiences, where calculability and predictability appear contradictory to our earlier definitions of adventure, but aspects of McDonaldization are increasingly obvious in some commodified forms of adventure experience. If we return to our example of bungy jumping, we can see that efficiency is needed to smoothly move people around the site, quickly sell tickets, and rapidly determine bungy to weight ratios. Calculability is used to foresee precisely how much income from the revenue streams will be gathered and what overhead costs exist. Predictability is essential for both customer satisfaction and sustainable business (an impeccable safety record is essential). Control over what staff and clients do is critical, as deviating from established operating procedures could be fatal. And, finally, technology is used to reduce the likelihood that staff and customers do not accidentally harm themselves. These are only some initial examples of how a theoretical framework can permit a much deeper analysis of social phenomenon.

A related, and equally illustrative, set of concepts exists in Eric Bryman's (2004) Disneyization framework. In 1999, Bryman first developed a complementary framework to McDonaldization, which brings additional and very useful concepts for interrogating the experience economy. Bryman (2004) defines Disneyization as 'the process by which the principles of the Disney theme parks are coming to dominate more and more sectors of American society as well as the rest of the world' (p. 1). According to Bryman, Disneyization has four principal features. First, there is *theming,* which refers to the overarching narrative that defines the experience. Indoor ski slopes with cafes named after iconic ski-hill names, food, wallpaper, staff uniforms, and antiques—all relating to the Swiss Alps—are an example of a place being themed, so that consumers are 'transported' to another place. Second, is *hybrid consumption,* 'which entails the buying of merchandise, food and drink while being engaged in the actual leisure activity' (Beames & Brown, 2017, p. 856). An example of this might be purchasing a baseball hat and video of the days' adventure, halfway through the river rafting experience. *Merchandising,* is the third feature, and concerns the goods directly related to the company logo being sold. This would include water bottles, t-shirts, sweatshirts, and other goods being sold on site. The fourth feature is *performative labour,* and refers to company employees following 'scripts' that dictate what they should say to, and how they should act in front of, paying customers.

❓ Discussion Questions

Indoor climbing walls, indoor ski slopes, and high-ropes courses are also often cited in relation to McDonaldization.

1. Consider one kind of adventure tourism, where clients pay for the experience (this could be for an hour or a month). To what degree can you find evidence of Ritzer's five themes of efficiency, calculability, efficiency, predictability, control, and replacement of human labour with technology?

2. Consider another kind of adventure tourism and consider the degree to which it is Disneyized. The four features are theming, hybrid consumption, merchandising, and performative labour.
3. Which of all of the above themes seems most prevalent to you in the kinds of adventure tourism that you've witnessed and experienced?

10.4 The Impacts of Commodification on Adventure Tourists

It should now be clear that providers of adventure experiences (where the ultimate responsibility for the outcome does not lie with the participant) put various measures in place to manage the inherent risks while creating the memorable experiences their customers want. The emergence of these services and experiences as distinct products which can be exchanged for money is called *commodification*. If you have read ▶ Chap. 5, you will see a subtle distinction in terms of what is being commodified in these different contexts. Note that in this tourism chapter, we are discussing the commodification of adventure *experiences*, whereas the capitalism and corporation's chapter explored the marketing and selling of adventure-related material *products*. Varley (2006) sought to make sense of how the more commodified forms of adventure tourism, as well as those which are apparently resistant to commodification, exist within a model that he called the 'adventure commodification continuum'. For Varley, the most commodified and rationalized products are simply 'adventure-flavoured' experiences (p. 175) that cater to consumers who may not be especially skilled and who seek a novel experience that is tightly orchestrated and managed by paid staff.

Contrastingly, adventurers operating at the 'deep' end of the continuum possess experience, skills, and knowledge and, because of this, are more responsible for their actions—even if being guided. This perspective provides an explanation for why increasingly rationalized 'packageable' adventures (such as indoorized adventures—see Van Bottenburg & Salome, 2010) have come to form such a large segment of the tourist market, and why more committing, less easily controllable and predictable activities (e.g. ice climbing coaching) remain more resistant to commodification.

If we think back to our discussions around identity (▶ Chap. 8) and risk (▶ Chap. 4) earlier in the book, we see how where adventure activities sit on this commodification continuum is directly related to our social and personal identities and our perceptions of risk. For someone who does not aspire to gain full membership to a particular adventure subculture, doing a bungy jump, getting the t-shirt, and sharing the photos on Instagram might consolidate their identity as a risk-taking extrovert within their relative social groups, whereas a skier interested in developing their own avalanche safety skills through a week of training with a guide may not necessarily be at all interested in the idea of a bungy jump. Both, however, are technically adventure tourists, but inhabit very different spaces on Varley's (2006) commodification spectrum.

Continuing this discussion on tourists' varying skill levels and motivations also involves perceptions of risk. Drawing on findings from his fieldwork in Queenstown, New Zealand, which is marketed as 'The adventure capital of the world', Carl Cater (2006) states that '[r]eal risk is quantitative, but perceived risk ... is an essence, and hence profoundly qualitative' (p. 322). From this perspective, the tourist experiences a feeling of riskiness or consequence that is greater than the objective risk (which is managed by the guide) and is left feeling that they have lived, negotiated, and survived an authentic adventure, which in turn feeds the myth of the hero that underpins much of the mainstream adventure tourism industry (see Kane, 2013). The feeling of riskiness and being on 'the edge' can be deliberately manipulated by the guide and her ability to orchestrate the route, setting, and level of challenge (Beedie, 2016). Beedie also notes that this kind of adventure management may have the converse effect of leading people to believe that they are safer than they actually are.

The *authenticity* of tourism experiences has been a core interest of tourism scholars for over 40 years (Wang, 1999), whether in relation to object-related authenticity (such as whether the vase that you see in a museum is the original, or a replica) or subject-related authenticity (Timm Knudsen & Waade, 2010), which, at its root, pertains to feeling as though you are being your most authentic self (Steiner & Reisinger, 2006). Due to its focus on lived bodily experience, subject-related (aka *existential)* authenticity is the kind of authenticity most often linked to adventure tourism. Some contemporary discussions position the opportunity to be (or perform) this authentic self through tourism as an escape from typical existences, where technology, social roles, and obligations to increasingly constant social networks limit individuals' opportunities just to *be* (Timm Knudsen & Waade, 2010).

Hopefully it should be clear now that this strand runs throughout this chapter, and to some extent, through our whole consideration of adventure: where people are participating in embodied activities that they find challenging and enjoyable, and through which they find respite from their everyday existence, they find spaces in which they can inhabit their adventure identities. As our lives become ever more busy and isolated from nature, these experiences become increasingly valuable, and commodified forms of adventure tourism have emerged to fill this economic niche; this shift may have consequences for both the consumers and producers involved in adventure tourism, as well as the corporations that have vested interests in the market.

10

Recently, *slow adventure* has been put forward as one response to the speed and connectedness of twenty-first-century life, due in principal to it being a form of adventure tourism that contrasts with the commodified and rationalized products that we have discussed above (Varley & Semple, 2015). Drawing on elements of Scandinavian outdoor life and increasingly popular 'slow movements' (see Honoré, 2004), slow adventure has been characterized as emphasizing four key elements of 'time, passage, comfort and nature' (Varley & Semple, 2015, p. 82). The slow food movement emerged in Italy in the 1980s, but is now influential across the world, and promotes the importance of local seasonal food, with an emphasis on community, enjoyment, health, and biodiversity as a very deliberately fashioned contrast to 'fast food' (Slow Food, 2015). If we continue the analogy first put forward by Loynes (1998)—relating to the McDonaldization of adventure—we can see slow adventure as a similar cultural response to the 'fast food' forms of adventure tourism.

This shift from fast to slow illustrates the cumulative effects of hypermodern living, with its emphasis on speed and connectivity, and shows that people are increasingly willing to pay to find retreat from this. Slower adventures give individuals time to catch up with themselves, others, and nature through time spent in culturally and environmentally distinct local places. Examples of this, which have emerged from a recent development project across Northern Europe, integrate sailing, yoga, kayaking, and cycling holidays with local food, foraging, and even art activities (Slow Adventure, 2017)—all of which demonstrate the increasing range of what comes under the banner of 'adventure tourism'.

Case Study: A Tale of Two Adventures

Over the course of this chapter, we have laid out the core elements of adventure tourism, and showed how these can be present in a broad range of settings and activities. In order to further illustrate this, we consider two contrasting adventure tourism experiences.

The Colorado River in a Wooden Dory

Compared to an inflatable raft journey, travelling through the Grand Canyon in flat-bottomed wooden rowboat (called a dory) is sold as being simultaneously more comfortable, relaxed, and thrilling.

Most commercial trips take at least a week, and involve sleeping under the stars every night after eating fresh food brought in an accompanying raft and prepared by your guides. Clients play no real part in the actual manoeuvring of the boat, and there is only one set of oars that is used by the expert river guides. As one client wrote on their blog, 'Our guides won't let us row. Why not? Because we couldn't row a dory if our lives depended on it. And our lives do depend on it …' (St. John, 2013, para. 10).

Clients variously enjoy technology-free camp life and lie back to watch wildlife on the flat sections, or hold still and keep calm as the guide skilfully navigates technical white-water rapids in order to avoid boat-devouring 'holes' and rocks that could smash the thin wooden hull. These guides are at the pinnacle of their field and have worked for years to build up the skills, knowledge, and experience required to convince their employer they can do the job at the required standard. As veteran boatman John Shocklee says, '[i]t's definitely easier to get a PhD than it is to get a dory here in the Grand Canyon' (Yeti, 2015, 1:35.)

It is not just about technical competency though, as one of the leading provider's website states, '[w]hat we're offering, really, isn't so much a trip as an experience. To most folks, the scenery, the thrills and the camp life are only a part of it. The rest of it comes from within' (Outdoor Adventure River Specialists, n.d., para. 29).

Point Five Gully on 'the Ben'

'Point Five Gully' on the north face of Ben Nevis is frequently named as one of the best winter climbing routes in the Scotland and is on many climbers' bucket list. While many will feel confident undertaking it independently with a climbing partner of similar ability, there are also numerous mountaineering instructors whose local knowledge, high skill level, and accredited certificate of competency are for hire.

A route like Point Five involves an early morning start, a long walk in before the sun rises, hours of technical climbing on frozen snow and ice, and a long descent (also probably in the dark). In order to even think about this sort of mountaineering, one would need to have significant experience in similar settings, which would demand big investments of time and money. The climbers who employ guides do so for a range of reasons, such as getting one-to-one coaching to develop their skills, the lack of a climbing partner, or a desire for the richer experience that comes from being with someone with local knowledge. This type of adventure tourist is far more likely to arrange their own travel and accommodation, and invest in hiring a well-known guide directly. Package deals for this kind of tourist experience would be very uncommon.

Because of the low ratios and the nature of the relationship and conditions, the guiding role can be demanding. For example, Mike Pescod, an International Federation of Mountain Guide Associations (IFMGA) guide recounts the challenge of balancing customer satisfaction, safety, and external variables such as the weather:

» Quite often my clients have time restrictions imposed on them by bus or flight timetables. With one such deadline of catching a bus at 1 pm, guiding Point Five Gully took just two and a half hours. It was the culmination of six days of climbing, enduring some prolonged thaw conditions before the weather and quality of the ice finally improved. (Pescod, 2017, para. 9)

— What are the key differences and similarities between the two above scenarios?
— How could you analyse these scenarios using one of the models that we have discussed in this chapter? For example, what does each scenario entail, in terms of client skill, experience, and commitment? How commodified is each scenario?
— Can you think of another adventure tourism experience that contrasts with both of them?

Chapter Summary

In this chapter, we have provided a brief historical outline of tourism in order to identify key factors that have had a direct influence on the more recent development of adventure tourism. These factors included the influence of Romantic sensibilities on European culture and tourists' desires to visit wild natural places as an alternative to their day-to-day lives; the emergence of interrelated products, services, and experiences in response to tourist demand; and the enduring desire of tourists to perform and represent their identities through what they do during their holidays. Adventure tourism is a distinct field that has more recently materialized from this history and is an increasingly significant sector within the global tourism industry. We defined it as a commercial exchange that typically takes place in a nature-related setting, with the focus on an activity experienced directly and perceived as adventurous by the paying customer, regardless of how much control they have over the outcome.

In order to understand how the market has responded to these developments, we introduced two key concepts: Ritzer's (1993) McDonaldization and Bryman's (2004) Disneyization—both of which have been used to interrogate adventure practices. These analyses demonstrate how profit often trumps authentic adventure, as rationalizing processes often control experiences that appear to be 'risky' on the surface. This also highlights the subjective nature of perceived risk, which has consequences for the forms of adventure tourism on offer, the ways that guide choreograph adventures, and how adventure tourism influences identity.

The wide range of adventure tourism experiences can be positioned on various spectra and continua depending on how we want to analyse them, and we have drawn on various perspectives to emphasize how more or less commodified and accessible forms exist which cater to a range of motivations, experience levels, and economic resources. Rather than attribute over-simplified value judgements to the different ends of the spectra, we encourage you to use these theoretical tools with a critical eye, as you seek to more deeply understand the different forms of adventure tourism that you encounter: Who are the main beneficiaries? Who may be less able to access certain practices? And, who (or what) loses out?

Key Reading

Varley, P. (2006). Confecting adventure and playing with meaning: The adventure commodification continuum. *Journal of Sport & Tourism, 11(2)*, 173–194.

References

Adventure Travel Trade Association (ATTA). (2018). *20 adventure travel trends to watch in 2018*. Retrieved from https://www.adventuretravel.biz/research/20-adventure-trends-to-watch-for-2018/

Arnould, E., & Price, L. (1993). River magic: Extraordinary experience and the extended service encounter. *Journal of Consumer Research, 20(1)*, 24–45.

Beames, S., & Brown, M. (2014). Enough of Ronald and Mickey: Focusing on learning in outdoor education. *Journal of Adventure Education and Outdoor Learning, 14(2)*, 118–131.

Beames, S., & Brown, M. (2017). Disneyization and the provision of leisure experiences. In K. Spracklen, B. Lashua, E. Sharpe, & S. Swain (Eds.), *The Palgrave handbook of leisure theory* (pp. 855–871). Basingstoke, UK, Palgrave MacMillan.

Beedie, P. (2016). Adventure tourism. In B. Humberstone, H. Prince, & K. Henderson (Eds.), *Routledge international handbook of outdoor studies* (pp. 463–471). Abingdon, UK: Routledge.

Bryman, A. (2004). *The Disneyization of society*. London: Sage.

Buckley, R. (2006). *Adventure tourism*. Wallingford, UK: CABI.

Buckley, R. (2010). *Adventure tourism management*. London: Butterworth-Heinemann.

Buzard, J. (1993). The grand tour and after – 1660-1840. In P. Hulme & T. Youngs (Eds.), *The Cambridge companion to travel writing* (pp. 37–52). Cambridge: Cambridge University Press.

Cater, C. (2006). Playing with risk? Participant perceptions of risk and management implications in adventure tourism. *Tourism Management, 27*(2), 317–325.

Chang, T., Teo, P., & Winter, T. (2009). *Asia on tour: Exploring the rise of Asian tourism*. London: Routledge.

Fletcher, R. (2010). The emperor's new adventure: Public secrecy and the paradox of adventure tourism. *Journal of Contemporary Ethnography, 39*(1), 6–33.

Holden, A. (2005). *Tourism studies and the social sciences*. Abingdon, UK: Routledge.

Holyfield, L., Jonas, L., & Zajicek, A. (2005). Adventure without risk is like Disneyland. In S. Lyng (Ed.), *Edgework: The sociology of risk-taking* (pp. 173–185). New York: Routledge.

Honoré, C. (2004). *In praise of slowness. How a worldwide movement is challenging the cult of speed*. New York: Harper Collins.

Humberstone, B., Prince, H., & Henderson, K. (Eds.). (2016). *Routledge international handbook of outdoor studies*. Abingdon, UK: Routledge.

Inglis, F. (2000). *The delicious history of the holiday*. Abingdon, UK: Routledge.

Kane, M. (2013). New Zealand's transformed adventure: From hero myth to accessible tourism experience. *Leisure Studies, 32*(2), 133–151.

Lomine, L. (2005). Tourism in Augustan society. In J. Walton (Ed.), *Histories of tourism: Representation, identity and conflict* (pp. 71–88). Clevedon, UK: Channel View.

Loynes, C. (1998). Adventure in a bun. *The Journal of Experimental Education, 21*(1), 35–39.

Loynes, C. (2013). Globalisation, the market and outdoor adventure. In E. Pike & S. Beames (Eds.), *Outdoor adventure and social theory* (pp. 135–146). Abingdon, UK: Routledge.

MacFarlane, R. (2003). *Mountains of the mind*. London: Granta.

MacNaghten, P., & Urry, J. (1998). *Contested natures*. London: Sage.

Martínková, I., & Parry, J. (2017). Safe danger: On the experience of challenge, adventure and risk in education. *Sport, Ethics and Philosophy, 11*(1), 75–91.

Outdoor Adventure River Specialists. (n.d.). *The dory experience*. Retrieved from https://www.oars.com/grandcanyon/dories/

Pescod, M. (2017). *Point to point*. Retrieved from https://www.jottnar.com/legend/point-point

Pine, B., & Gilmore, J. (2011). *The experience economy*. London: Harvard Business.

Pomfret, G., & Bramwell, B. (2016). The characteristics and motivational decisions of outdoor adventure tourists: A review and analysis. *Current Issues in Tourism, 19*(14), 1447–1478.

Ritzer, G. (1993). *The McDonaldization of society: An investigation into the changing character of contemporary social life*. Newbury Park, CA: Pine Forge Press.

Sharpley, R. (2003). *Tourism, tourists and society* (3rd ed.). Huntingdon, UK: ELM.

Slow Food. (2015). *About us*. Retrieved from https://www.slowfood.com/

Slow Adventure. (2017). *Slow adventure*. Retrieved from http://www.slowadventure.scot/

St. John, R. (2013). *Down the Grand Canyon in dories*. Retrieved from http://www.richardstjohn.com/blog/down-the-grand-canyon-in-dories/2013/07/07/

Stebbins, R. (2007). *Serious leisure: A perspective for our time*. London: Transaction.

Steiner, C., & Reisinger, Y. (2006). Understanding existential authenticity. *Annals of Tourism Research, 33*(2), 299–318.

Swarbrooke, J., Beard, C., Leckie, S., & Pomfret, G. (2003). *Adventure tourism: The new frontier*. Abingdon, UK: Routledge.

Swarbrooke, J., & Horner, S. (2007). *Consumer behaviour in tourism*. Oxford, UK: Elsevier.

Timm Knudsen, B., & Waade, A. (2010). *Re-Investing authenticity: Tourism, place and emotions*. Bristol, UK: Multilingual Matters.

United Nations World Tourism Organization (UNWTO). (2018a). *Methodological notes to the Tourism Statistics Database*. Retrieved from http://statistics.unwto.org/news/2018-03-23/methodological-notes-tourism-statistics-database-2018-edition

United Nations World Tourism Organization (UNWTO). (2018b). *UNWTO Tourism highlights* (2017 edition). Retrieved from https://www.e-unwto.org/doi/pdf/10.18111/9789284419029

Van Bottenburg, M., & Salome, L. (2010). The indoorisation of outdoor sports: An exploration of the rise of lifestyle sports in artificial settings. *Leisure Studies, 29*(2), 143–160.

Varley, P. (2006). Confecting adventure and playing with meaning: The adventure commodification continuum. *Journal of Sport & Tourism, 11*(2), 173–194.

Varley, P. (2012). Max Weber: Rationalization and new realms of the commodity form. In E. Pike & S. Beames (Eds.), *Outdoor adventure and social theory* (pp. 34–42). Abingdon, UK: Routledge.

Varley, P., & Semple, T. (2015). Nordic slow adventure: Explorations in time and nature. *Scandinavian Journal of Hospitality and Tourism, 15*(1–2), 73–90.

Wang, N. (1999). Rethinking authenticity in tourism experience. *Annals of Tourism Research, 26*(2), 349–370.

Weiss, T. (2004). Tourism in America before World War II. *The Journal of Economic History, 64*(2), 289–327.

Yeti. (2015). *Yeti presents: In current*. Retrieved from https://youtu.be/qkApB-W1GC80

10

Adventure and Sustainability

© The Author(s) 2019

S. Beames et al., *Adventure and Society*, https://doi.org/10.1007/978-3-319-96062-3_11

Chapter Aims

After reading this chapter, you will be able to:

- Describe the environmental costs that come from adventure equipment manufacture and air travel
- Outline the key labour rights issues associated with the manufacture of outdoor clothing and equipment
- Critically consider the ethical imperatives for adventures that come with a deeper understanding of the ecological and human rights costs inherent in them
- Understand how the notion of seeking 'authentic' and 'sustainable' adventures within broader contexts of capitalism, technology, and social media is highly problematic

Three central issues persist as we explore notions of adventure and leisure in the twenty-first century. The first issue revolves around the environmental costs associated with outdoor equipment manufacture and air travel. All of our adventures come with ecological price tags and, as such, demand ethical consideration. The second issue considers the humanitarian side of adventure practices—in particular, the degree to which dominant concepts of adventure (fostered by the Global North) can offer something to all humans, without excessive harm to any kind of 'other'. The third and final issue is more philosophical and identity-oriented, as it ponders to what extent it is possible to find sustainable 'authentic adventures'—or 'purist' type adventures—that are unfettered by the larger structures and belief systems of greater society. The chapter (and book) closes by highlighting how the world of adventure is remarkably complex and must be examined simultaneously through interrelated analytical lenses, such as identity, capitalism, and sustainability, in order to work towards social and environmental justice.

11.1   The Ecological Price Tag of Adventure

All of our actions have ripple effects that influence ecosystems and communities throughout the world. Some of these influences may be very obvious, such as cutting down a section of hedge to build a mountain bike ramp, and others may be hard to perceive, such as the influence of buying an iPhone on miners in the Congo (see Merchant, 2017). Scientist and deep ecologist, Fritjof Capra (1997), outlined what he called a 'holistic worldview' and explained how all phenomena in our world are fundamentally interdependent. Humans, he argued, needed to see 'the world as an integrated whole rather than a dissociated collection of parts' (p. 6). This notion of the interdependence between everything is central to understanding how adventuring and sustainability influence each other.

As with most topics that we have covered in this book, there are lots of different ways to understand 'sustainability'—depending on your theoretical perspective and cultural background. As global society has become increasingly aware of the impacts of human behaviour on the planet in the last 60 years, sustainability has become a concept that influences people's behaviours to greater or lesser degrees across a wide range of contexts. Attempting to distil the core elements of the term, Thiele (2016) explains that, '[s]ustainability is the practice of satisfying current needs without sacrificing future wellbeing by preserving core values and relationships while managing the scale and speed of change' (p. 4). At its simplest, this means not using more of a resource than a system can support. For example, taking water from a well at a rate faster than it naturally refills is not sustainable, nor is using modes of transport that depend on the extraction of ancient fossil fuels and lead to the emission of greenhouse gases that the planet's natural systems cannot process fast enough. Historically, sustainable solutions have been framed in terms of social, environmental, and economic elements, but Thiele urges us to also consider *cultural creativity* as a fourth pillar, as this helps to ensure that sustainable solutions respond to people and place.

Given this broad range of views on what should be valued most highly and the different ways of working towards sustainability, an equally wide spectrum of approaches has emerged. *Sustainable development* is one such approach and comprises principles and practices that can be marshalled to address issues of sustainability in many spheres of life across the globe. For example, the United Nation's most recent Agenda for Sustainable Development (UN, 2015a) sets out 17 goals to be met by 2030 and includes such big picture, transformational aims as 'ensure sustainable consumption and production patterns' and 'take urgent action to combat climate change and its impacts' (p. 14). The UN Educational Scientific and Cultural Organization (UNESCO) highlights that sustainable development is about 'the will to improve everyone's quality of life, including that of future generations, by reconciling economic growth, social development and environmental protection' (2014, p. 3). The growing field of Education for Sustainability is a movement overseen by UNESCO (2014) that, through education, has the principal aims of 'reconciling economic growth, social development and environmental protection' (p. 2). Thus, we can see that if it is to be effective, sustainable development needs to be integrated into all forms of public and private citizenship.

Living in sustainable ways has arguably become a human imperative, and is seen by many as one that needs to be actively practised and constantly improved upon (Thiele, 2016). Figuring out how to live sustainably can be very challenging for adventurers and non-adventurers alike, because so many of the sustainability issues in our lives comprise multiple, interwoven, highly complex, interdisciplinary, and even 'wicked' problems (Rittel & Webber, 1973), where trying to fix one aspect may have unpredictable knock-on effects on others. Consider the complexity surrounding buying a new fleece sweater. Should you buy the cheapest one, the one that is from recycled material, the one made in your own country, the one manufactured in a factory with strict labour laws, or the one from the company that only uses factories with low CO_2 emissions? Maybe we should not buy synthetic fleece at all!

As we can see, even the most basic example of trying to live sustainably requires higher-order reflection and critical thinking skills, which enable us to deeply consider the various arguments surrounding the consumer activity that is an inescapable part of our adventure practices.

Dennis Soron (2010) argues that our consumer habits are deeply intertwined with our identities (see more in ▸ Chap. 8). He cites Alan Durning, who in 1992, claimed that consumption had become a 'primary means of self-definition' (p. 8). Soron explains how the 'quest for sustainability' (p. 173) is hugely limited by people of relative privilege who are unwilling to let go of their patterns of consumption. Ultimately, dominant consumer identities lie in opposition to ecological identities (Elgin, 1981). This shift in thinking (and buying!) from one to the other is so wrapped up in non-rational values, emotions, and socio-cultural influences, that individual behaviour change towards environmentally friendly practices can be very difficult to effect and sustain (Soron, 2010).

The sustainability and consumption discussion takes on another level of complexity when we consider 'green consumption'. Green consumption refers to acts of buying 'conscience soothing goods', which can include everything from free range eggs to electric cars, and is generally associated with affluence (Soron, 2010). Affluent people have the ability to make choices about what they buy, which, of course, makes them targets for profit-making companies who want to sell them their green products. This arrangement is further complicated by the inestimable costs associated with the disposal of old products and the manufacture of new ones.

For example, most of us now know that the microplastics from our fleeces and the poly-fluorocarbons (PFCs) in our waterproofs are bad for the environment. However, even though some people can afford to replace them with organically farmed wool layers or PFC-free garments, the chemicals, plastics, and associated carbon would still exist in the ecosystem, and they are hard to recycle. This raises the crucial question of whether it is more ecologically harmful to purchase new products, even if they are more environmentally friendly, or make do with what we have until we really need to replace them. There is a danger of green consumerism becoming the unwitting driver of the production of endless amounts of 'eco-junk' (Monbiot, 2007). Indeed, it is strongly argued that human beings' rampant consumerism (green or otherwise) will effectively 'kill the planet' (Leonard, 2010, p. xiv). The answer to living more sustainably lies not only in consuming greener products but also in consuming fewer products, as has been highlighted in the UN's Sustainable Development Goal 12 (UN, 2015b).

Our consumption patterns are much more involved, far-reaching, and multi-stepped than many of us realize. In broad terms, first, there is the extraction of resources from the land; second, there is the manufacture of the product; third, is the packaging; fourth, is the transport and distribution of the finished goods from the sites of production to the seller; fifth, is the actual buying of the product; and sixth, is the eventual disposal of the product.

> ### ❓ Discussion Question
> Consider a material good that is part of your 'adventure world' which you have bought in the last three months. On a rough scale of 1 to 10 score, how ecologically harmful you think the following stages of its life were (and will be)? (10 would be the most harmful).
> - Extraction
> - Production
> - Packaging
> - Transportation (before, during, and after manufacture)
> - Disposal

In the last decade, the world of adventure recreation has been criticized for its relatively narrow view of sustainability. Many adventurers love 'gear', and this love has changed adventure and wilderness recreation into a global industry that 'extends from alpine summits to urban retail outlets, open ocean shipping lanes, factory floors in developing nations, and oil fields around the world' (Simon & Alagona, 2009, p. 19). The authors explain how, since the 1970s, many of the products 'required' by the burgeoning adventure market have been synthetic materials that are derived from petroleum. This includes everything from waterproof breathable jackets to Vibram rubber soles to wetsuits and from plastic canoes to nylon tents. As noted in ▶ Chap. 5 on capitalism, the gear we buy for our adventures is not only designed for certain adventurous pursuits, but is created to sell as many units as possible through marketing tactics that 'evoke sentiments and arouse desires' (p. 20).

This creates something of a paradox: superficially, outdoor adventure activities are environmentally wholesome, but responsible action in one area of your life does not necessarily transfer to other (perhaps more dominant) areas. Simon and Alagona (2009) discuss this in relation to the Leave No Trace (LNT) movement, which they state has 'become widely accepted as a popular, common sense, and uncontroversial environmental ethic' (p. 18), and which represents an officially sanctioned way of acting in the wilderness. The authors argue that the seven LNT guidelines allow many adventurers to demonstrate exemplary low-impact camping practices while in the backcountry, but do this without effectively reducing the high levels of consumption of fossil fuels and electronics, for example, in their home lives. They highlight, in the title of their 2012 paper, that 'Leave no trace starts at home'. In this view, adventurers are at risk of 'divorcing themselves from their actions as consumers outside wilderness' areas (Turner, 2002, p. 479), despite the fact that the 'outdoor recreation industry that helped to create the LNT program, also participates in global circuits of capital' (Simon & Alagona, 2009, p. 25).[1] The contexts in which many campaigning groups and non-governmental organizations operate are complex and often tied up with consumption and corporate social responsibility (see Thorpe & Rinehart, 2013, and ► Chap. 5 in this book).

While acknowledging these grassroots/corporate relationships and the inherent contradictions present in unsustainable consumption associated with participating in some adventures, it is important not to downplay the power of membership organizations and issue-driven campaigns, which can often embody the mantra 'think global, act local'. Shared experiences, or even the mere *idea* of cherished environments that are important to adventure communities, can bring people together. Surfers Against Sewage (SAS), for example, has grown from a local campaigning group of a dozen surfers fed up with the pollution of their local breaks into one of the more influential environmental charities in the UK (Hines, 2015). It has played a role in improving water quality and beach cleanliness around the country since 1990 (SAS, 2015). The SAS members' aims are not just trying to enhance their own surfing experience; Wheaton's (2007) consideration of SAS suggests that environmental campaigning linked to adventure sports can extend beyond self-interest and play a role in developing wider political engagement, as well as facilitating the increasingly complex identities discussed throughout this book. As local communities around the world become increasingly aware of threats to environments that they care about and more easily mobilized through social media, we are likely to see more of this type of voluntary campaigning. Hines (2015) suggests that surfers, climbers, and other adventure practitioners who 'interact with the natural environment in its raw state' (p. 248) are uniquely

---

1   It is worth noting that Simon and Alagona's paper has generated much fascinating debate, and some of this has been captured through position papers in the journal *Ethics, Policy and Environment*.

positioned and motivated to act for positive social and environmental change.

The final topic that we consider in this section on the ecological cost of adventure shines the spotlight on air travel. Transcontinental cyclist and environmental philosopher Kate Rawles is a campaigner for low-carbon adventures. Rawles (2013) summarizes the environmental condition as follows:

> » We have taken carbon, formed from long-dead plants and stored for millions of years under the surface of the earth in the form of oil, coal and gas, and burned it. This has given us a vast new source of energy and the many, undeniable, life-transforming benefits of industrialization. It has also released immense amounts of carbon dioxide into the atmosphere, where it and other 'greenhouse gases' trap heat from the sun. At the same time, we have destroyed millions of acres of forest that would otherwise act as a carbon sink; this adds up to an appalling double-whammy. (p. 151)

Drawing on work from the World Bank Group (2012) and George Monbiot (2006), Rawles (2013) explains how we need to limit individual carbon footprints to under two tonnes per year. What does this mean? Well, the average American has a carbon footprint of 13 tons (Carbon Brief, n.d.). It stands to reason that all humans—adventurers and non-adventurers alike—need to find ways to significantly reduce their carbon footprints. Long-haul air travel is a major 'carbon culprit', and Rawles (2013) implores adventurers to ask themselves whether the aims of their adventures can be achieved without it. She challenges the ethical positions of adventures that involve high amounts of air travel and minimal public or ecological benefit, such as climbing the highest peak on all seven continents. Such a position suggests that some adventures are inherently incompatible with sustainability. Unsurprisingly, Rawles advocates either choosing closer to home adventures or finding ways to travel to your adventure site in a carbon light way (which, in itself, could be adventurous!).

Working to reduce the greenhouse gas emissions, which carbon footprints help to measure, is important, especially as the global community attempts to minimize the extent to which global temperatures might rise in the coming years. The most recent agreement of the United Nations Framework Convention on Climate Change (UNFCCC), ratified in Paris in 2015, aims to keep the rise in global temperature 'well below 2°C above pre-industrial levels' (UN, 2015b, p. 3) and work towards 1.5 °C. This is an immense challenge for the world, but even 0.5 °C difference in global temperature increases will have a significant impact on what life looks like in the coming century, especially for developing countries (Schleussner et al., 2016).

While the international policy focus is thus, rightly, on global climate change, alternative measures of environmental sustainability have been put forward, which may be useful to our discussions around the multifaceted nature of sustainability issues in adventure. One such tool is the Ecological Footprint, which 'measures human demand on nature, expressed as a single, easy-to-understand number that's scalable from an individual to a global level' (Global Footprint Network, 2018, para. 3). This measure has been developed from the early work of Mathis Wackernagel and William Rees (1996). It starts from the standpoint that ecosystems provide services (e.g. forests simultaneously sequester carbon dioxide and provide sources of timber) and uses the economic concepts of *deficit* (when demand outstrips supply) and *reserve* (when supply exceeds demand). Using these factors, ecological footprints allow us to calculate whether a person, country, or region is existing within the capability of the earth's systems. At present, our global ecological footprint is equivalent to 1.7 Earths (Global Footprint Network, 2018), meaning that we are using more of the Earth's resources than can be naturally regenerated. It follows that, in order to 'balance the books' and establish a truly sustainable way of life (which only requires one earth), we need to reduce consumption and restore or enhance natural systems. You can measure your own Ecological Footprint at ▶ www.footprintcalculator.org.

What is implicit from the above critical perspectives is the ethical imperative for all adventurers to consider 'How much stuff do we really need to adventure?' (Rawles, 2013, p. 154), and where does that stuff come from? The climate change context demands that all of us examine the far-reaching costs of our adventures in relation to the personal, educational, or social benefits.

11.2 The Human Costs of Adventure

While the first section of this chapter focused on the ecological costs of adventure practices, the second section looks at the unintended and, too often, unnoticed human costs of adventure. Our discussion places a specific focus on 'global others' who lead marginalized lives, yet manage to indirectly support and subsidize adventure practices in the Global North.

We have all heard of the manufacturing 'sweat shops' that exist in Southeast Asia and Central and South America (among other places). These shops, which are characterized predominantly by long working hours and low pay, often feature in the manufacture of adventure sports clothing (O'Connor, 2015).[2] Perhaps unsur-

2   Adventure sports technical equipment (e.g. ropes and carabiners) is most often made in the Global North, where quality standards are easier to monitor.

prisingly, much of the extraction and manufacture of many of the goods we consume is performed by people who are forced by financial hardship to work for low pay, in appalling conditions. Seen this way, the 'dark side' of having 'nice things' relies on dominant patterns of consumption which may be harming people and places on the other side of the world from us. This is also discussed in ▶ Chap. 5 on capitalism.

In 2015, *Outside Online* published a story that examined the manufacture of adventure garments from a labour rights perspective (O'Connor, 2015). While critics have been examining the rights of garment workers for years (see, e.g., Ross, 1997), this interrogation of the outdoor sports clothing industry specifically has been relatively recent. O'Connor spoke to Verite, an organization that advocates for workers' rights, and learned that almost 21 million workers around the world are victims of forced labour—most of whom are in the textiles, agriculture, and fishing industries.

The vast majority of these workers are migrants, as they have moved from their homes in order to find work. In the *Outside* article, Verite CEO Dan Viederman explained, for example, how 'Taiwanese factories tend to bring in Filipino, Thai, Vietnamese, and sometimes Indonesian workers' and 'Malaysian factories tend to bring workers in from Burma, Nepal, and Indonesia' (para. 13). Some migrants find work through 'brokers', but many of the brokers are malicious and offer desperate workers high interest loans that are impossible to pay off. These people effectively become prisoners who are unable to leave, in what is called 'debt bondage' (Hepburn & Simon, 2013).

The more we 'peel back' the outer layers of adventure practices to what goes on behind the thrilling video of the skiers cruising the couloir or the climbers hanging off the giant icicle, the more the ethical argument grows to critically examine the arrangements that make our adventures possible. To 'cherry pick' words from Simon and Alagona (2009), too many adventure-related organizations, corporations, and individuals fail to respond to the 'exploitative labor conditions in less developed nations' and the landfills and chemical pollution that are by-products of the 'manufacturing process' (pp.19–20).

Viederman, from Verite, urges consumers to do their own research by visiting their favourite brands' websites and investigating whether or not the 'labour rights risks' in every step of their supply chain is disclosed. He finishes by stating that 'if you aren't confident the product you're buying has been made ethically, chances are it hasn't been' (O'Connor, 2015, p. 38).

In ▶ Chap. 5, we highlighted the discrepancy between the 'haves' and 'have nots' in the increasingly capitalistic adventure world, where a disproportionately large number of vulnerable and disadvantaged (usually from the Global South) are effectively supporting adventure-based existences for privileged others. It may be that in our quest to have the next 'cool' or 'required' piece of equipment, clothing or Instagram-able adventure experience, we fail to consider the environmental and humanitarian impacts of our lifestyle choices.

This distinction is closer to the surface in some adventure contexts than others, and may be a factor in how certain industries or sports respond to sustainability and human rights issues. For example, surf tourism in the Global South has existed since the 1960s, but increasing numbers of surfers travelling in search of the four-featured 'surfing Nirvana' of perfect waves, uncrowded conditions, and pristine tropical environment (see Ponting, 2009) have led to unsustainable development and the exploitation of local communities and resources. However, as can be seen in many of the cases presented by Borne and Ponting (2015) in 'Sustainable Stoke: Transitions to Sustainability in the Surfing World', the international surf community has increasingly had to face up to ecological damages and human oppression and is now working to develop creative solutions that involve a more diverse range of stakeholders. This surfing example highlights ways in which financially powerful individuals and organizations must work hard to increase cross-cultural understandings and engagement with those from adventure destination communities (O'Brien & Ponting, 2013).

11

Case Study: Alastair Humphreys' Microadventures

Following a run of international, physically demanding adventures that included a four-year bike ride around the world, rowing across the Atlantic, and walking across India, Alastair Humphreys turned his attention to more localized activities that could be conducted by everyday practitioners and integrated into family and work life. The result was a new buzzword and social media-fuelled push for new forms of adventure.

In 2011, Humphreys set out to explore his home country in a year of 'microadventures', starting off with a 120-mile circumnavigation of the M25, the motorway which encircles London, to show that even the most apparently mundane, close to home landscapes could

be settings for extraordinary experiences. According to Humphreys, a microadventure is 'an adventure that is short, simple, local, cheap – yet still fun, exciting, challenging, refreshing and rewarding' (n.d., para. 1). When surrounded by strong support systems and cultures, which, for example, ensure equitable responsibility for childcare and a healthy work/life balance, these can potentially serve to tackle some of the constraints to participation in adventurous activities that we have discussed elsewhere in the book.

Over time, and with the support of a strong social media following, this concept has been distilled to encompass everything from multi-day trips through lesser known areas of

your home region to '5–9' overnights, which squeeze as much adventure into the time between finishing work in the evening and starting work the following morning. This could be something as comfortable as walking to a nearby beach or hill with family or friends to spend the night in a tent, or more intense, like Chris Mackie's recent midsummer mountain bike ride with a friend that was structured to fit around looking after young families: leave after the kids are in bed, ride until it gets as dark, sleep in a bivvy bag near a mountain stream for three hours, then get up and ride home in time for breakfast and a day of looking after the kids starting from 7 a.m.! As Humphreys states in a short video summary, microadventures are not about 'diluting' adventure but coming up with 'a concentrated form, distilled, like a shot of espresso' (Humphreys, 2016, 04:10).

For adventurers like Humphreys, simple acts of low-impact adventure like this also offer a space to challenge some of the dominant values held by our consumption and work-driven culture: what do we value most if we aim to come into work more tired and uninspired on the Monday than when we left on the Friday? Is it so radical for families to value time spent together in natural environments with few financial transactions, over other, more consumption-driven pursuits?

11.3 In Search of Authentic Adventure in the Twenty-First Century

While the first two sections of this chapter featured some rather challenging (and perhaps concerning) material on the ecological and human elements of adventure and sustainability, the following section is more philosophical and identity-oriented in nature. In recent years, a significant amount of attention has been paid to notions of participant authenticity in a range of adventure domains (see, e.g. Beal & Weidman, 2003; Fletcher, 2008; Poulson, 2016; Telford & Beames, 2016). Something to consider is whether—given our extensive discussions on the influences of capitalism and transnational corporations (▶ Chap. 5); technology and social media (▶ Chap. 6); multiple, fluid, and social-driven identities (▶ Chap. 8); and contradictory ways that sustainability has been invoked and practised by adventurers (this chapter)—we might come to a consensus regarding what it means to undertake adventures that are 'authentic'. Furthermore, to what degree do our 'authentic' adventures reflect or come into conflict with key principles of sustainability?

On one hand, philosopher Charles Taylor (1991) explains that every human has a particular 'way of being' (p. 28) and that authenticity is about 'following a voice of nature within us' (p. 27). This harkens back to our earlier idea from ▶ Chap. 8 regarding a highly personal or 'core' sense of self. Within this notion is an assumption that people can attempt to live authentically when 'they make decisions about their lives that are not overly shaped by external influences' (Beames & Brown, 2016, p. 51). This may seem reasonable enough, but how can we follow our own way of being in the face of the barrage of social, corporate, and technological influences? These latter influences, according to many social scholars and philosophers, cannot help (at some level) but determine what we think and what we do. In ▶ Chap. 8, for example, we referred to the structural arguments put forth by philosophers such as Antonio Gramsci and Michel Foucault, who both suggested that societal forces greatly impacted our identities, belief systems, and life practices.

These discussions of authentic contemporary adventures become further complicated as we consider the increasing reach of new online and virtual applications into our worlds of adventure. Following discussions in ▶ Chap. 6 on technology and social media, to what degree do we consider drone flying and other 'adventure by proxy' practices authentic representations of adventure sports?

We authors are fascinated by the proliferating notions of what it means to be an authentic adventurer, and what features these authentic adventures comprise (see the virtual adventure section in ▶ Chap. 6). Although, as noted three paragraphs earlier, authenticity has been a key feature in much adventure scholarship, there are now so many evolving, changing, and even contradictory ways that participants attempt to claim and experience 'authenticity' in adventure. We suggest that it is our responsibility to ponder how these emerging identities and practices may or may not be commensurate with what can be seen as a global ethical imperative to live more sustainably; perhaps the ways in which we negotiate what constitutes a personally authentic adventure need to sit more firmly within discourses of what is not only in our best interests but also in the best interests of 'global others' and the planet that sustains us.

❓ Discussion Question

It will be interesting to see if there is a move away from high-carbon adventures in faraway places that have no public benefit, towards low-carbon, self-funded, local, microadventures. Is one more authentic than the other?

Conclusions

If we look back to key elements of the material covered in this book, several of them seem to rise above the others as being central to any consideration of adventurous practices in the twenty-first century. These key elements are capitalism, technology, identity, equalities and sustainability (i.e. ▶ Chaps. 5, 6, 7, 8, and 11). We can now reveal one of this book's shortcomings that we have identified (you may have others!): it is almost impossible to examine adventure practices through only one theoretical lens at a time. This kind of approach tends to render sociological analyses of all kinds into reductionist, oversimplified, and narrow academic exercises.

Because of the high degree of overlap between the different forces at play, a more fruitful, but much more demanding, approach to examining adventure is to consider how multiple features interact with each other. This 'systems' view is well articulated by the Centre for Eco-Literacy (2012):

» A system is a set of interrelated elements that make a unified whole. Individual things—like plants, people, schools, watersheds, or economies—are themselves systems and at the same time cannot be fully understood apart from the larger systems in which they exist. (para. 3)

» Systems thinking is an essential part of schooling for sustainability. A systems approach helps young people understand the complexity of the world around them and encourages them to think in terms of relationships, connectedness, and context. (para. 4)

In a similar way, this systems view is also helpful as we seek to gain a 'big picture' view of adventure. For example, it is very limiting to discuss identity without also considering the influences of social structures, such as global capitalism and social media, upon it.

The principal focus of this chapter has been to help you understand general conceptions of sustainability, critically interrogate the ecological and human costs of our adventure practices, and to provoke creative thinking about how we can have morally excellent adventures. It is important to note that we are not making a blanket statement that adventure harms the environment and other people, but we are definitely saying that some consumption practices do.

If we have a rallying cry, it is for adventurers around the world to deeply examine their adventure practices and consider how they might adversely affect people and places, especially on the other side of the world. This involves using our unique understandings of people and place in order to help affect meaningful and enduring social change.

❯ When we look at the sustainability of adventure, we must do so deeply and broadly enough to reveal the social, cultural, economic, and environmental conditions and consequences that permit our adventures. Ultimately, the big questions we must answer are:

1. Who in society are advantaged and disadvantaged by changing adventure practices that are being driven by an increasingly globalised world?

2. How are we going to address these unjust social arrangements?

We believe that adventure can be re-positioned as a societal asset, which can be used as a tool to create more equitable communities and healthier ecosystems. Adventurous experiences do not just offer opportunities for 'respite' or 'escape' from the pressures of late modern society, but instead can be spaces which allow for experimentation and encounters that might be harder to achieve in other social contexts. This might involve, for example, using adventure to welcome migrants from war-torn countries, or to extend invitations to those who might normally be excluded from activities that seem 'boundaried' by class, sex, race, sexual orientation, and ability. From this perspective, communities of adventurers can become shining examples of what a caring, inclusive, and environmentally conscious group of people can bring to society.

Key Readings

Humphreys, A. (2014). *Microadventures: Local discoveries for great escapes.* London: William Collins.

Rawles, K. (2013). Adventure in a carbon-light era. In E. Pike & S. Beames (Eds.), *Outdoor adventure and social theory* (pp. 147–159). Abingdon, UK: Routledge.

References

Beal, B., & Weidman, L. (2003). Authenticity in the skateboarding world. In R. Rinehart & S. Sydnor (Eds.), *To the extreme: Alternative sports inside and out* (pp. 337–352). New York: SUNY Press.

Beames, S., & Brown, M. (2016). *Adventurous learning: A pedagogy for a changing world.* New York: Routledge.

Borne, G., & Ponting, J. (2015). *Sustainable stoke: Transitions to sustainability in the surfing world.* Plymouth: University of Plymouth Press.

Capra, F. (1997). *The web of life: A new synthesis of mind and matter.* London: Flamingo.

Carbon Brief. (n.d.). *Five facts about Europe's carbon emissions.* Retrieved from https://www.carbonbrief.org/5-facts-about-europes-carbon-emissions

Centre for Eco-Literacy. (2012). *Systems thinking.* Retrieved from https://www.ecoliteracy.org/article/systems-thinking

Durning, A. (1992). *How much is enough? The consumer society and the future of the earth.* New York: W.W. Norton & Company.

Elgin, D. (1981). *Voluntary simplicity: Towards a way of life that is outwardly simple, inwardly.* New York: Morrow.

Fletcher, R. (2008). Living on the edge: The appeal of risk sports for the professional middle class. *Sociology of Sport Journal, 25*(3), 1–23.

Global Footprint Network. (2018). *Our work.* Retrieved from https://www.footprintnetwork.org/our-work/ecological-footprint/

Hepburn, S., & Simon, R. (2013). *Human trafficking around the world: Hidden in plain sight.* New York: Columbia University Press.

Hines, C. (2015). Surfing can change the world. In G. Borne & J. Ponting (Eds.), *Sustainable stoke: Transitions to sustainability in the surfing world* (pp. 248–259). Plymouth: University of Plymouth Press.

Humphreys, A. (n.d.). *Microadventures inspiration.* Retrieved from http://www.alastairhumphreys.com/microadventure-inspiration/

11

Humphreys, A. (2014). *Microadventures: Local discoveries for great escapes.* London: William Collins.

Humphreys, A. (2016). *Microadventures.* Retrieved from https://vimeo.com/136917267

Leonard, A. (2010). *The story of stuff: How our obsession with stuff is trashing the planet, our communities, and our health -- and a vision for change.* London: Constable.

Merchant, B. (2017). *Were the raw materials in your iPhone mined by children in inhumane conditions?* Retrieved from http://www.latimes.com/opinion/op-ed/la-oe-merchant-iphone-supplychain-20170723-story.html

Monbiot, G. (2006). *Heat: How to stop the planet burning.* London: Allen Lane.

Monbiot, G. (2007). Ethical shopping is just another way of showing how rich you are. *The Guardian,* p. 27.

O'Brien, D., & Ponting, J. (2013). Sustainable surf tourism: A community centred approach in Papua New Guinea. *Journal of Sport Management, 27*(2), 158–172.

O'Connor, M. (2015). The dirty secret hiding in our outerwear. *Outside Online.* Retrieved from https://www.outsideonline.com/1999281/dirty-secret-hiding-our-outerwear

Ponting, J. (2009). *Consuming nirvana: The social construction of surfing tourist space.* Saarbrücken, Germany: VDM Verlag.

Poulson, S. (2016). *Why would anyone do that?: Lifestyle sport in the twenty-first century.* New Brunswick, NJ: Rutgers University Press.

Rawles, K. (2013). Adventure in a carbon-light era. In E. Pike & S. Beames (Eds.), *Outdoor adventure and social theory* (pp. 147–159). Abingdon, UK: Routledge.

Rittel, H., & Webber, M. (1973). Dilemmas in a general theory of planning. *Policy Sciences, 4,* 155–169.

Ross, A. (1997). *No sweat: Fashion, free trade and the rights of garment workers.* London: Verso.

Schleussner, C., Lissner, T., Fischer, E., Wohland, J., Perrette, M., Golly, A., et al. (2016). Differential climate impacts for policy-relevant limits to global warming. *Earth System Dynamics, 7*(2), 327–351.

Simon, G., & Alagona, P. (2009). Leave no trace starts at home: A response to critics and vision for the future. *Ethics, Policy & Environment, 15*(1), 119–124.

Soron, D. (2010). Sustainability, self-identity and the sociology of consumption. *Sustainable Development, 18,* 172–181.

Surfers Against Sewage. (2015). *Making waves since 1990: 25 years of cleaner oceans.* Retrieved from: https://www.sas.org.uk/news/campaigns/making-waves-since-1990-25-years-of-cleaner-oceans/

Taylor, C. (1991). *The ethics of authenticity.* Cambridge, MA: Harvard University Press.

Telford, J., & Beames, S. (2016). Bourdieu and alpine mountaineering: The distinction of high peaks, clean lines, and pure style. In B. Humberstone, H. Prince, & K. Henderson (Eds.), *Routledge international handbook of outdoor studies* (pp. 482–490). Abingdon, UK: Routledge.

The World Bank Group. (2012). CO_2 emissions (metric tons per capita). Retrieved from http://data.worldbank.org/indicator/EN.ATM.CO2E.PC

Thiele, L. (2016). *Sustainability.* London: Polity Press.

Thorpe, H., & Rinehart, R. (2013). Action sport NGOs in a neo-liberal context: The cases of Skateistan and surf aid international. *Journal of Sport and Social Issues, 37*(2), 115–141.

Turner, J. (2002). From woodcraft to 'leave no trace': Wilderness, consumerism, and environmentalism in twentieth century America. *Environmental History, 7*(3), 462–484.

United Nations (2015a). *Transforming our world: The 2030 Agenda for Sustainable Development.* Retrieved from http://www.un.org/ga/search/view_doc.asp?symbol=A/RES/70/1&Lang=E

United Nations (2015b). *The Paris agreement.* Retrieved from https://unfccc.int/sites/default/files/english_paris_agreement.pdf

UNESCO. (2014). *The DESD at a Glance.* Retrieved from http://unesdoc.unesco.org/images/0014/001416/141629e.pdf

Wackernagel, M., & Rees, W. (1996). *Our ecological footprint: Reducing human impact on the earth.* Gabriola Island, Canada: New Society.

Wheaton, B. (2007). Identity, politics, and the beach: Environmental activism in surfers against sewage. *Leisure Studies, 26*(3), 279–302.

11

Supplementary Information

S. Beames et al., *Adventure and Society*, https://doi.org/10.1007/978-3-319-96062-3

Index

Printed by Printforce, the Netherlands